MRS. GASKELL

Mrs. Gaskell
(from the portrait by George Richmond)

MRS. GASKELL

The Basis for Reassessment

EDGAR WRIGHT

London
OXFORD UNIVERSITY PRESS
NEW YORK   TORONTO
1965

Oxford University Press, Amen House, London E.C.4

GLASGOW NEW YORK TORONTO MELBOURNE WELLINGTON
BOMBAY CALCUTTA MADRAS KARACHI LAHORE DACCA
CAPE TOWN SALISBURY NAIROBI IBADAN ACCRA
KUALA LUMPUR HONG KONG

*Printed in Great Britain
by Hazell Watson & Viney Ltd.
Aylesbury, Bucks*

Contents

The portrait of Mrs. Gaskell by George Richmond is reproduced
as a frontispiece by courtesy of the National Portrait Gallery.

Preface

I HAVE set out to provide a basis for the overdue reassessment of Mrs. Gaskell. The earlier chapters have been used to examine what seem to me to be the main themes and interests which determine the nature of her work, and in these chapters I am particularly concerned with the early novels. The later chapters follow up the discussion of themes and interests by relating them, through detailed reference to particular books, to her development as a novelist. Had either a completely chronological or a completely thematic method been attempted, it would not have been possible to show so clearly how this development occurred. The discussion of technique, although given its own chapters, is also related closely to the discussion which precedes it.

I have had to be selective in my choice of the work dealt with. Mrs. Gaskell wrote seven novels, five 'nouvelles', twenty-two short stories, eleven articles or essays some of which are lengthy, a major biography and some odds and ends of poetry and prefaces. An account of all these (with the inexplicable omission of the short article 'An Italian Institution') is to be found in Miss Hopkins' *Elizabeth Gaskell, Her Life and Work*, a survey which I have constantly referred to. But a number of the items are of minor importance while a few are best forgotten. I see Mrs. Gaskell's longer work as being the more important, and I have therefore concentrated on the novels and the 'nouvelles'. We have no adequate term in English for the very long short story or short novel; I use the term 'nouvelle' for 'Mr. Harrison's Confessions', 'The Moorland Cottage', 'Lois the Witch', 'A Dark Night's Work', and *Cousin Phillis*. Two of these strike me as being major works both in themselves and for my argument, and they have been treated accordingly. *My Lady Ludlow* I count as a novel, although it really splits completely into a nouvelle and a short story.

The short stories are of varying length and quality. A few are memorable examples of the form, a number of others are interesting. But to have considered them in detail would have conflicted with my intentions and added enormously to the length. I have therefore referred to them only as they illustrate my argument.

The articles have been drawn on when they are relevant. One of them, 'Company Manners', is important not only for this reason but because it is also an unfairly neglected example of that generally neglected form, the long essay, and one which deserves to be better known. I devote part of a chapter to *The Life of Charlotte Brontë*, but this is confined to looking at its place in her development as a novelist.

The edition I have used is the Knutsford, edited by A. W. Ward. This edition had the authority and help of Mrs. Gaskell's daughters, and as we have details of its provenance which give information about the novels themselves as well as the edition, it is worth while recording them.

Reginald Smith, of Smith, Elder and Co., secured the co-operation of Mrs. Gaskell's daughters by promising that comment, critical and biographical, would be kept on a factual basis and would not intrude on the personality or privacy of their mother:

To Mr. Arnold was entrusted the revision of the text and the re-grouping of the stories. For example, the text suffered from very long paragraphs which required breaking up. Some extended to a page and a half. The probable reason for this appears from an early letter of Mrs. Gaskell to George Smith. She explains that she writes steadily across her papers, dialogue and all, leaving it to the printer to break up. Among peculiarities of diction or slips occurred the "isle" of a church. Was this, as the Miss Gaskells thought, a printer's error, or was it a survival of the old spelling, the latest example of which in the New English Dictionary is dated 1836, twenty years earlier? As to the existing grouping of the stories, Mr. Aitchison, for many years manager to Smith, Elder, being appealed to, remembered that "when the collected edition came into being, the plates on which many of the stories were printed were brought together from various publishers, and they were re-arranged more according to length than to any thought of chronology. So that 'Wives and Daughters,' which *was* last, *is* first."

To the scheme as outlined by Reginald Smith's persuasive pen, the Miss Gaskells gave a cordial consent, and promptly offered to lend any pictures, drawings, MSS., or original editions, among which they named a "rough sketch of the plot of 'Mary Barton,' drawn out before a word of the book was written, but strangely adhered to in the writing —a water-colour drawing of a picturesque little farm in the Green Hays Fields, the scene of its opening, etc."

"We would," Miss Gaskell added, "name the very few *places* which can be identified as having been described; but we want to make a dead set against the tendency to identify the *characters* in my mother's books with so-called 'originals'. The way in which, in spite of our reiterated assurances, Knutsford claims to be the original of 'Cranford' and pretends to recognise the originals of all the characters in it, has annoyed us more than I can say. It seems to belittle her genius and imagination.

"This tradition has now so firmly established (itself) at Knutsford, that we have at length almost ceased trying to overcome it" (May 1902).

For the critical and biographical work it was impossible to secure either Leslie Stephen, or Canon Ainger, to whom merely abstract and impersonal criticism did not appeal, or Mr. John Morley, who was approached as he came to the end of his "Life of Gladstone."

Finally, Dr. (afterwards Sir) Adolphus Ward, of Peterhouse, despite misgivings about the pressure of other work, accepted the task at the end of 1903. His long-standing friendship with the Gaskell family and with his collaborator added a special sympathy to his scholarly qualifications.

On the death of Mr. Arnold, Dr. Ward took over his chronological list and his notes, so far as completed, on the separate stories. For the edition he planned a duplex chronological arrangement; the long stories in right sequence of date, and the short stories similarly, but interplaced among the former series according to the exigencies of space.

Plans once settled, the correspondence shows Reginald Smith constantly ready to lend help with his practical judgment in literary details, such, for instance, as the doubtful ascription to Mrs. Gaskell of "One of Our Legal Fictions," which appeared anonymously in *Household Words*. And Dr. Ward at the end of his difficult task, found "all difficulties lightened by his confidence," and his "unfailing kindness and consideration."

As is generally the case with a special collected edition, the question
of a name took long to decide. A baker's dozen of suggestions were
considered, from the Biographical Edition to the North and South,
from the Cranford, which might perhaps clash with the Cranford
Series, to—Miss Gaskell's preference—either the Ward or the Queen's,
a title recalling the Queen's interest in "Mary Barton" and its social
problems.

Finally came "a little Cinderella of an after-thought"—"there is also
the Knutsford Edition." The shoe fitted at last; Cinderella was the
instant elect of editor and publisher.[1]

Ward's labours were more than editorial. He succeeded tactfully
in producing, in his prefaces to the individual works, what is
still a shrewd and enlightening critical commentary, based on a
detailed knowledge of the period and an enviable range of
miscellaneous information about Mrs. Gaskell's subjects and intentions. I have often gone back to see what Ward says on a
particular point, and while I may not have agreed with him, I
have always found him interesting and helpful.

Certain items of the text I have checked against MSS., first
editions and the original Smith, Elder edition in seven volumes
of 1873. There are occasional differences, mainly in punctuation—
for Mrs. Gaskell was liberal with her punctuation, as her letters
show—but they are small and do not affect critical comment. I
have touched on the question of serialization and book publication
in the appropriate sections. But this does not set out in any way
to be a textual study.

The other collected edition is that edited by Clement Shorter
for The World's Classics. It contains one or two of the minor
items which are not in the Knutsford edition, and I have consulted
the prefaces, but my major debt to Shorter's work is to the
material, now in the Brotherton Library, that he collected towards a projected critical biography. I have also used *The Life of
Charlotte Brontë* which he prepared for the Haworth edition.
Both of the collected editions are out of print and hard to come
by; individual works have been reprinted but there is need for

---

[1] (Leonard Huxley), *The House of Smith, Elder*, printed for private circulation, 1923,
pp. 205–7.

a fresh edition if Mrs. Gaskell is to reach the reading public again.

There is no collected edition of her correspondence, although one is being made. Many of her letters are however available in print, and I have seen a number of holograph collections.

I am grateful to Professor Geoffrey Tillotson for first suggesting to me that Mrs. Gaskell would repay a detailed critical examination, and to his keen eye for error and infelicity. Mr. Charles Richards put his wide knowledge of Victorian literature and of theology at my disposal, together with a personal library hardly to be expected in Nairobi. To librarians in many places I am grateful for their courtesy and help. The University of Leeds, the Huntington Library, The University of California, Los Angeles, and the John Rylands Library have kindly permitted me to quote from material in their collections. Much of Chapter 7 first appeared in slightly modified form in *The Review of English Literature*, January 1965. My friends Mrs. Barbara Ratzeburg and Mrs. Eileen Bowman typed the drafts and produced order in them. My work was helped by a research grant from the University College, Nairobi.

Abbreviated References

The following abbreviated titles have been used for certain works.

Chadwick — Ellis H. Chadwick, *Mrs. Gaskell: Haunts, Homes and Stories*, Pitman, 1913.

Haldane — Elizabeth S. Haldane, *Mrs. Gaskell and Her Friends*, Hodder and Stoughton, 1930.

Hopkins — Annette B. Hopkins, *Elizabeth Gaskell, Her Life and Work*, John Lehmann, 1952.

Letters — *Letters of Mrs. Gaskell and Charles Eliot Norton, 1855–1865*, edited Jane Whitehill, O.U.P., 1932.

Rylands — *Letters Addressed to Mrs. Gaskell by Celebrated Contemporaries*, edited R. D. Waller. Reprinted from *The Bulletin of the John Rylands Library*, Vol. 19, No. 1, Jan. 1935.

Tillotson — Kathleen Tillotson, *Novels of the Eighteen-Forties*, Oxford Paperbacks, 1961.

Reference to all work by Mrs. Gaskell, with the exception of the *Life*, are to the Knutsford edition, reprinted by John Murray 1919–20, from the Smith, Elder first edition of 1906, and are given under the title of the particular volume in which they appear; e.g. a reference to 'Morton Hall' would be given to *Cranford*, the title story of the volume in which this story appears.

I have abbreviated slightly the titles of the volumes. The abbreviations used, with the full titles, are given below. Other items in a volume are included in brackets. *Mary Barton* contains also the editorial preface and a short bibliography.

Mary Barton — *Mary Barton and Other Tales* (Libbie Marsh's Three Eras, The Sexton's Hero, Clopton House)

Cranford — *Cranford and Other Tales* (Christmas Storms and Sunshines, Lizzie Leigh, The Well of Pen Morfa, The Moorland Cottage, The Heart of John Middleton,

Disappearances, The Old Nurse's Story, Morton Hall, Traits and Stories of the Huguenots, My French Master, The Squire's Story)

Ruth — *Ruth and Other Tales, etc.* (Cumberland Sheep-Shearers, Modern Greek Songs, Company Manners, Bessy's Troubles at Home, Hand and Heart)

North and South — *North and South*

My Lady Ludlow — *My Lady Ludlow and Other Tales* (Round the Sofa, An Accursed Race, The Doom of the Griffiths, Half a Lifetime Ago, The Poor Clare, The Half-Brothers, Mr. Harrison's Confessions, The Manchester Marriage)

Sylvia's Lovers — *Sylvia's Lovers, etc.* (An Italian Institution)

Cousin Phillis — *Cousin Phillis and Other Tales* (Lois the Witch, The Crooked Branch, Curious if True, Right at Last, The Grey Woman, Six Weeks at Heppenheim, A Dark Night's Work, The Shah's English Gardener, French Life, Crowley Castle, Two Fragments of Ghost Stories)

Wives and Daughters — *Wives and Daughters, an Every-Day Story*

References to *The Life of Charlotte Brontë* are to the Haworth edition, Smith, Elder, 1914, and are normally abbreviated to *Life*.

CHAPTER I

Introduction

THERE has been relatively little serious examination of the works of Mrs. Gaskell, yet she is one of the most firmly 'placed' of all Victorian novelists. I mean by that, that there is an almost unanimous expression of opinion, when it is necessary to say something about her, which stresses her simplicity and sense of compassion, admits that she had talent, is ready to admit also if pressed that some explanation must be found for the diverse nature of her production, and notes finally that because of certain books (the choice may vary within a limited range) she is definitely an important minor novelist. There is generally added a reference to her charm, femininity and some vague quality that is better felt than analysed. Yet any close reading of her work reveals qualities that merit closer attention, and should make us realize that until her art and mode of thought are given a closer examination we lack the criteria necessary for a reassessment.

Because of the strength of what has become a traditional method of approach, one which is still current, it is wise to look at how this approach has become established before a detailed examination takes place. This is not to say that the accepted conclusions are always wrong, but they are almost certainly too limited in range. Current work on the Victorian novel, both in general and as regards individual authors, has given us more insight into and sympathy for the achievement of the Victorians and the methods they used, while Mrs. Gaskell's own powers of survival indicate that her achievement has been glossed over and simplified. The accepted opinions, and some idea of the reason for them, must be clearly seen before any reassessment can be made.

One reason is undoubtedly that some of her novels have been too easily and conveniently labelled for extraneous reasons. *Mary*

Barton for instance has long been the possession of the social historian, occasionally borrowed for exhibition in the 'social realism' or 'social reform' sections of the history of the novel. Its literary qualities have tended to receive a superficial examination and its relation to the other novels which fall outside of this category have been rather cursorily dealt with. Here we can trace a tradition dating from the time of publication of *Mary Barton* when W. R. Greg, to take the best known example, concentrating on whether the picture of Manchester life was fair to all concerned, devoted the weight of his critique to exposing the misguided view of the industrial situation which he claimed it represented, noting that:

there was nothing in the extremity of their Manchester destitution, which the Davenports, immigrants from Buckinghamshire, are described as dreading so much, as to be sent back to their rural home.[1]

Mary Barton, North and South and (linked with problems of moral decency) *Ruth* became documents in the social reform struggle of the mid-Victorian period, taking their place with the novels of Kingsley and Disraeli. A result has been that her non-controversial work has come to be considered mainly as a change of direction, although whether for better or worse depends on the importance given by any critic to the subject matter. Comments ranging from:

very imperfect as *Mary Barton* (1848) and *North and South* (1855) are, it is on these novels that her reputation mainly rests.[2]

to

. . . her later masterpieces, such as *Cousin Phillis* and *Wives and Daughters* . . . Not itself [i.e. *Mary Barton*] a great novel, it is the first novel of a great novelist . . .[3]

are found. And we may already note in passing the divergent views on Mrs. Gaskell's achievement.

The change of direction—we can allow the phrase for the moment as a convenience—has itself been glossed over in rather

[1] W. R. Greg, Review of 'Mary Barton', *Edinburgh Review*, Vol. 180, April 1849, p. 434.
[2] Walter Allen, *The English Novel*, Penguin, 1958, p. 183.   [3] *Tillotson*, p. 203.

simple terms. There is no argument but that Mrs. Gaskell does have impulses that pull in different directions; *Cranford* and *Ruth* were being written at the same time, while a powerful study of the supernatural, 'The Old Nurse's Story', was also produced in the same period. Any serious consideration of her art will need to consider the pattern into which works so apparently different in content, form and method can be fitted. We need to look for the unity behind the dissimilarity. The traditional approach has been to rest it solely on some criterion such as personality or sensibility, shrugging off any necessity to look very hard with the excuse that the carriage is not worth the labour. But if Mrs. Gaskell is a novelist worthy of serious consideration this attitude is no longer possible.

Reference to *Cranford* raises a particular point within the general issue of the unity of her work. *Cranford* has undoubtedly been the most popular and the most consistently well known of all her novels, yet it is obviously of rather loose construction and is widely regarded as a series of episodes given a slenderly factitious structure though possessed of a pervasive 'tone'. A compromise view of her ability therefore develops which leads to her:

being regarded merely as a writer of social criticism in novel form, or at best as the author of *Cranford*.[4]

and the attempt to see her as a serious novelist is further bedevilled by the esteem in which one early book is held.

Changes in taste and fashion must also be taken into account. The changes in both theory and practice during the early part of the twentieth century have altered opinion about what a good novel should be, although the reaction against the wholesale acceptance of, for example, the Jamesian credo as the one and only Simon Pure is now setting in. As a result the Victorian novelists are being reassessed, and the validity of their methods can be more clearly understood. The question of taste is rather more important. After all, relatively few novel readers are much affected by rigid views of how a novel should be constructed,

[4] G. D. Klingopulos, 'The Literary Scene', *The Pelican Guide to English Literature*, 1958, Vol. 6, p. 106.

whereas individual features may well strike them as distasteful. The authorial commentary for example is a convention, and as with most conventions we can get used to it. But the religious sentiment is no longer to the public taste; we are probably embarrassed when we meet with it and so become over-conscious of it. We do not stop to ask how much there is of it, or what its purpose is, let alone attempt to acquire the taste in order to find out how it balances or enhances other flavours.

Biographical reference has also been less than helpful to Mrs. Gaskell's reputation because of the undertone so often present. What are we to expect of a writer who, we are told:

Apart from her writing . . . had a full life as the wife of a Unitarian minister in Manchester and the mother of a large family . . .[5]

Such references, intentionally or not and irrespective of factual accuracy, are pejorative. The stereotype of the moderately cultured amateur with a nostalgic affection for childhood traditions and a talent for story-telling, when she could spare the time from maternity and good works, has been since her death a hindrance to a just appreciation of her work. This attitude has been coupled with an emphasis on her femininity, especially when she has been compared to George Eliot, or to Charlotte and Emily Brontë, all of whom can be shown to be exceptional. So we get comments such as this:

In the placid dovecotes of Victorian womanhood, they were eagles.

But we have only to look at a portrait of Mrs. Gaskell, soft-eyed, beneath her charming veil, to see that she was a dove.[6]

Too much of the critical reference to Mrs. Gaskell has tended to centre itself on the biographical material and to stress disproportionately the element in her work which draws on the early Knutsford days. The Life has cast its shadow over the Work, obscuring the literary qualities by which the autobiographical element (quite as important in the work of George Eliot and the Brontës) has been transmuted into fiction.

If I seem to have stressed the superficiality of elements in the

[5] Allen, op. cit., p. 182.
[6] David Cecil, *Early Victorian Novelists*, Constable, 1935, pp. 197–8.

critical opinion that has crystallized about Mrs. Gaskell, and in doing so to have neglected unfairly those critics who have demanded a revision of that attitude, it is because the conventional view is still deeply entrenched. One more quotation may show just how strong this generalized acceptance is, and how firmly Mrs. Gaskell has been bedded into the minor league of novelists. It is taken from a leading article in *The Times Literary Supplement* (August 11th, 1961). The writer was dealing with the way in which some overseas critics have tried to prove the merits of their native literature by a comparison with accepted British authors, a method which:

took the form of asserting that Australian X was as good as English Y . . . only minor English writers could be matched—no one had the temerity to entice even Mrs. Gaskell or Swinburne into the field . . .

The 'even' speaks for itself; positions in the major and minor leagues are regarded as beyond argument. (One could wish Swinburne were alive to reply!) The mandarin rigidity of such a pronouncement is a warning of the extent to which we need to be aware of the persistent critical tradition and its influence.

The interesting thing is that her contemporaries had no difficulty from the very beginning in recognizing her artistic merit, though admittedly the conventions of fiction and the primary moral assumptions were largely shared. Thackeray's daughter, Lady Ritchie, noted that:

my own father, and Dickens, and Carlyle, and Kingsley, and all the leading critics of those days recognised her great gifts at once and with warm plaudits.[7]

W. R. Greg in the same review in which he attacked the false economics and harmful attitude of *Mary Barton* had no hesitation in beginning his article with praise for the unusually high literary merit of the anonymous author. Young Henry James, reviewing *Wives and Daughters*:

cannot help thinking the late Mrs. Gaskell has added to the number of those works of fiction—of which we cannot perhaps count more than

[7] Quoted in *Hopkins*, p. 81.

Mrs. Gaskell

a score as having been produced in our time—which will outlast the duration of their novelty and continue for years to come to be read and relished for a higher order of merit.[8]

happily unaware that his own theories would play a part in its later neglect: The collected editions of Ward and Shorter show that down to the turn of the century her quality was appreciated. Miss Hopkins does well to remind us that:

A reconsideration of Mrs. Gaskell's place among the Victorian writers of fiction which has been long overdue, would do well to give weight to Gosse's observation that *Cousin Phillis* and *Wives and Daughters* are "among the most faultlessly constructed novels in the language."[9]

We need not go all the way with Gosse, but there is certainly an era of neglect to make up for.

This summary view of the critical reputation of Mrs. Gaskell's novels will have made obvious the confusion of approach as well as the varying estimates not only of her work as a whole but of individual novels. The way out of the confusion, and towards a firmly based assessment of her achievement, can only be through a closer examination of what she actually wrote and of her methods as a novelist. Much of the preliminary work will be a clearing of the bush, but at least it will provide the chance for a clear view of the reality. The Chevalier Bunsen wrote of her, with reference to *Ruth*:

I admire the courage as much as the genius of the noble-minded authoress.[10]

The attempt must be made to reverse the terms of the proposition; to admire her genius as much as her courage.

[8] *Notes and Reviews by Henry James*, Dunster House, Cambridge, Mass., 1921, originally in *The Nation*, 22 Feb., 1866.
[9] *Hopkins*, p. 332.
[10] Quoted in Margaret J. Shaen, *Memorials of Two Sisters*, Longmans, 1908, p. 99.

CHAPTER II

The Basis for Reassessment

MISS HOPKINS concluded her biography of Mrs. Gaskell, published in 1952, with the claim that the time had come to revalue that writer's work. One response was the stimulating but one-sided article by H. P. Collins,[1] but on the whole little was changed. When Mrs. Gaskell has been mentioned, the conventional judgement and approach have carried on. One or two good comments have appeared on special aspects of her writing, or on her relation to the social background of the period.[2] A break with conventional opinion occurred with the publication of Professor Kathleen Tillotson's *Novels of the Eighteen Forties* in 1958, which contained a long criticism of *Mary Barton* based on a detailed general introduction to the literary and social conditions of the time. And here once again, implicit in that criticism, is the belief that Mrs. Gaskell's novels will repay a closer critical attention than they have so far received.

One reason for the lack of attention is undoubtedly that it is almost impossible to become excited by Mrs. Gaskell as an individual, while Miss Hopkins's biography has probably exhausted the biographical detail for a long time. The essential quietness, respectability and overt domesticity of her life leave hardly a crevice for any sensation other than moral approval to take root in; she would seem to defy even the wilder fringes of the psychoanalytical school. Most of the eminent Victorians were in the dust of public combat; Mrs. Gaskell rarely was, and then unwillingly: a good many of the Victorians have private lives which are still being disinterred; information about Mrs. Gaskell's was meticu-

---

[1] H. P. Collins, 'The Naked Sensibility', *Essays in Criticism*, Vol. 3, No. 1, Jan. 1953.
[2] e.g. Raymond Williams: *Culture and Society 1780–1950*, Penguin, 1961. See Part 1, Chap. 5.

lously destroyed (if it ever excitingly existed) by her daughters'
obedience to her wish that she wanted no biography and no papers
left hanging about. Even quiet Victorians could explode intellectual mines—who was quieter than Darwin? But Mrs. Gaskell is
highly intelligent without being intellectual and is overshadowed
in this respect by George Eliot, with whom she has a good deal
in common.

This is the accepted traditional view, repeated and reinforced
by a century of criticism, and by the fact that her best known
work is still *Cranford*. *Cranford* has to quite an extent been responsible for the picture of Mrs. Gaskell as a dealer in charm, nostalgia
and gentle humour. And the introductions to *Cranford*, as well
as the references in standard histories of the novel, or of English
Literature, add their further quota of information about Mrs.
Gaskell as the Unitarian Minister's wife, the busy mother, etc.
It is possibly unfortunate, from this point of view, that the only
private diary (printed by Clement Shorter) turned out to be a
record of the early years of her daughter Marianne.[3] Now it
would be easy enough to show briefly, as Miss Hopkins has shown
in detail, that this is an unbalanced picture. The controversies over
Mary Barton, *Ruth* and *The Life of Charlotte Brontë* (the two
latter in particular) raised dust enough. The Minister's wife was a
European traveller, the friend of the literary great of the time. She
had a will of her own to underlie the charm.

Still, if any genuine reassessment is to take place—and I am
firmly convinced that it ought to—it must begin with her work;
closer acquaintance with that will have its effect in turn on our
view of the author. And here we have to take more particular
note of two of the obstacles in the way. The first is the lack of
comment by the author herself. She is not a literary critic, not
much—in her surviving correspondence—of a self-critic. Yet
there is, if we look for it, quite a lot of indication that she thought
seriously about her work and was a conscious craftsman. The
second point is that traditional criticism has set up its conventions

[3] *My Diary*, privately printed 1923. The diary is, however, useful in explaining certain
attitudes towards children and moral development which were held by Mrs. Gaskell and
were part of the Victorian ethos.

about her work as much as about her character. The core of these
is that she was an intuitive novelist who really began writing at
a mature age (35 years—*Mary Barton* was published in 1848
when she was 38 years old) and that although she displays a great
variety of talent she doesn't really develop. She writes two or
three novels of social reform, some charming and humorous
novels of traditional small town or country life, a historical
novel, some ghost stories, some articles. But there is no development in theme, style, etc., no essential unity can be discovered.

Other writers have begun writing, or begun publishing late.
Other writers have written varied types of novel and article.
Conrad, we note, also first published at the age of thirty-eight,
wrote articles, sea stories, novels of social analysis, etc. (Admittedly Conrad had a romantic background and an exciting career, but
if ever a writer was set in his opinions and mature in his attitudes
before he published his first novel, Conrad was that man. The
nature of his development as a *novelist* is a different matter.) If
then we can point to some line of development in Mrs. Gaskell's
work, some evidence of maturing as a novelist and an observer
perhaps, or the slow discovery of an essential direction for her
thoughts and powers, we shall do two things: we shall help to
eliminate a conventional judgement and we shall demonstrate
the existence of at least one of the qualities that we expect to find
in a novelist of stature.

Development may be considered in several ways when a
novelist is being discussed. In terms of attitude there may be a
change that can be charted, or a growth of maturity—in itself a
special form of change. Intellectual powers may grow or become
more forceful, habits of analysis and depth of penetration may
increase. Along with changes of attitude and intellectual development may go changes in general or specific interests. All the
impacts of experience may play a part in modifying opinion and
belief. As far as elements of craftsmanship are concerned, development or change of style, a growing ability to manipulate structure
and to move more freely within the limits of a chosen form, these
are now standard points of reference when the art of a novelist is
under discussion. I shall choose two aspects, one broadly con-

cerned with attitude and subject matter, the other more narrowly concerned with techniques, to demonstrate that Mrs. Gaskell's work can be seen to have a unity and a development. The first concerns her attitude to society, the second her growing skill in the handling of narrative techniques.

Mrs. Gaskell is best considered, properly considered I would say, as a social novelist, but in using the term 'social novelist' I am far from thinking solely of her so-called novels of reform, those that Cazamian deals with under the title of 'L'Interventionnisme Chrétien'.[4] Mrs. Gaskell was always concerned with how people lived and the social structure that groups of them formed. Her range embraces two extremes, at one end the shifting fabric of society in the industrial England of the times, at the other end the traditional and stratified pattern of social classes which was still the accepted theory, and which existed in the country areas with little impact from industrialization. She knew both in terms of personal experience. Her childhood at Knutsford was spent in a completely stable, small country town in which every social group had its accustomed place and moved easily by custom within the social pattern. Her married life in Manchester gave her first-hand experience of the unease in society as new forces overcame caution; she was not so conscious of the political forces and economic theories as of the shift of population out of the customary social routine and of the formation of new social patterns on a large scale in which ease of communication between the sections had broken down and the sense of being part of a comfortably related whole no longer existed. The stable had given place to the unstable. We know that for her first novel she had considered, because of her 'deep relish and fond admiration for the country', writing a historical tale 'the period of which was more than a century ago, and the place on the borders of Yorkshire', but that she had turned instead to 'the romance of some of those who elbowed me daily in the busy streets of the town in which I resided.'[5] Collins has pointed out her reliance on her sensibility and her strong sympathy for human emotion and

[4] L. Cazamian, *Le Roman Social en Angleterre (1830–1850)*, Vol. 2, Didier, Paris, 1935.
[5] *Mary Barton*, p. lxxiii.

affections; the point to which I wish to draw attention is the admission, in talking of her first novel, that she felt compelled to write of what was close to her and observable. It is in this sense—of observing human beings as they behaved and felt in the social scene—that she is a social novelist, and this interest is fundamental to all her serious work. *Mary Barton*, the novel in question, is a picture of one large social group in Manchester, the mill workers. It does not try to give a comprehensive picture of Manchester society; the masters appear only as they are necessary to the plot, and the few pages devoted to their way of life—as seen in the household of the Carsons[6]—are almost a burlesque in the exaggeration that her unskilled pen produced for the sake of contrast. Other social groups are virtually absent. Though the influence of Carlyle is strong,[7] political and economic motivation is laboured by comparison with the sympathetic insight into the consequences for the individuals and the mill-hands as a class. The Chartist movement, when it is brought in, is introduced by a section that opens with a sort of newspaper cum blue-book résumé whose style is out of key with the general tenor of the novel, and interest quickly moves to:

this feeling of alienation between the different classes of society.[8]

The demand for reform legislation, so prominent in Kingsley's *Alton Locke*, is quite lacking. The rare references to reform of working conditions—Jane Wilson's accident with unfenced machinery, a comment on child labour—are introduced without comment.[9] The whole emphasis of the novel is in its account of the way of life of one class, and its feeling of insecurity and isolation. We must endorse, with certain reservations that will appear later, Professor Kathleen Tillotson's comment that:

It would be better then to remove from *Mary Barton* the old tag of 'novel with a purpose', implying social, extra-artistic purpose. It was indeed, more perhaps than any other of the time, a novel with a social *effect*, but Mrs. Gaskell wrote, then as always, not with her eye on the effect, but as one possessed with and drenched in her subject.[10]

[6] See especially Chap. 6.
[7] See *Tillotson*, especially Introductory Section 20. Further examples can be found.
[8] *Mary Barton*, p. 95.   [9] ibid., pp. 98 and 100.   [10] *Tillotson*, p. 222.

Her next novel, *Ruth*, is similarly a picture of a social group: this time with its limits slightly extended. Apart from the introductory material which introduces Ruth's background and the history of her seduction, we are confined to a cross-section of a small part of Eccleston society, the wealthy Unitarian tradesman's circle (the Bradshaw family) and the Unitarian minister's household (the Bensons). It is the *mores* and behaviour of these groups which are Mrs. Gaskell's interest, together with their relationship and the strains within each group. The conflicting standards within the Bradshaw family get considerable attention on their own. As with *Mary Barton*, other social groups get little of this detailed attention, though a fair amount of *space* is necessary for the aristocratic Bellingham because of his part in the plot. Once again we can note that he and his way of life are presented in an artificial manner; as necessary contrasts and plot devices.

While *Ruth* was being written *Cranford* was appearing in periodical form in *Household Words*.[11] At first sight *Cranford* would appear to have little in common with *Mary Barton* and *Ruth*; in fact an essential element of the three is that they are based on familiar experience of a small social group. Because of its origins and methods of publication the apparent contrast of tone and content—small country town as against industrial city; gentle humour as against melodramatic seriousness—is reinforced by the difference in form.[12] Yet what we have in the three novels is in fact an exploration of the extremes mentioned earlier; the society and standards in flux at one extreme, the society and standards in stable and traditional form at the other. Mrs. Gaskell 'brackets' her objective, which is the social group with the standards of its component smaller groups and individuals. The rest of her work is a ranging between these extremes as she develops her central interest in observing and analysing the various aspects of individual emotion and behaviour, as controlled by social custom and belief, that combine to form a unified or disorganized society. She never extends her bounds very far, but by the time her final

[11] A preliminary sketch, 'The Last Generation in England', was published in the U.S.A. in *Sartains Union Magazine*, July 1849.

[12] Although, as the series continued, Mrs. Gaskell began to develop a plot structure and narrative links.

novel, *Wives and Daughters*, is written, she is able to take as her field a complete cross-section of a small society, from the aristocratic household in the Towers to the farm-labourers of Squire Hamley. She can now operate from a central viewpoint, that of the country surgeon on good terms with all levels (Mr. Gibson and his household), taking in respectable villagers, yeoman gentility, governesses and estate agents. The range is still not very wide, but there is a confident handling of several groups within the total society and at last the feeling that symptoms of change can be absorbed by society without unsettling it unduly.

I do not wish at this stage to do more than indicate the paths which lead from *Mary Barton* and *Cranford* to *Wives and Daughters*. It is obvious that Mrs. Gaskell is convinced of the need for all members of society to have beliefs and attitudes in common; these to her are something more than glues to stick society together, they are in the nature of a life-blood circulating through the body social and preserving its organic unity. Tradition, custom, tolerance, respect for the affections and, above all, religion are the main elements which she selects from her own experience, personal tastes and acquired attitudes as primary ingredients. These prove to have a good deal in common with each other, even while they act as correctives to undue emphasis on any one particular quality. We have noted *Mary Barton* and *Cranford* as extremes respectively of the fragmented and stable societies of the period; it is apparent also that while religion is the suggested cohesive agent in *Mary Barton*, tradition and custom are emphasized in *Cranford*. The reconciliation element which has been frequently commented on as the all too obvious climax of many Gaskell plots is an inevitable outcome of this feeling for unity and human brotherhood. But having recognized these ingredients we can look briefly and more closely at the paths which lead from Knutsford and Manchester.

The line through *Cranford* is fairly clear. 'The Moorland Cottage' and 'Mr. Harrison's Confessions', immediately precede it; Mrs. Browne and Maggie in 'The Moorland Cottage' are forerunners of Mrs. Kirkpatrick and Molly Gibson in *Wives and Daughters*, the relationship of Maggie to Frank Buxton fore-

shadows that of Molly to Roger Hamley. *My Lady Ludlow* is a
large-scale and on the whole successful attempt (if one discounts
the disastrous interpolated story of the French Revolution) to show
what we may call the Cranford ethos facing up to the necessity
of change as new beliefs and attitudes infiltrate. This was a
significant advance. Another was that, whereas in *Cranford* the
life was observed and its ethos more or less left to be recognized
by the reader, in *My Lady Ludlow* an analysis of the various individual virtues which make a responsible member of society
is attempted. These are summed up—using religion as a standard
—through the eyes of three of the main characters, Mr. Horner, the
family estate steward, Lady Ludlow herself and Mr. Gray, the
new-style clergyman with a sense of personal and social (but not a
muscular-Christian) responsibility for his flock:

The answer in the Catechism that Mr. Horner was most fond of
calling upon a child to repeat, was that to, "What is thy duty towards
thy neighbour?" The answer Mr. Gray liked best to hear repeated with
unction was that to the question, "What is the inward and spiritual
grace?" The reply to which Lady Ludlow bent her head the lowest, as
we said our Catechism to her on Sundays, was to, "What is thy duty
towards God?"[13]

In the meantime *Mary Barton* had been followed by *Ruth* and
then by *North and South*, accompanied by shorter stories such as
'Libbie Marsh's Three Eras' (before *Mary Barton*) and 'Lizzie
Leigh'. All of these explored in one way or another the Manchester background, all of them contain injections of religious
didacticism. Yet the element of 'message' steadily diminishes as
the novelist of the individual and his relationships becomes more
aware of her natural bent as a social observer.

There is another probable reason for the diminution of the
'religious message' element. Although the effects of industrialization and urbanization were growing, the fear of violent upheaval
that permeated the 1840's was nearly dead. As it became obvious
that social adjustments, however distasteful, would come naturally,
so the compulsion to suggest means to mutual understanding

---

[13] *My Lady Ludlow*, p. 52.

diminished, and the capability of viewing change—and the resistance to change—with a more detached attitude became possible. It also became possible for the comic as well as the pathetic aspects of an over-rigid attitude to change to be exploited, fortunately for Mrs Gaskell's sense of humour.

The Life of Charlotte Brontë is vital in Mrs. Gaskell's development, for it forced her to concentrate on the individual, her surroundings and background in an objective manner. *My Lady Ludlow* appears after it, a novel probably written in reaction to and as a relaxation from the intense strain which the rapid production of the *Life* entailed. And we should note the reintroduction of the objective narrator, who recounts the events as a reminiscent and partly episodic biography. The effect was adventitiously helped by the controversy roused by the *Life*. After *Mary Barton* and *Ruth*, each of which had provoked comment, the *Life* was third time unlucky. Mrs Gaskell never again ventured on controversial ground, she stuck to observation and more and more allowed actions and characters to speak for themselves.

While these aspects of two different experiences of social attitudes (Knutsford and Manchester) were being developed, a third miscellaneous group of stories and articles were being produced. Discounting the more obvious pot-boilers (Dickens was a demanding editor and *Household Words* followed a well-defined 'party-line') we can see Mrs. Gaskell exploring small social situations and traditional behaviour in other areas, such as North Wales and France. She has a good deal of the zest and inquisitiveness of the sociologist and cultural anthropologist, whether discussing the *mores* of salon etiquette or the temperament of the Cumberland statesman.[14] The objectivity and interests of the social historian are rapidly becoming dominant, as is apparent in her handling of the New England witchcraft trials in 'Lois the Witch', which appeared in 1859.

There is a long gap—five years—between *My Lady Ludlow* and her next novel, *Sylvia's Lovers*, published in 1863. By now the social historian is in the ascendant. The story is set back sixty

---

[14] 'Company Manners' and 'Half a Life-time Ago' are respectively examples of each.

years, the social background carefully and skilfully depicted and though the final section contrives the religious element somewhat didactically again, this is now noticeably out of key with the tone and manner of the earlier powerful sections, and is at least partly attributable to the fact that her technique had still not finally resolved the problem of shaping a satisfactory plot conclusion. But by now she was prepared to forgo dramatic plots in her work. (Two more stories for Dickens in *All the Year Round*, which are still melodramatic, are well below her possible level and are obvious potboilers.)[15] With *Cousin Phillis* Mrs. Gaskell emerges as the detached yet sympathetic observer of the small social group whose activities—and, in terms of plot, actions— spring naturally from character and social background. The time —near contemporary—is just sufficiently distanced to avoid irrele- vant doubts about the validity of events or matters of transient interest; in settling finally for the country town and country set- ting she by-passes the more immediate political and economic problems of industrial change. Yet she can use the advent of the railway as the medium for hinting at change and, more impor- tantly, for bringing in a 'modern' character—the engineer Holds- worth—as the disruptive element dropped among the more con- servative, more strongly principled Holman family. Within this narrow compass, and with a native love of the background she describes, she can dispense with melodrama while watching the acutely observed reactions of the small group.

The ground is prepared for *Wives and Daughters*, the extension to a large-scale work of this type of observation. The setting is now finally chosen, country rather than town, but with the out- side world moving in and beginning to modify the local world of the Hollingford inhabitants. The Cranford type is represented, but is only a part—an eccentric, respected and loved but slightly absurd part—of the community. The aristocracy of the Towers has both the paternal outlook of Lady Ludlow in the parents, and the modern awareness of contemporary life represented by their

[15] 'A Dark Night's Work' and 'Crowley Castle'. Mrs. Gaskell by this time was placating Dickens with occasional stories and reserving her good writing for the *Cornhill*, which allowed a free hand in composition and content.

children. The industrial world of Manchester exists only as a hint; it was impossible to regard it with the detachment necessary for the social observer but the experience gained in depicting its social groups and their interactions was used. The result is a fully conceived and executed study of a small society. Society is changing, for the surgeon's daughter will marry the squire's son, who is a scientist and a friend of the heir to The Towers, and she is herself on friendly and unpatronized, if not familiar, terms with the daughter of The Towers. The new generation is moving up behind the old, but not pushing it, not disturbing the essential stability of the social fabric or the principles which maintain it, only accepting the elements of change and weaving them into the tradition. And with this achieved ability to observe and analyse in a detached manner, the need to proselytize for religion has also disappeared. Change is to be expected, but fear for ultimate social stability has gone; the ironic as well as the sympathetic viewpoint is possible.

The development of a novelist is just as much a matter of the growth of artistic control and powers and methods of expression as it is of the growth of imaginative insight and self-knowledge, or the gradual clarifying of aims and themes. Mrs. Gaskell was a fluent writer and natural story-teller from the beginning, but she began as an uncertain novelist. Much of the discussion about the gradual realization of her true bent and interests, and of her development to the mature social novelist of *Wives and Daughters*, has implied a necessary, parallel, artistic development.

As far as style is concerned, Mrs. Gaskell had the natural gift of narrative ease and fluency—perhaps too much fluency. Her letters and her predilection for Mme. de Sévigny can be produced in evidence. But she had also an ear for speech rhythms and a genuine interest in problems of narration. 'They knew,' she says of Mme. de Sablé's friends:

They knew how to narrate, too. Very simple, say you? I say, no! I believe the art of telling a story is born with some people, and these have it to perfection; but all might acquire some expertness in it, and ought to do so, before launching out into the muddled, complex, hesitating, broken, disjointed, poor, bald, accounts of events which

have neither unity, nor colour, nor life, nor end in them, that one sometimes hears.[16]

Comments on the use of language abound in her stories—'if I
live in a factory town,' says Margaret Hale, 'I must speak factory
language when I want it.'[17] And of course *Mary Barton* is an early
experiment in the serious use of dialect. A certain facility and
abundant flow were never quite controlled, though she improved greatly.[18] The experienced novelist's sense of taste—for the
correct nuance, the correct detail—was slower in coming; there
are unfortunate lapses, particularly in the areas of pathos and
passion, until very late in her career.

The control of a plot structure is in evidence from the beginning, but with a taste for melodrama and showing the influences
of many conventions jumbled together. The shift to more precisely
controlled and detailed character motivation, along with a concentration of the story line round fewer and more closely
integrated sub-plots that have a direct bearing on the social theme,
is another aspect of development. Mrs. Gaskell had also to learn
to make her skill in narrating an episode subserve the needs of the
novel as a whole; I have already mentioned the digression in *My
Lady Ludlow*.

The most important development is probably in the gradual
shift away from the use of authorial commentary. Recent critical
works on Victorian novelists have drawn attention to the use and
importance of this method in Victorian fiction. Mrs. Gaskell,
when writing *Mary Barton*, accepted and used the convention to
the full to expound her views about social and individual understanding as well as for narrative links, character analysis, and
comment on action and emotion. But this method is unsuitable
to the presentation of a community through the behaviour and
speech of its members, particularly if behaviour and speech are
themselves to carry ironic implications. She was by nature a

---

[16] 'Company Manners', *Ruth*, p. 508.   [17] *North and South*, p. 281.
[18] The MSS. of Mrs. Gaskell that I have seen have all been remarkably clean and appear
to have been written with an extraordinarily steady flow. It is possible that these were fair
copies, but the MS. letters show the same fluency and command of detail, the same absence
of correction or second thoughts.

descriptive writer, describing places and people, the society in its setting; she concentrates more and more on letting the scene and its occupants speak for themselves, and on absorbing herself in the subject. The attempt to persuade, guide and influence her readers went against the grain of her natural abilities. She writes to Norton in 1858:

I *can* not (it is not *will* not) write at all if I ever think of my readers, & what impression I am making on them. 'If they don't like me, they must *lump* me' to use a Lancashire proverb. It is from no despising my readers. I am sure I don't do that, but if I ever let the thought or consciousness of them come between me & my subject I *could* not write at all.[19]

Authorial commentary demands, or is a product of, continual thinking about one's readers. Thackeray is an example. While writing the earlier 'novels with a purpose' Mrs. Gaskell had felt that it was necessary to explain both the background and her views about it, but this direct injection of a personal comment into the narrative was, I have suggested, unsatisfactory. Her real interest as a novelist was in the individuals and their background; the humanitarian gloss on them led on to lack of balance, particularly where it gave openings for the author's sensitivity to the emotional and the pathetic.

In *Cranford*, however, written for personal pleasure and to suit her own interests, such commentary is almost totally absent. Instead the device of the narrator/character speaking from within the scene is successfully employed and the society of Amazons is left to present itself, which it does very well as Mrs. Gaskell is thoroughly at home in its idioms and customs. Another device used in some of the shorter stories is to begin with the narrator describing a setting she knows, and then going on to recount a tale about the place; this method again allows of impartiality and knowledge, though more liable to the occasional intrusion of authorial comment.[20] The short stories, mediocre as some of them are, are further important because in them Mrs. Gaskell is able to

---

[19] *Letters*, p. 20, 10 May 1858.
[20] e.g. 'The Well of Pen Morfa', 'The Doom of the Griffiths'.

forget herself in the process of writing up an exciting or moving
episode; the practice obtained over several years was valuable.

By the time that *Sylvia's Lovers* was written, the author as
personal commentator, as distinct from the author as narrator,
has more or less vanished from the scene, taking with her much
of the pious and sentimental comment that modern taste finds
unpalatable. Not all of it goes; even if the duty of bearing witness
to God in public has now given place to the novelist's sense that it
would 'come between me and my subject' there is still an element
of explanation which the sociological spirit of Mrs. Gaskell is
impelled to favour. Comparison between past and present can
still bring her on to the stage with her pointer:

In looking back to the last century, it appears curious to see how little
our ancestors had the power of putting two things together, and
perceiving either the discord or harmony thus produced. Is it because
we are farther off from those times, and have, consequently, a greater
range of vision? Will our descendants have a wonder about us, such
as we have about the inconsistency of our forefathers, or a surprise at
our blindness . . .? It is well for us that we live at the present time, when
everybody is logical and consistent.[21]

I have quoted the passage at some length for two reasons. In the
first place it shows that the author is now appearing in person
because the central theme—social contrast and individual contrast—is at issue. The second reason is that the author is taking her
role as commentator less gravely; irony is contained in the body of
comment while the conclusion turns the ironic gaze on to the
present as well as the past. Mrs. Gaskell the novelist and ironical
observer (she has not the sustained intensity of satire of a Jane
Austen to qualify as a social satirist)—the essential Mrs. Gaskell
of the novels, I have suggested—has moved into what is left of
the commentator's chair.

The author as omniscient narrator remains; Henry James was
old enough to review *Wives and Daughters* favourably but the
Jamesian revolution was still to come. Yet even this narrator is
far more retiring than in earlier novels; dialogue, internal thought

21 *Sylvia's Lovers*, pp. 71–2.

and direct description have assumed far more importance; the story is carried along by the actions and comments of the people in it. Moral points and attitudes are now voiced by individuals; we are left to judge them by our knowledge of the character.

The process is in fact a continuous one from *Mary Barton* onwards; the development of control of structure grows along with concentration on the story itself and on its characters as vehicles of the author's attitude to replace the author's personal intrusion. And though one hesitates to talk about 'point of view' at what is still an early stage in the development of the novel, there can be little doubt, from the internal narrative method of *Cranford* and the 'defined narrator' method of some of the other stories, that Mrs. Gaskell was aware of the problem of narration. It was solved easily enough in the short story or episode, the three-volume novel demanded more handling.

The story of the origin of Mrs. Gaskell's first novel is well enough known—that her husband suggested that she write something to take her mind off the death of their only son when still a baby. The suggestion was made to a natural story-teller; the first novel led to many others. It took Mrs. Gaskell time to bring into focus the things she really wanted to write about; yet having something she wanted to write about, she developed her technique as she sharpened the focus and discarded elements which, however important to her as a sincerely religious and humane woman, were irrelevant finally to her as a novelist, or could not be introduced in the raw state without upsetting the balance of the total novel. The necessary attitudes and opinions were absorbed into the characters of the books until she was able to stand aside and, having selected her central character, work through her to reflect the surrounding social scene. Form and content develop together. In *Mary Barton*, Mary is often considerably off-centre. Manchester is presented to us separately much of the time. By the time *Wives and Daughters* is written we have a heroine—Molly Gibson—who is squarely and alertly at the centre; Hollingford and its characters emerge through her eyes and standards, yet distinct in their individual variation.

Joyce Cary says of art in general that:

the work of art as completely realised is the result of a long and complex process of exploration, as well as construction.

and later adds that:

novelists discover new aspects of their theme, and also new limitations of their technique, as they work.[22]

The exploration of theme and technique go together. Where there is little or no exploration of theme, it is possible for a writer still to refine his technique, but I doubt whether it is in any way possible for technique to stand still while the 'complex process of exploration' of theme is carried on. Criticism of Mrs. Gaskell in the past has largely neglected to consider her technical artistry, and in neglecting it has ignored also a good deal that would give more insight into her aims and themes. Certainly the nature of her achievement has not yet been evaluated. There is evidence for believing that the view, still widely held, that she is an intuitive novelist, relying on her natural insight and a natural gift for storytelling, is a very mistaken one.

[22] Joyce Cary, *Art and Reality*, C.U.P., 1958, pp. 86–7.

CHAPTER III

Religion and Purpose

IN order to understand what a writer of fiction is achieving, or failing to achieve, it is necessary to grasp clearly the nature of the elements which go to make up the 'world' of his novels. It is related to reality yet not a copy of it; as Warren puts it:

The great novelists all have such a world—recognizable as overlapping the empirical world but distinct in its self-coherent intelligibility.[1]

This world may be, as Warren goes on to point out, pre-eminently physical or spiritual; Hardy's Wessex or Graham Greene land; its characteristic is a quality which distinguishes the whole of a writer's output (or all that is important). We might add that the social world may also deserve recognition as a separate element. It is a useful starting point to realize that any novelist worth considering will impress us at one and the same time with the general validity of the standards of his world, and the individual nature of it as represented through viewpoint and the process of selection. We recognize common elements in the worlds of Thackeray and Dickens without ever confusing the two, for the contemporary empirical world is firmly shaped by the viewpoint and art of each. We need further to bear in mind that some elements of the past which have been blurred to recent critical vision by prejudice or ignorance may come to be seen more clearly as changes occur in awareness and taste. This is indeed what has been happening with the Victorian novelists; a redefinition of their empirical world is under way, with consequent adjustments to the distinct worlds of the novelists who interpret it. The redefinition embraces artistic methods and moral values.

[1] R. Wellek and A. Warren, *Theory of Literature*, Harvest Books, New York, 1960 p. 203.

It becomes necessary then to see whether such a world is discoverable in Mrs. Gaskell's novels; a world in part shared with her fellow Victorians, in part shared only with those of her immediate society and background, and given a distinctive quality by her individual feelings, attitudes and talents.

The most superficial reading of her work shows that regional, social, and spiritual interests are each important, and we need to be clear about the nature of these. But we must also note that the balance and treatment of such interests alter, and that in the course of her career this shift of emphasis affects the nature of her work as has already been suggested in general terms. For our purpose it will suffice to examine in some detail certain of the key elements which throw light on her development as a novelist and which can be accepted as important enough—not merely in her work but in terms of general interest—to be of major significance for any reassessment. While pursuing this aim we should not forget, as strong presumptive evidence in her favour, the point made by Dr. Johnson in his *Preface to Shakespeare*:

To works, however, of which the excellence is not absolute and definite, but gradual and comparative; to works not raised upon principles demonstrative and scientifick, but appealing wholly to observation and experience, no other test can be applied than length of duration and continuance of esteem.[2]

Before discussing the use which Mrs. Gaskell makes, as a novelist, of religion, it is necessary to know just what the term 'religion' means as far as her novels are concerned. There are two possible meanings concealed in it, each controlled by a number of factors:

(a) There is the precise nature of the faith held by the individual (which may in itself be a personal interpretation of an accepted body of belief), distinguishing it from other current faiths or overlapping with them.

(b) There is the field of influence or behaviour covered by the term, i.e. the extent to which religion is not confined to the notion of a specific faith but subsumes areas of morals, ethics, etc.

[2] Walter Raleigh, *Johnson on Shakespeare*, O.U.P., 1931, p. 9.

The distinction is not always easy to make, and about as difficult as it can be in Mrs. Gaskell's case. She was a Unitarian, and Unitarianism is about as undogmatic a religion as Christianity allows, one which places its emphasis largely on ethics and conduct. At least, this was so of the leading Unitarians of the time when Mrs. Gaskell lived, and of the circle she moved in; it is this religion that I shall discuss, not the narrower, more fanatical versions that have also been seen.

It is extraordinarily difficult to give any precise definition of Unitarianism in the nineteenth century. As Holt points out, 'The older Unitarians prided themselves on being unsectarian and having no creed. The opening number of their weekly periodical *The Inquirer* stated this point of view quite clearly in 1842.'[3] As its name implies, a belief in the unipersonality of the Godhead instead of the Trinity, and in Socinianism (a denial of Christ's divinity) were in the tradition of its foundation, but the old-established English congregations had moved away from any doctrinal emphasis.

The importance of faith in God, the appeal to the individual heart and judgement, the ignoring of official elements, all show its roots to be in the nonconformist tradition. Its lack of sectarian bile is striking. Its great reliance on the Bible will become obvious when the novels are discussed, and the Bible's importance as providing an ethic and a code of conduct is fundamental.

In a sermon published a few years after his marriage, the Rev. William Gaskell preached against intolerance by Protestant theologians, and defended Unitarianism on the principle of liberty of interpretation of the Scriptures and on the grounds that no man can claim infallibility for his views. He sets out the task which he sees:

As liberal Christians, I should say, that the work to which we are more immediately called is . . . in labouring to bring them [our Protestant Brethren] to a fuller recognition of the great fundamental principles in which we all profess to be agreed.[4]

[3] Raymond V. Holt, *The Unitarian Contribution to Social Progress in England*, Allen and Unwin, 1938, p. 339.
[4] *Protestant Practices Inconsistent with Protestant Principles*, R. Hunter, St. Paul's Churchyard, 1836, p. 8. The term 'liberal' to mean free from prejudice was current. (See *O.E.D.*)

and his view of the Gospel is that:

It is simply the highest teacher of humanity.[5]

In a later sermon he argues that one cannot accept any particular view as correct. As a Unitarian he is not prepared to accept all bible interpretation as merely speculative, although he does not deny that good may exist outside of his own beliefs. His point is that error induces deterioration, and that errors of belief are bound finally to lead to errors of conduct.[6] In a still later sermon, with a title suggestive for a later stage of my argument, *Unitarians Called to Bear Witness to the Truth*,[7] while reaffirming his view that errors of interpretation need to be fought against, he points out that intelligent artisans reject stupid orthodoxy and religion altogether because of it. He then goes on to attack the popular interpretations which present a religion based on fear:

It is a thing of gloom and terror, not of light and love; that which is kept in view as a last resource, rather than cherished as a constant presence of comfort and joy.[8]

The relevance of these comments to Mrs. Gaskell's work will be seen to be obvious. Their importance is twofold; they represent the official Unitarian view put by one of the leading Unitarian authorities, and they are at the same time the views of a husband who was also an adviser and critic for at least the earlier novels. Mrs. Gaskell was a Unitarian by birth and upbringing; these would have been views that she accepted. At the moment we can note certain points. These are briefly the playing down of sectarian differences and the stressing of general Christian principles; the importance of the Bible as the source of truth; the relation of belief to conduct; the stress on comfort and love as the chief attributes. The shrewd comment on 'the intelligent artisan' is more of a special reference to the Manchester experience, but it does denote a view that one's religion should be rationally as well as emotionally satisfying, its reasonableness residing in its connection with common sense and normally accepted decent

[5] ibid., p. 19.
[6] *Some Evil Tendencies of the Popular Theology*, West Riding Tracts, 1847.
[7] Published by Edward T. Whitfield, Strand, 1862.   [8] ibid., p. 13.

behaviour and feeling, not in intellectual subtleties or dogma. 'One God, no Hell and twenty shillings in the Pound,' as it was later summed up,[9] or as Darwin's grandfather had contemptuously called it, 'A feather-bed to catch a falling Christian'.[10]

It must be added that Unitarianism was very far removed socially from the conventicles and bethels of Dissent. It was, when Mrs. Gaskell knew it, a religion rooted in a tradition that was partly Anglican, worshipping in churches that were often as venerable as many of the local Anglican ones. Its membership inclined to the solid middle-class or wealthier upper-class; manufacturers and professional men with some pretensions to taste and culture (the Wedgewoods, Darwins, Turners and Hollands were connected by marriages; Mrs. Gaskell's mother was a Holland), and such people mixed easily with the accepted social world at this level. There were poor Unitarians, as there were poor Anglicans, ministers and congregations; the modest circumstances of Mr. Benson are reputedly copied from those of the Newcastle minister, Mr. Turner, with whom Mrs. Gaskell had stayed,[11] but by and large her own experience of it was as a traditional and comfortable world. In Manchester itself the Unitarians were socially and culturally in the leading stratum, while the intellectual and independent quality of Unitarian training and teaching was well known. It is not badly summed up by J. A. Froude when he calls it 'that latest form of orthodoxy'.[12] There was nothing in this background to tempt towards thoughts of radically reforming the social or governmental structure—the Christian Socialism of Kingsley's novels is far more outspoken—or to the type of satire directed by social or political animus. Mrs. Gaskell was of the ruling party, at least in her realm of Manchester, nor

[9] Quoted in R. H. Mottram, *Portrait of an Unknown Victorian*, Hale, 1936, p. 269.

[10] Francis Darwin, *The Autobiography of Charles Darwin*, Dover (N.Y.), 1958, p. 213. For fuller accounts of Unitarian doctrine in the nineteenth century see K. Scott Latourette, *Christianity in a Revolutionary Age*, Vol. 2, Chap. 28, Eyre and Spottiswoode, 1960; L. E. Elliott-Binns, *Religion in the Victorian Era*, Lutterworth Press, 2nd Ed., 1946; and S. C. Carpenter, *Church and People 1789–1889*, Vol. 3, S.P.C.K. Seraph Books, 1959. Articles in the *Oxford Dictionary of the Christian Church*, and the major Encyclopaedias are also useful. The impact of rationalism and biblical scholarship came too late to affect Mrs. Gaskell's version of Unitarianism.

[11] *Chadwick*, p. 103.

[12] W. H. Dunn, *James Anthony Froude: A Biography 1818-1876*, O.U.P., 1961, p. 99.

was there any residue of bitterness from childhood or youth to
be worked out of her system. We find instead that religion is
regarded as a conciliating and stabilizing force, teaching acqui-
escence and patient endurance as well as a sense of human rights
in matters of industrial and social conditions (though there is a
growing realization, especially in the field of personal emotions
that occupies her more and more, that cause and effect do not
operate so demonstrably as the neat solutions of the earlier novels
would suggest). Carlyle was an influence in her early work and
Carlyle's broad unsectarian outlook did not clash with the tolerance of her own views.

Before going further we can place Mrs. Gaskell in her contemporary world. Behind the individual religion lies the general
body of Victorian religiousness. Sectarian distinctions and
squabbles merge into a larger whole of:

the immensity of the effort made in the middle of the century by
religious Englishmen from every Church, Dissenting Protestant, Roman
Catholic and Church of England, to evangelize and civilize those who
seemed to have been deprived of the Christian message by the growth
of the population, by the results of the wandering of the people or the
failures of the previous centuries.[13]

We are apt in thinking of Victorian England to recall, whether
approvingly or not, its religious ambience; or at least to recall the
'honest doubt' that troubled the mind of Clough and raged more
hectically into the controversies of the time. But the religious
census of 1851 showed statistically what many observers already
knew from experience, that nearly half the population of England
had little or no contact with religion at all.[14] The urban areas
were particularly notorious. Disraeli's account of the see of the
'Bishop of Wodgate' where:

No church there has yet raised its spire; and, as if the jealous spirit of

[13] G. Kitson Clark, *The Making of Victorian England*, Methuen, 1962, p. 176. To these
factors we can add intellectual doubts from various causes, leading to attitudes ranging
from Latitudinarianism to Atheism. Causes and attitudes are both to be found in Mrs.
Gaskell's work.
[14] ibid., p. 149 and notes. A detailed analysis can be found in Elliott-Binns, op cit.

Woden still haunted his ancient temple, even the conventicle scarcely dares show its humble front in some obscure corner.[15]

is echoed in Dickens's picture of a Coketown where the inhabitants

lounged listlessly, gazing at all the church and chapel going as a thing with which they had no manner of concern.[16]

The knowledge that much of England's population was more in need of the light than the so-called heathen added urgency to a general religious revival already given momentum by such forces as the Evangelical and Tractarian movements. And it united with the goadings of a tender and rapidly developing moral and social public conscience.

It is against this background that a good deal of Mrs. Gaskell's work has to be seen. Even without considering what niceties of character and shades of belief prompted her to speak out—and she was a shy woman where making public statements was concerned[17]— we can see her as adding her contribution to the growing volume of protest about the condition of England. The question is, what particular aspect of the condition was she hoping to treat? The social or the religious?

The answer must be, I think, the religious. It would be futile to claim that she was unaware of the social problem in Manchester, just as it is important to bear in mind that religious, moral and social movements formed part of one larger movement in which the energies of all three united. To write about Manchester, for anyone possessed of a conscience and a sense of responsibility—let alone someone strongly influenced by Carlyle—meant inevitably writing about conditions in Manchester. My argument is that Mrs. Gaskell began writing with an awareness of the need to bring religion actively and purposefully into the lives of those who either lacked it or had been led to doubt it, or who only superficially professed it. The importance of religion could be dramatized in terms of a conflict that did in fact exist, between workers and employers; though the normally stated terms of the conflict

[15] B. Disraeli, *Sybil*, Penguin, 1954, p. 162.
[16] Charles Dickens, *Hard Times*, O.U.P., 1955, p. 23.
[17] See the letters to F. J. Furnival quoted on p. 241.

were social and industrial. Mrs. Gaskell knew by experience quite enough about the conflict and its local setting to recognize a mass of material ready made for transformation into a novel. But her emphasis is on the need for religion, not for social reform; she sees the latter as one desirable outcome of the former when she begins to write. The essential change, in other words, has to be made in the souls and hearts of individuals.

The short preface to her first novel, *Mary Barton*, makes two main points. The first is that conditions of life in Manchester created bitterness between suffering workers and prosperous employers. The second is the need to do something to lessen the feeling of isolation that the workers felt. She concludes her comments on the first point by stating that:

> It is enough to say, that this belief of the injustice and unkindness which they [the workers] endure from their fellow-creatures taints what might be resignation to God's will, and turns it to revenge in many of the poor uneducated factory-workers of Manchester.[18]

Having thus made her point that religion is in danger (and that society is being endangered because of it; the final paragraph of the Preface refers to the 1848 revolutions) she briefly gives her suggestions on how to improve matters. But the matters she wishes to improve have little to do with the basic causes of the suffering. Her attitude in the Preface, and the novel bears it out, is that the greatest suffering is the sense of isolation, the feeling that nobody cares:

> the agony of suffering without the sympathy of the happy, or of erroneously believing that such is the case.[19]

Consequently the remedy she proposes is to show the sufferers that people do care, and to try by public and private effort:

> to disabuse the workpeople of so miserable a misapprehension.[20]

In this sense *Mary Barton* originated as a moral deed, as the earnestly careful style of the Preface underlines. It was a task peculiarly suited to Mrs. Gaskell's sensitivity to individual feeling

---

[18] *Mary Barton*, pp. lxxiii–lxxiv.　　　[19] ibid., p. lxxiv.　　　[20] ibid., p. 8.

and to the social nuances of the classes she knew. What she failed to realize at the time was that the moral duty, genuinely felt though it was, acted as a cloak in which the creative urge could assert itself. Part of the history of her development as a novelist lies in her reluctance to discard the shelter of the cloak.

The concern for a stable society and sympathy between 'fellow creatures'—the phrase 'resignation to God's will' is appallingly informative—is what governs the emotional slant of the novel, and religion is the operating agent suggested. Barton's first outburst leads up to the comparison that:

we are to live as separate as if we were in two worlds; ay, as separate as Dives and Lazarus . . .

putting the social grudge in biblical terms. The comparison is continued when Wilson waits at Carson's door for help, the poor man waiting for the crumbs of comfort, and the direct reference is repeated after Barton's return from the abortive Chartist march in London, 'Still at the old parable of Dives and Lazarus!'[21]

The main story in *Mary Barton* is that of the honest, proud and intelligent working man so embittered by circumstances and lack of sympathy that he finally murders a mill-owner's son as an act of representative vengeance. In growing embittered he becomes as a natural consequence more isolated in his community; both humanity and faith lose their power to guide him. Mary Barton, his daughter, really loves Jem Wilson, who is arrested after having threatened the murdered man for trying to seduce Mary, and it is her efforts that produce the melodramatic last-minute evidence that saves him. John Barton, sick from self-imposed hardship and the pangs of hunger and conscience realizes how mistaken his attitude has been, and in a chapter fittingly (in later editions) entitled 'Forgive us our Trespasses' dies in the arms of the murdered man's father while Mary prays with them. Various subplots and sub-themes are worked into the fabric of the story.

[21] *Mary Barton*, p. 112. The 'Dives and Lazarus' treatment of the distinction between rich and poor is carried through the novel; see notably pp. 195 and 425. Disraeli's phrase 'the Two Nations' probably fathered the 'two worlds', though *Sybil* does not appear to have been an influence on *Mary Barton*.

These include a number of exemplary histories; those of Barton's sister-in-law Esther who is led by vanity through seduction into prostitution, of old Alice Wilson who keeps her simple faith and love in the hardest conditions, of her sailor nephew Will who falls in love with Margaret, Job Legh's niece, herself going blind but retaining her courage and hope. And constantly present as an essential setting for the characters and the complicated plot is Manchester, Carlyle's 'Sooty Manchester . . . built on the infinite Abysses;'[22] or in her own paraphrase:

Ugly, smoky Manchester; dear, busy, earnest, noble-working Manchester . . . where God had cast their lives, and told them to work out their destiny.[23]

Organized religion does not exist in this world, is so remote that it does not even warrant comment. Although the characters are shown as living at times in such conditions that 'they only wanted a Dante to record their sufferings',[24] no priest or minister is ever mentioned. The very rare references to churches show that they exist vaguely in the background as buildings, but not as a force. A church clock strikes, the 'Oud Church' is used as a concert-hall or for getting married, the statement that a minor character has been to church turns out to be a method of drawing attention to the time scheme.[25] Only once in the whole book is religion linked to formal worship in any way. That is when old Alice is dying and her memory wanders back to childhood, far away from Manchester:

with old scraps of ballads, or old snatches of primitive versions of the Psalms (such as are sung in country churches half draperied over with ivy, and where the running brook, or the murmuring wind among the

---

[22] *Past and Present*, Book 3, Chap. 15, Chapman and Hall, 1905, p. 196. The whole chapter is an outburst against the confusion of religion with creed, and for that matter with reform. The comment, 'Fancy a man, moreover, recommending his fellow men to believe in God . . . that the Manchester Operative be got to spin peaceably!' must have given Mrs. Gaskell pause.

[23] 'Libbie Marsh's Three Eras', *Mary Barton*, p. 477.

[24] The reference is an echo of Carlyle's reference to the story of Ugolino in the proem to *Past and Present*. Pp. 94–6 of *Mary Barton* which deal with the depression period of 1839–41 owe a debt to the account in the proem of conditions in Stockport.

[25] *Mary Barton*. The page references are to 150, 53, 100 and 315 respectively.

trees, makes fit accompaniment to the chorus of human voices uttering praise and thanksgiving to their God) . . .[26]

Simpler times, rural communities, a natural life in natural surroundings, these are the suggested conditions in which a church could embody the religion of those who lived around it. Urban Manchester had no connexion with nature or with natural life, there was little enough to offer praise or thanksgiving for. But the impulse to religion, the true feeling in the individual heart, could still exist even though organized religion had by implication nothing to offer save its necessary conventions for marriage and death. Just as the opening chapter shows the impulse to get out into the country as being still a strong one, so that:

the artisan, deafened with the noise of tongues and engines, may come to listen awhile to the delicious sounds of rural life.[27]

so the purpose of the novel is to show that religion has a similar freshness and goodness to offer in the conditions of industrial life. It is the simplest essence of Christianity, the love of man for man within the love of God, that controls the feeling behind *Mary Barton*. It is expressed by Mrs. Wilson as she comforts Mary after her father's death; the cadences and echoes of the Bible adding force and authority to the personal statement:

Thou'rt not alone; so donnot take on so. I'll say nought of Him who's above, for thou knowest He is ever the orphan's friend; but think on Jem! nay, Mary, dear, think on me! I'm but a frabbit woman at times, but I've a heart within me through all my temper, and thou shalt be as a daughter henceforward, as mine own ewe-lamb. Jem shall not love thee better in his way, than I will in mine; and thou'lt bear with my turns, Mary, knowing that in my soul God sees the love that shall ever be thine, if thou'lt take me for thy mother, and speak no more of being alone.

To which the author adds her own comment:

Mrs. Wilson was weeping herself long before she had ended this speech, which was so different to all she had planned to say, and from

[26] *Mary Barton*, p. 312. The description is of the Unitarian chapel in Knutsford. The influence of Knutsford recollections will be dealt with separately.
[27] ibid., p. 2.

all the formal piety she had laid in store for the visit; for this was heart's piety, and needed no garnish of texts to make it true religion, pure and undefiled.[28]

The primary appeal of religion is then through the 'heart's piety', in itself surely a verbal echo of Wordsworth's 'natural piety' and a reminder that the Wordsworthian ethos, as interpreted by the Victorians, is an influence to be reckoned along with that of Carlyle.[29]

It is important to note that in this, her first novel, the basic assumption of an inherent goodness in humanity that can be given direction and fortified by faith is the major principle. The theme that faith provides individual support and a sure guidance permeates *Mary Barton*. Davenport, the workman whose death from fever and starvation is made the peg for one of Mrs. Gaskell's most vivid descriptions of the horrifying conditions in which so many families lived, is shown as supported by his faith. Wilson recalls a letter Davenport wrote home when looking for work:

It were as good as Bible-words; Ne'er a word o' repining; a' about God being our Father, and that we mun bear patiently whate'er He sends.[30]

and this reliance on God, with its accompanying duty to accept affliction and help others, is illustrated constantly throughout the novel as well as being reinforced by authorial comment.

But the crucial issue is John Barton's own loss of faith as he sees the disparity between the Christian ethic of common humanity and the daily facts of human selfishness and contrasting conditions:

John Barton's overpowering thought, which was to work out his fate on earth, was rich and poor; why are they so separate, so distinct,

[28] ibid., p. 439.
[29] This influence is examined in Humphry House's 'Wordsworth's Fame', *English Critical Essays, Twentieth Century, Second Series*, O.U.P., 1958. Carlyle is influenced by Wordsworth, as Basil Willey shows in his *Nineteenth Century Studies*, Chatto and Windus, 1949. Mrs. Gaskell was widely read in the Romantics and she quotes from Wordsworth. The descriptive influence is more immediately obvious, but compare her story 'The Crooked Branch' with Wordsworth's 'Michael' for a direct debt in theme and to some extent plot.
[30] *Mary Barton*, p. 72.

when God has made them all? It is not His will that their interests are so far apart. Whose doing is it?[31]

This comment receives its gloss in Barton's dying words:

At last I gave it up in despair, trying to make folks' actions square wi' th' Bible; and I thought I'd no longer labour at following th' Bible mysel. I've said all this afore, maybe. But from that time I've dropped down, down—down.[32]

What we have been reading, in other words, is the history of a man who in discarding his religion discarded the rules of conduct and sense of purpose which had sustained him in an otherwise grim environment where natural goodness and love for one's fellows were submerged in the struggle for existence, reducing man to the level of Tennyson's:

> dragons of the prime
> That tare each other in their slime.

As Mrs. Gaskell remarked, anticipating Hardy's memorable comment on the fate of Tess:

Oh, Orestes! you would have made a very tolerable Christian of the nineteenth century.[33]

Faith begets conduct but faith stands first. It is clear that in her first book Mrs. Gaskell was concerned with the importance of faith; not of any particular faith but of faith itself, and with its genuine lodgement in the individual heart rather than in its apparent manifestation through church attendance or religious authority. Faith equated with Christianity of some sort, faith in God implied acknowledging the spirit of Christianity. When Carson, father of the murdered man, imputes Barton's loss of faith to his being an Owenite, Job Legh ridicules the idea. The masters pay too much attention to sterile facts and not enough to Christianity:

Now, to my thinking, them that is strong in any of God's gifts is meant to help the weak,—be hanged to facts![34]

The author's own conclusion, in which she draws the moral that many of the current reforms in Manchester sprang from the new

[31] *Mary Barton*, p. 195.   [32] ibid., p. 431.   [33] ibid., p. 247.   [34] ibid., p. 448.

attitude in Carson after his talk with Legh, is a straight summary
of the argument as it affected the mill-owner:

that the truth might be recognised that the interests of one were the
interests of all, and, as such, required the consideration and deliberation
of all; that hence it was most desirable to have educated workers,
capable of judging, not mere machines of ignorant men; and to have
them bound to their employers by the ties of respect and affection, not
by mere money bargains alone; in short, to acknowledge the Spirit of
Christ as the regulating law between both parties.[35]

The judicious use of Benthamite commonplace to propound the
Christian message does not disguise that Christianity is the all-
important factor, but is worth noting as supporting the view that
'the interest of all' is best served by following the 'regulating law'
of Christianity. As Professor Kathleen Tillotson points out, 'the
hope of betterment lies not in this or that reform, but in the persistence, against all odds, of humanheartedness'. But it is not
quite, as she goes on to suggest, 'as simple, and as remote from
"political economy" as that'.[36] Mrs. Gaskell is shrewd enough
(and probably employer enough) to see that she can strengthen
her argument by suggesting that one of the end-products will be
better relations with better work, just as she is Christian enough
to reject the idea that suffering is necessarily a good incentive to
religion. She realizes that humanheartedness itself needs support
if it is to persist.

Her aim and method place her at the outset fairly in the stream
of evangelicalism, in its broad, non-sectarian sense. It is in this
light that she is to be seen as one of the voices of the moral conscience of mid-Victorian England; recognizing the connexion between the reform of men's hearts and their conditions, but in-
sisting with the conviction born of faith that the soul is more important than the reason for beginning the task. She brings to the
task all that was best in the Unitarian conscience that was at
its influential and confident prime in mid-nineteenth century
England.

Sectarian attitudes have no part in Mrs. Gaskell's work. The
most religious character in *Mary Barton* is Alice Wilson, who is

[35] *Mary Barton*, p. 451.   [36] *Tillotson*, p. 212.

Church of England; more important perhaps is the fact that the novel has no stated representative of nonconformity in it. It is true that in her next novel, *Ruth*,[37] the 'hero' and the one who sets the standard is a Dissenting minister, Thurstan Benson, who with his sister, Faith Benson, presents us with the example of the Christian in action. But the Pharisee of the story, the rich merchant Bradshaw, is also a Dissenter, while Ruth herself is the grand-daughter of a poor curate in Norfolk. If it is a fair presumption that she adopts the religion of her rescuer when she is taken into the Benson family, no specific reference is made to it. Sally, the Benson's faithful maid and the type of crusty warm-heartedness, is belligerently orthodox in her belief, proudly proclaiming:

I'm a parish-clerk's daughter, and could never demean myself to dissenting fashions . . .

(note the implication of snobbery) though she excludes Benson from her comic derogation of dissenting habits of prayer, and significantly adds:

God forbid I should speak disrespectful of Master Thurstan and Miss Faith, though; I never think on them as Church or Dissenters, but just as Christians.[38]

It is not what people call themselves but how they behave that is the criterion of real Christianity. So witch-hunting Puritans are the background to 'Lois the Witch', Cagot-persecuting Roman Catholics provide the material for 'An Accursed Race', a sycophantic Church of England clergyman is satirized in *My Lady Ludlow*.

---

[37] *Ruth* was published in January, 1853, by Chapman and Hall. It tells the story of an orphan seduced by the aristocratic Bellingham, abandoned, and finding a home with the Bensons who protect her and her child by saying that she is a widow. Ruth is offered work as a companion in Mr. Bradshaw's house until, after five years, her secret is discovered. The Bensons stand by her and her child, Leonard. Bellingham returns but Ruth refuses him. She finally becomes a heroine nursing the victims of a cholera outbreak, catches the cholera from Bellingham whose life she saves, and dies 'redeemed'. A secondary plot concerns the Bradshaws and their children; the spoilt son embezzles Benson's money.

The book was bitterly attacked, even burnt by outraged moralists. Mrs. Gaskell fell ill from the angry criticism.

The title may have been taken from the same tale, Crabbe's 'Ruth', that she used for *Sylvia's Lovers*. Its heroine is left pregnant and defenceless.

[38] *Ruth*, p. 165.

Examples of sympathetic treatment of the three religions can equally be found, for example, in *Ruth* as we have seen, in *Wives and Daughters* and in *My Lady Ludlow* again. But to catalogue instances of Mrs. Gaskell's fairness of treatment and lack of prejudice would be wearisome. If any further proof is wanted it may be found in the *Life*, not merely in the account of Charlotte herself, whose rather rigid Anglicanism made an exception of Mrs. Gaskell for the sake of friendship, but in the handling of Charlotte's husband, the Rev. Mr. Nicholls, to whom Dissent was anathema and who was prepared to break the friendship. All shades of belief find their place in her work and receive judgement of praise or blame in so far as the individual practice can be equated to the generally accepted principles of Christianity.

An amusing sidelight on this attitude is given by an anecdote Mrs. Gaskell repeats in 'French Life', the published version of the diary she kept on a holiday in 1862. The anecdote, capped with a flick at one of the bastions of orthodoxy in England, is worth quoting, though it is too long to give in full. It concerns a young aide-de-camp after the Napoleonic wars, who has refused to stay in the room given to him because it had once belonged to Madame de Sévigné:

> "Pardon me, sir; but it appears to me that you forget that Madame de Sévigné was a Jansenist, and that I am a Montmorenci, of the family of the first Baron of Christendom."

To which Mrs. Gaskell adds:

> The young man was afraid of the contamination of heresy that might be lingering in the air of the room. There are old rooms in certain houses shut up since the days of the Great Plague, which are not to be opened for the world. I hope that certain Fellows' rooms in Balliol may be hermetically sealed, when their present occupants leave them, lest a worse thing than the plague may infect the place.[39]

[39] *Cousin Phillis*, p. 646. She knew Jowett of course, and what he had to put up with because of his views. The refusal to give him a worth-while salary as Professor of Greek was well known, as was the bitterness directed against him for his writing, especially after *Essays and Reviews* in 1860. She wrote to Norton about Oxford's refusal to give him permission to marry, and Norton replied that 'Mr. Jowett may congratulate himself that he lives three centuries too late to be burned.' *Letters*, p. 60.

It will be realized that much of the writing, fiction and non-fiction, already mentioned deals with historical and not contemporary religion. Her historical sense and wide general reading were further important in reinforcing the sense of tradition and enabling her to see individual religions calmly and in perspective, aware of the good and bad in the history of each. This aspect will be dealt with in more detail when her interest in history and social customs is considered.

It is hardly surprising to find that the work of an author steeped in and alive to the traditions of Dissent should reveal a marked preference for individual judgement and conscience, or that the manner in which this preference is expressed shows clearly how integrity of principle is placed before accepted convention. Job Legh, the intelligent artisan of *Mary Barton*, is a portrayal of non-dogmatic integrity, but the aristocratic Anglicanism of Lady Ludlow and the desperately sincere Evangelicalism of Mr. Grey in *My Lady Ludlow*, are both in contrast to Legh's approach yet presented with equal sympathy. Those who earn Mrs. Gaskell's scorn are those whose principles are elastically accommodated to circumstance, whatever their creed. *My Lady Ludlow* is in every way a useful exponent of this attitude. It contains the sharply told anecdote of the flattering family chaplain made to eat a tough old rook and enjoy it, and it deals lightly yet pointedly with the current prejudice against Dissent:

Why can't they believe as we do? It's very wrong. Besides, it's schism and heresy and, you know, the Bible says that's as bad as witchcraft.[40]

says Lady Ludlow about Brooke, the retired baker and successful farmer. But by the end of the story her agent has married his daughter and the Brookes have had an invitation to the Hall. We may note in passing that Mrs. Gaskell seems to have felt it necessary to play down, to some extent, any direct praise of Unitarianism or Dissent. She often refers jokingly to prejudice against it, but praise is indirect, by showing praiseworthy conduct, as in the case of Minister Holman and his family in *Cousin Phillis*. And this is a further, if minor, incentive to placing the focus of attention

[40] *My Lady Ludlow*, p. 209.

on conduct rather than on belief, a development which is of
major importance in her work.

There is, however, a conflict inherent in this view of religion,
the eternal one between good intentions and doctrine on the one
hand, human weakness and affection on the other. Christianity
may be claimed as 'heart's piety' but this will not necessarily co-
incide with normal standards of piety, and may clash with
fundamental principles. Mrs. Gaskell is too honest to avoid the
issue and a good enough novelist to take advantage of its potential. She uses as a plot mechanism the well-intentioned action
contradicting a fundamental principle; Benson's invention of a
fictitious husband for Ruth, and Philip Hepburn's concealment of
the fact that Kinraid is still alive in *Sylvia's Lovers* are two variations. It is a sign of Mrs. Gaskell's realism as well as of her sensibility
that she recognizes the futility of attempting to control or circum-
scribe natural goodness in favour of any theoretical virtue (she
does, of course, deal with the necessity of disciplining it and
refining it). She had on the whole, as Collins comments, 'no
faculty for distortion.'[41] When it comes to the push it is the human
impulse to love and feel affection that is important. So Lady
Ludlow, when she hears of the death of her last surviving son, is
deaf to the injunction of Mr. Gray that 'The Lord gave and the
Lord taketh away.'

> But my poor lady could not echo the words. He was the last remain-
> ing child.[42]

When the two fellow ministers similarly come to console Holman
as his only daughter is apparently dying, they quote Abraham's
willingness to sacrifice Isaac:

> "Take example by him, Brother Holman. Let us hear you say, 'The
> Lord giveth and the Lord taketh away. Blessed be the name of the
> Lord!' "
> There was a pause of expectancy. I verily believe the minister tried
> to feel it; but he could not. Heart of flesh was too strong. Heart of
> stone he had not . . .

[41] op. cit., p. 61.   [42] *My Lady Ludlow*, p. 167.

and Holman adds shortly afterwards:

"I hold with Christ that afflictions are not sent by God in wrath as penalties for sin."
"Is that orthodox, Brother Robinson?" asked the third minister, in a deferential note of inquiry.[43]

The question is not answered, but the answer is implicit.

The problem is as old as religion itself. It is posed in the *Antigone*, by Sophocles, who carries the dilemma to its ultimate stage by putting the laws of God and the laws of man in conflict. Mrs. Gaskell does not carry the dilemma to its extreme, though she touches on it in *Sylvia's Lovers* when old Daniel Robson is hanged for rioting. There is no condemnation of the law, but all the force of the narrative is in sympathy with Robson. To deal openly with such a problem would have carried her into the realms of tragedy, and she is not a tragic writer. Nor did her view of life, based on optimism and love, allow of it. The most that she can do is to indicate that had she ever to make a decision on the issue she might have put the laws of man in second place. The vicar who preaches the sermon at the funeral of the sailor killed defying the Press Gang stutters into silence:

. . . the discord between the laws of man and the laws of Christ stood before him; and he gave up the attempt to do more than he was doing, as beyond his power.[44]

The Bible is the central and essential, if often unmentioned, guide to faith and to conduct; it is read, referred to, quoted and preferred as guide, philosopher, friend and spiritual authority throughout Mrs. Gaskell's work. It enabled the author to maintain a steady view of society and its morals over eighteen years of authorship, and to condemn, if not the laws of man, certain unchristian unwritten laws of Victorian society such as the one that damned the fallen woman without hope. It is seen as the necessary element of daily life, not as the weekly exhortation from the pulpit reserved for a different, Sabbath way of life. It is more particularly, in Mrs. Gaskell's work, the New Testament with its

[43] *Cousin Phillis*, pp. 104–5.   [44] *Sylvia's Lovers*, p. 71.

message of forgiveness and love, and its figure of Christ as the supreme example of human conduct.[45] This aspect is conveniently shown in a short story, 'The Heart of John Middleton', a rather deliberately moral Christmas story written for Dickens's *Household Words* in 1850.

It is the story of a rough and ignorant mill-hand who owes his salvation to falling in love with a gentle girl. She helps him to learn, he becomes acquainted with the Bible, by precept and example a moral regeneration is begun. But the girl is injured by the mill-owner's son, who has always been his enemy. Middleton marries her but nurses revenge, and the chance finally offers itself when the enemy, now an escaped convict, unwittingly takes refuge in his house. It is actually a better story than the sketch of the melodramatic plot suggests, well written and with insight into the type of mentality she is describing. Through it runs the thread of John Middleton's moral education. It begins with hearing about God and learning to read the Bible. So far, so good, but he still has a revengeful nature. When he learns about Christ's life and death:

I longed to have been there, to have avenged Him on the wicked Jews . . . But I got the Bible myself, and read the mighty act of God's vengeance, in the Old Testament, with a kind of triumphant faith that, sooner or later, He would take my cause in hand, and revenge me on mine enemy.[46]

The persuasion of his wife, with lessons of hunger and suffering, soften him a little, but the thought of his wrongs still has the power to harden his heart:

I took Nelly's Bible, and turned, not to the gracious story of the Saviour's birth, but to the records of the former days, when the Jews took such wild revenge upon all their opponents.[47]

It needs further suffering and the plea of his dying wife, carried through the appropriate storm when his enemy is at his mercy, to change him. The result is final peace for the soul:

---

[45] Unitarians do not regard the doctrine of the Trinity as essential, and the view that Christ was human (Socinianism) was widely held.
[46] *Cranford*, p. 395.   [47] ibid, p. 398.

. . . what I teach is, how Christ lived and died, and what was Nelly's faith of love.[48]

We have already seen that Mrs. Gaskell views religion as coinciding as far as possible with natural feeling. Where feeling requires guidance, it is towards cultivating the love which is present, even if only as a seed, in every soul. This attitude receives powerful support from the New Testament emphasis, and the selection from it of the doctrine of love as the key one. The individual, as has been pointed out, is seen as the arbiter of his own conscience and responsible directly for his own faith. The Bible is there to sustain him, but when precepts for conduct and standpoint are concerned, the Old Testament is rejected as dangerous. Mrs. Gaskell's world is not merely a Christian one, it is a selectively New Testament one, discarding the Hebraic element which gave religion much of its authority in the Victorian period. Furthermore, a religion of love is necessarily a religion that must rely heavily on example and influence; the emphasis is again thrown on conduct. Such a point of view will tend naturally to themes and plots involving reconciliation, which is what we find in her novels.

The tendency of Mrs. Gaskell's beliefs is then to attract her attention to individual conduct, and we can now enlarge the idea of 'conduct' to social behaviour, conduct in relation to the society one lives in. My contention is that Mrs. Gaskell is primarily a social novelist, concerned however not with society at large but with small communities in which individual conduct and feeling are important, and which will serve at the same time to illustrate universal standards. The corollary is that her work develops to demonstrate this. A long look at her religion and the expression of it has been necessary because of the degree to which it supplied the moral system by which she worked, and because it was a religion that reinforced her bent as a novelist. The behaviour of her characters and the comments that guide the reader's attitude to that behaviour cannot be fully understood without realizing the extent to which conduct, even when not overtly religious, is

[48] *Cranford*, p. 409.

nevertheless an aspect of the 'good' man, who is basically the religious man as she understood him. He is also, I must emphasize, something very different from the 'pious' man.

Yet it is the behaviour more than the religion which really interests the novelist in her, and we can now expand a little on the earlier comment that her work shows a progressive falling-off of direct interest in religion as such, accompanied by an increasing difficulty in integrating it successfully in the development of plot and character. The treatment of the religious element as a component of her work changes. I am not suggesting that she became herself less immediately concerned with religion, though one could infer from her work that she became less zealously so; the concern here is with the writer. Much of the evidence on this aspect overlaps with discussion of technique and with the analysis of the social element, but certain comments are necessary now.

The early work contains a good deal of direct exhortation, much of it mediated through the comments of characters but supported also by direct comment. The plots have as an essential element the transformation of the main character under the influence of religion; religion itself being for all practical purposes the guidance and teaching of whoever causes the change, with the Bible as the ever-present support. Examples are the influence of the preacher David Hughes on the embittered Nest Gwynn in 'The Well of Pen Morfa'; the reclamation of the prostitute Lizzie Leigh by her mother ('Thou hast not forgot thy Bible, I'll be bound, for thou wert always a scholar,')[49] and the earlier, more obviously sentimental 'Libbie Marsh's Three Eras' and 'The Sexton's Hero'. These carry the same pattern as is contained in the larger treatment of *Mary Barton* or the more tightly concentrated narrative line of *Ruth*.

With *North and South* the centre of interest has definitely shifted. It now lies squarely in the conflict and contrast of social relationships and conventions at various levels, linked with individual feelings caught up in patterns of behaviour and opinion. The evangelized character still appears—Nicholas Higgins, the intelligent and agnostic artisan—but he is a secondary figure. The

[49] *Cranford*, p. 239.

saintly figure is also there—his daughter Bessie—but peripheral to the story, and endowed with a stock pathos and frenetic piety quite out of keeping with the more controlled and deeper studies of the main characters. The effect is of a tract straying into the narrative, and this is virtually what has happened. The felt duty to testify to religion has failed to accommodate itself happily to the more objective study of behaviour.

The short stories of this period show the same sort of pattern. The powerful tale 'Half a Lifetime Ago', for example, concentrates successfully on the background and character of the Westmorland 'stateswoman' Susan Dixon. Religious reference has no part in it, the story depends solely on the accurate description of scenes, events and character, and on the highly dramatic but factually presented theme of the emotions involved when a woman renounces her lover to care for an idiot brother. But— and this is the point to note—the *patterns* of the conduct, the moral standards and the principles involved are those subsumed in the direct religious reference of the earlier stories, and inferred in:

the grave, solid books brought round by the pedlars (such as "Paradise Lost" and "Regained," "The Death of Abel," "The Spiritual Quixote," and "The Pilgrim's Progress"), which were to be found in nearly every house.[50]

The outcome, however, is a study in practical Christianity. Susan obeys 'God's will' in her mother's dying request, and follows the biblical precept 'Nought but death shall part thee and me!'—the only direct connexions made between precept and practice.

In between *North and South* (1855) and *Sylvia's Lovers* occurred a relatively non-productive period, the major effort going into the biography of Charlotte Brontë which occupied the first two years of it. The *Life* forced her to examine closely the individual conduct of a narrowly Anglican woman in an area which contained a population divided between the Church of England and various dissenting sects. And, of course, she was constantly studying the thoughts and methods of a writer of genius who herself

[50] *My Lady Ludlow*, p. 280.

had tackled problems of feelings and conduct boldly, honestly and with some unconventionality. Only one aspect of this influence concerns us here. Mrs. Gaskell was led to study diverse views and attitudes to religion in action, to see religion not as some ideal solvent of social and personal problems, or as some higher and transfiguring influence, but as an ingredient in the total pattern of life. To come across a statement such as:

Certainly, the *soi-disant* Christians who forcibly ejected Mr. Redhead at Haworth ten or twelve years before, held a very heathen brother-hood with the *soi-disant* Christians of Heckmondwike, though the one set might be called members of the Church of England and the other Dissenters . . .[51]

is to be made to realize how far she had travelled from the relatively idealized view of religion presented in *Mary Barton*. The germ of this sort of comparison was always there, witness the comment on Orestes and the later satirical sketches of hypocrisy that have been referred to. But this is comment on conduct without any saving gloss, with comparison of religions added as a secondary feature. It would seem more than coincidence that the work of the following two years produced, as the only other important items, two stories (*My Lady Ludlow* and 'Lois the Witch') which are also to some extent comparative studies dealing directly with religion as a function of social conduct.

In *Sylvia's Lovers* (1863) the dilemma facing Mrs. Gaskell is clearly revealed. The didactic element springing from the desire to do something for religion, or do something for people through religion, militates against the interest in people and conduct for their own sakes which has developed as the legitimate material for the novelist. Technically, she is still a little insecure, and having chosen a subject that does not arise from within her own experience she is unable to follow the conduct of her characters through naturally to the end. The result is that she brings in religion as a solution not only to the problems of the characters but to the technical problems of the novel itself. Every critic who has commented on this novel, for good or for bad, has had to

[51] *Life*, p. 116.

admit that the final section, with its repentances and excessive piety, is false to the manner of the rest. Some of the difficulty is created by the fact that she is still exploring, in the characters of the Hepburn group, the inconsistencies between belief and conduct, though the novel turns more decidedly to the problem of the conflict between feeling and principle. It is therefore necessary that Philip Hepburn, the main character after Sylvia herself, should talk in the terms of and with the direct references to religion that are natural to a professing Quaker. As Pollard says of one of his speeches on forgiveness:

In isolation this may seem very pointedly didactic. It springs, however, from the serious religious feeling which pervades the book . . .[52]

The difficulty was to allow this feeling to pervade the novel while preventing it from spilling over into the over-emphatic or didactic, which shows up in terms of contrived conduct.

The concluding stage in Mrs. Gaskell's development is the dropping of the didactic element. If we compare *Ruth* with *Cousin Phillis* as novels both of which have ministers as the central character, and in both of which we may therefore expect to find religion as a necessary ingredient of normal life and dialogue, we find that in *Ruth* the didactic element is so strong as to be a primary force, in *Cousin Phillis* we do not think about didacticism at all. Our concern is with the characters and their feelings.

This change can be equated with the technical one of a move away from authorial comment. The dropping of such comment means that the reader is not going to be buttonholed by the author, a proceeding which can make a reader aware—if only through annoyance—of the subject of the commentary. But a growing interest in exploring and presenting situations and social relationships will diminish the desire to gloss events from a religious or moral viewpoint. And we find in fact that the type of comment made by the characters themselves shows this trend equally. The religious content of Mrs. Gaskell's work is a dimin-

[52] Arthur Pollard, 'The Novels of Mrs. Gaskell', *Bulletin of the John Rylands Library*, Vol. 43, No. 2, March 1961, p. 418.

ishing quantity, and in her last novel, *Wives and Daughters*, the life we enter is as free from religiosity as is normal life itself. Let us be clear on this point. What has vanished is surface reference. The behaviour of the characters is as Christian as could be desired, or is wrong or superficial by Christian moral standards. But we are in a world which is the normal world of daily life, in which the human being is not always pulling his principles and beliefs out of his pocket to refer to them; he knows them by heart. There is a time and a place. Minister Holman himself upholds this view when he refuses to interrupt people doing their work in order to call on them officially:

> . . . they are all at their business, their shops, or their warehouses; they ought to be there. I have no fault to find with them . . . I judge them by myself. If there are clouds in the sky, and I am getting in the hay just ready for loading, and rain sure to come in the night, I should look ill upon Brother Robinson if he came into the field to speak about serious things.[53]

A fuller treatment of the religious element in Mrs. Gaskell's work would have to note other points. It is, for example, grossly unfair to a writer with such a delicate observation of the irony and comedy in daily life to give the impression that the world of her novels is a deadly serious one. It is fundamentally serious, but the humour is always there. The principles are never in doubt. But religion is manifested in conduct, conduct results from people, and people and conduct are the material (given the viewpoint) for social comedy. Her treatment of clergymen, to take one instance, is not basically so very different from that of Jane Austen. They are characters holding a place in society and living by certain standards in that society; they are not regarded as set apart from social pressures or human weaknesses. The result differs from Jane Austen's partly because Mrs. Gaskell writes of a different order of society, and of a different pattern of clergyman in society. Leaving aside differences in technique and temperament, between the two writers lie the evangelical revival and the troubles of the Forties; it has become impossible—as Trollope's

[53] *Cousin Phillis*, p. 29.

novels show—for a clergyman to be written about as though his religion could be ignored. The type of clergyman had changed; so had the type of reader.

Many of Mrs. Gaskell's novels therefore contain 'religion' automatically because the characters are consciously religious or are clergymen. It is probably true to say that her ministers are somewhat idealized, at least when they are main characters, although the context of situation in which they are placed becomes steadily more personal and less 'professional'. A Chadband or a Slope would be unthinkable in her environment; the possibility that such an attitude to religion could exist would be a threat to religion itself. I suspect that Mrs. Gaskell is held back from becoming a major satirist in the Jane Austen sense because she cannot accept hypocrisy beyond a certain degree as comic. Her world is less mundane, more morally strenuous and conscious of a duty to God as well as society, though not in any way attempting deliberately to oppose the two.

Such an attitude has its compensations for the novelist. The presentation of good behaviour comes more naturally and credibly to Mrs. Gaskell than to almost any other novelist; it retains its humanity, its humour and its standards without effort. When Thackeray for example puts an emotional crisis in Amelia Sedley's way—her parting with her son, George—the occasion is highlighted and solemnified by the introduction of conventional piety as she reads the Bible story of the parting of Hannah from Samuel to him. The reader is meant to be conscious that this is rather a special occasion. When Mr. Holman is faced with a crisis, the probable death of his daughter, his religion and his humanity are so much a part of each other that he can reject conventional piety, as has been shown, without the reader feeling that there has been any loss of either; indeed, the touch of the ridiculous in the behaviour of his fellow ministers adds to the genuineness of the emotions involved. Mrs. Gaskell is at ease with religion, Thackeray is not.

It will be possible to look more closely at the implications of some of the points that have been raised when other facets of her work and development are examined. For we come back to the thesis that the change in treatment of and emphasis on religion is a function of Mrs. Gaskell's development as a novelist, though we can now see that the fundamental premisses of her religion do not alter. It is first necessary to look at other salient features of her world; an easier task now that its basis in religion is clear.

CHAPTER IV

Family and Stability

WHEN Mr. Gibson marries again he does so to carry out
a duty. Molly at seventeen needs a type of guidance and
an orderly domestic background which he feels he cannot fully take care of. Much of the irony of the novel lies in the
fact that his choice is unfortunate. Mrs. Kirkpatrick's principles
are too frivolous, her understanding too superficial, to provide the
right sort of influence; her concern is with outward behaviour.
We are shown in the end that it is the training Molly received
from her father which finally carries her through her trials. In
addition Mr. Gibson himself acquires a step-daughter nearly
ruined by the way she has been brought up. We are in the world
of comedy, so although the ill-effects of neglect and poor example
can never be completely remedied, a reasonable salvage is possible. And Cynthia recognizes this when she blurts out to Mr.
Gibson:

Oh, sir! I think, if I had been differently brought up, I shouldn't have
had the sore angry heart I have now.

though Mrs. Gaskell is wise enough to let her continue:

. . . I should always have wanted admiration and worship, and men's
good opinion.[1]

Looking at Cynthia's outburst in another way we can note
that it is her 'heart' that is sore and angry; her nature has been
successfully appealed to by means of the sympathy and affection
which her own mother had failed to give her. We can turn for
comment on this to Ruth's position when first her beloved mother

[1] *Wives and Daughters*, p. 638.

and then her feckless but amiable father died. She is left to the care
of a guardian who was:

a sensible, hard-headed man of the world; having a very fair proportion of conscience as consciences go . . .[2]

but who looks at the business of doing the best for Ruth as a
matter of common sense and rational investment. Her scanty
capital is used to apprentice her to a reputable milliner, and:

Ruth's loving disposition, continually sending forth fibres in search of
nutriment, found no other object for regard among those of her daily
life to compensate for the want of natural ties.[3]

The connexion between love and goodness is a close one in
Mrs. Gaskell's world. We have seen that love in one of its aspects
is to be considered by the very nature of her underlying faith as an
active moral principle. A corollary is that it becomes an essential
ingredient in matters of sound upbringing. The question of upbringing is thus linked directly with character and behaviour. But
more is involved than this.

If we look at the families which provide the main characters in
Wives and Daughters a peculiar pattern emerges. The Gibson
family consists of father and daughter. The Kirkpatrick family
is mother and daughter. The Hamleys to begin with have mother,
father and two sons, but the mother is a delicate invalid who dies
fairly early in the proceedings, leaving Squire Hamley with the
feeling of being adrift. Of the two sons, one is secretly married and
finally dies, leaving in turn a widow and a baby. We find in fact
that the pattern 'family' in Mrs. Gaskell's novels bears little relation to the stereotype of the Victorian family that we—perhaps
wrongly—normally think of. It is the one Frederick is so conscious of in *North and South* when he says to his sister Margaret,
'we are curiously bare of relations.'[4] There is no hint of the
swarming life that continuously bursts through in Dickens's
novels; the Toodles, the Cratchetts, ('we're thtrong in the Fairy
business and the Nurthery dodge' as Mr. Sleary says of his Circus

[2] *Ruth*, p. 37.   [3] ibid., p. 38.   [4] *North and South*, p. 211.

and its families);[5] all, in fact, that House summed up as 'the careless fertility of his women'.[6] Hers is the very minimal family unit and subject to calamity, it is the family on the verge of dissolution, or with its ties and affections made more intense by the realization that only the one parent or child exists; indeed it sometimes appears only as a reference, not as an actuality; a tender memory of a happiness that existed before the story begins its existence in time. The typical heroine of Mrs. Gaskell's novels and stories (and we need to bear in mind that it is the heroine rather than the hero who is her main interest) is the only child of an only surviving parent, or a complete orphan. There are variations within the framework; parents may die in the course of the story, there may be a brother who has left the family group, but to all intents and purposes the pattern is impressively dominant.[7]

Before dealing with the significance of this pattern it is necessary to note as a fact that Mrs. Gaskell is repeating in her novels the pattern of her own life. Her mother died when the daughter was thirteen months old. Her father married again, but she went to her Aunt Lumb and was brought up by her. Mrs. Gaskell rarely saw her father before his final illness and we know that she disliked her stepmother. Although she was one of eight children, only one brother survived childhood, and he disappeared mysteriously at sea while she was still young. The extent to which the family situations she portrays are variations on her own experience is immediately obvious, but certain caveats have to be introduced. As far as we know her own childhood and

---

[5] Dickens, *Hard Times*, p. 280.

[6] Humphry House, *The Dickens World*, Oxford Paperbacks, 1960, p. 76.

[7] How striking and dominant it is may be judged from a brief analysis of the heroine's situation in her major work: all the heroines are only children. *Mary Barton*: Mother dies early, father left; *Ruth*: Orphan; *North and South*: Mother and father die before the end; 'Lois the Witch': Orphan; *Sylvia's Lovers*: Father and later mother die by half way; *Wives and Daughters*: Father only. The only family with any resistance to mortality is in *Cousin Phillis*; Phillis herself is an only child. *Cranford*'s heroine is elderly, but Miss Matty is an orphan whose 'mother-figure' sister dies after the first episode. (Her brother Peter finally returns after having vanished for about forty years. Margaret Hale in *North and South* also has a brother who is permanently abroad.) This pattern dominates the slighter stories as well. The only exception of any importance to this pattern apart from *Cousin Phillis* is possibly the Cumnor family in *Wives and Daughters* and the Bradshaw family in *Ruth*. They are not at the centre of the plot, although they have their own significance. Otherwise even the background families share this parental inability to survive.

youth was a happy period, spent in an atmosphere of affection, comfort and security. Her own marriage was again, as far as we know, a happy one, with four children growing up in an atmosphere of cheerful domesticity, although these children were daughters, the only son dying before he was a year old. The manner in which the pattern emerges in her novels, however, suggests that the sense of deprivation was far stronger than she ever admitted; in particular the stress which is laid on the father-daughter relationship from the beginning (*Mary Barton*) to the end (*Cousin Phillis* and *Wives and Daughters*) of her writing career suggests that the sense of deprivation in this respect was exceptionally strong.

Our concern however must be with the imaginative use to which the experience was put, and what emerges is the overwhelming emphasis on the part played in upbringing by the absence of that sense of security and affection which a complete and well-principled family life alone can give. She takes therefore, as her range, the various situations in which this sense of security is frail, may be endangered or is absent, and concentrates her attention on the ways in which the behaviour of her characters is affected by the upbringing they have received. The result is to link the whole problem of moral standards and social behaviour with parental duty—and one might add that not the least important part of that duty would appear to be the duty to survive. The basis for stability which we have seen is fundamentally a matter of individual belief and principle, character is regarded as dependent to a degree on the immediate social unit of the family, which is itself part of the larger concept of society. Mrs. Gaskell assumes without demur the proposition that 'The greater and better part of English society accepted the social structure and moral objective of the nation, as a community of families . . .'[8] What distinguishes her as a novelist is the instinct with which she fastens on the cases where the structure is weak, and the skill with which she examines the possible consequences, working from the effect on the individual and his relationship to the society around. To a novelist concerned with the interplay of characters and

[8] G. M. Young, *Portrait of an Age*, O.U.P., 1953, p. 13.

emotions and the training of the development of character, these
are fruitful circumstances.[9]

Stability of character is, then, linked with emotional stability
and social stability in the family unit, it is a conflation that suits
Mrs. Gaskell's interests admirably and whose use she develops
steadily. The early work relies a good deal on personal experience
because the amateur novelist will normally turn to such experience. *Mary Barton* is in every way as personal a book, in this
sense, as *Cranford*; its details and reminiscences draw heavily on her
past. But the contemporary setting and the sense of purpose have
tended to obscure this quality, while the Cranford scene and content throw it into relief. Yet *Mary Barton* is shot through with
references to the importance of the family element. We can take
only a few examples.

We have seen John Barton explain his downfall by his loss
of faith. But he is also shown as a man whose roots are being cut
away. His only boy has died as a baby,[10] his wife's sister Esther
has run off with a lover, shortly afterwards his wife dies in labour:

One of the ties which bound him down to the gentle humanities of
earth was loosened, and henceforward the neighbours all remarked
he was a changed man.[11]

He still has his daughter, Mary, but too many of his affections have
withered or turned sour on him. While this one tie is still strong
he is capable of responding to other appeals, as when he helps the
Davenports. But circumstances in general combine to embitter
him, and Mary is not dependent enough on him nor close enough
to his confidence to supply the sufficiency of love and sense of
parental duty which could have pulled him away from the fatal
preoccupation with his bitterness. Conversely, Mary lacks the
continuing guidance which would have prevented her from ever
listening to the seductive temptations of Henry Carson, although

[9] The abundance of widows, widowers and orphans may also reflect an aspect of
Victorian life as common as fertility—the mortality rate.
[10] This emotional echo of the death of her own son—an echo often repeated—is one
instance of personal experience being brought in to supply emotional realism in support
of the social realism which was absorbed into her fiction. But see Chapters XI and XII.
[11] *Mary Barton*, p. 22.

she has been sufficiently well brought up (we see her, one Sunday afternoon, alternating between watching passers-by from behind the window blind 'in the intervals of reading her Bible, which lay open before her')[12] to wrench herself free before she falls into the trap which snared the misguided and wilful Esther. Barton has unconsciously wriggled out of much of his duty by apprenticing Mary to a dressmaker; the existence of this alternate authority, not based on affection, inevitably slackens the tie. Similarly Ruth's guidance is handed over on a contract basis.

The comparison between this father–daughter relationship and that of Mr. Gibson and Molly hardly needs pointing out, although detailed discussion of the way in which Mrs. Gaskell varies the handling of basically similar themes must properly be left until later. The tie of affection between Mr. Gibson and Molly is strong and continuous, and there are no social or economic worries to cloud the domestic scene. (One of the strongest elements in the social aspect of *Mary Barton* is found in the passionately felt and emotionally described scenes which show how family life and family affections suffer and deteriorate in poverty.) When Molly learns of her father's approaching remarriage, the threatened intrusion of a stranger to interrupt the long and easy pattern of affection is shattering; all Mrs. Gaskell's feelings about the reliance of a child on the security of its parents' affections are concentrated in the comment she makes:

It was as if the piece of solid ground on which she stood had broken from the shore, and she was drifting out into the infinite sea alone.[13]

Upbringing is the key to a stable character, and the weaker the character the more the need of a stable domestic environment to supply the example and training and to bring love in to support principle. We have seen that Mrs. Gaskell believes in the existence of some good in every heart; she is aware as we have noted that material circumstances may affect it, but her concern is primarily with the moral environment. Even Sally Leadbitter, the loose-principled girl who acts as pander to Henry Carson, has

[12] *Mary Barton*, p. 92.   [13] *Wives and Daughters*, pp. 125–6.

'this seed of the future soul', which shows in her care for a bed-ridden mother:

But the mother was lightly principled like Sally herself,[14]

we are told, and the failure by the parent to provide moral example and training is rubbed in, while Henry Carson's own failings—and by implication his death—can be traced to his being spoilt. Similarly Richard Bradshaw's lapse into feeble crime is attributed directly to poor upbringing; this time because he is tainted by the hypocrisy underlying his father's stern profession of principles, and reacts against the lack of any affection to accompany them. He is expected to be perfect and his father makes no allowance for humanity.[15] Bellingham succeeds in seducing Ruth because he can take advantage of her naïvety when she has no-one to support her own prompting to escape. He is himself another example of the character whose viciousness is due to a spoilt upbringing, this time to his mother's capricious use of her wealth instead of genuine love and training to hold his affection.

The story of Sylvia's home life in *Sylvia's Lovers* shows clearly the influence of the home and the example of the parents. Sylvia Robson is the only child (there is the almost inevitable mention of an infant son who died) and is spoilt by her parents, in particular by her father Daniel. The opening scenes in which we first meet Sylvia show how Mrs. Gaskell prepares for the development of major events from slight beginnings. Sylvia is shown as a high-spirited and impetuous girl, forgetting to sell the butter in the excitement of watching the first whaler of the season return; choosing the showy red material for her cloak against the advice

---

[14] *Mary Barton*, p. 102

[15] Dickens seems to have drawn on the episode of Bradshaw and his son's forgery for *Hard Times*. Just as Bradshaw's rigid principles and lack of affection and humanity drive Richard to the secret pursuit of pleasure, and so into debt and finally into forgery, Gradgrind's doctrinaire methods drive Tom along the same road and to the same end. In both cases an essentially weak character is given the wrong twist because he cannot act naturally and under sympathetic guidance. It is symptomatic of the different views held by Mrs. Gaskell and Dickens that she gives us an ending in reconciliation and optimism with the hope of a reunited family (prosecution is avoided) whereas Dickens lets Tom be driven abroad and, though ultimately repentant, die on his way home again. Dickens also seems to have used the elder Bradshaw as a model for Bounderby.

of her more sober cousin and the known wishes of her mother. It is an attractive and natural picture, one designed to gain the sympathy of the reader. But the hints of insufficient control are there. Sylvia is too used to getting her own way, almost too secure in the admiration and affection of parents, and she gets round her mother's disappointment at her choice of material with a kiss:

at the end of which her mother had adjusted her cap with a "There! there! ha' done wi' thee," but had had no more heart to show her disapprobation.[16]

As life in the farm-house is developed, we see that her father Daniel is, if kind-hearted and generous, obstinate and capricious; not properly educated, easy-going, occasionally drunk, averse to any controls on his own pleasures. Religion is as may be imagined, only superficially present. Mrs. Gaskell has shown what is the daily example of authority and conduct. Episode after episode shows his want of depth of character; there is no evil, simply no positive striving to be better. His wife, Bell, is the stronger character but inclined to spoil her only child. Sylvia's education is neglected—she cannot read or write—and when Philip Hepburn tries to teach her they give in to her pleas that the work is too difficult and unnecessary. How important her 'education' is to be we shall see. So when the catastrophe occurs, with Daniel hanged for rioting, Bell become 'dateless' and the farm allowed to be sold, Sylvia is adrift; without the necessary moral and religious training which would have guided her, she is unfitted to face adversity or to distinguish right action. No question of evil is raised here, except in so far as the consequences produce their own evil. Sylvia's character is naturally a good one, and her parents are by normal standards good people. Mrs. Gaskell's implied point is that though they are good people they are bad parents. When the stability of family life is shattered, there is no preparation for individual character to take the strain. In particular Mrs. Gaskell presses home her point as she traces Sylvia's progress in adversity. She finds immediate security by marrying her cousin Philip, although she loves the missing Kinraid. In his

[16] *Sylvia's Lovers*, p. 43.

family she is first brought into close and prolonged contact with religious people and we realize that she is ignorant of any real knowledge of religion. Her education is significantly linked with her gradual realization of religious standards and belief in God by the device of having the Bible used as the primer in which she learns to read. (We may compare Sylvia with Lois Barclay, whose home and security vanish just as completely, but who faces jealousy, persecution and finally death with her faith and her confidence unbroken.) Mrs. Gaskell is, however, too good an observer of human nature—and she develops into too good a novelist—to rely on an easy formula that equates good upbringing with religion. It is an essential basis, which comes out with painful obviousness in the two tracts she wrote for the Sunday School Penny Magazine[17] or in such an early story as 'The Sexton's Hero', in which the youth who refuses to fight reveals his true bravery when drowned saving his rival's life, and whose Bible proved to contain:

many a text in the Gospel, marked broad with his carpenter's pencil, which more than bore him out in his refusal to fight.[18]

But, as I have stated, the religious element is kept out of *Wives and Daughters*, and Phillis's recovery in *Cousin Phillis* is based on the essential soundness and affection of her background rather than on any suggestion of especial piety because her father is a minister.

Types of upbringing account for certain types of behaviour. For example, with Bellingham and Richard Bradshaw we may class Benjamin Huntroyd in 'The Crooked Branch' and Edward Wilkins in 'A Dark Night's Work', of whom Mrs. Gaskell comments that he was:

not one to be spoilt by the course of indulgence he had passed through; at least, if it had done him an injury, the effects were at present hidden from view.[19]

Nest Gwynn in 'The Well of Pen Morfa' is another spoilt girl. There are those who, like Philip Hepburn or the Puritans in 'Lois

---

[17] 'Hand and Heart' and 'Bessy's Troubles at Home'.   [18] *Mary Barton*, p. 500.
[19] *Cousin Phillis*, p. 406.

the Witch', have had the moral upbringing but have lacked the
necessary accompaniment of humane and sympathetic affection.
The desirable balance between affection and moral training is
sometimes shown by a reversal of position, when the child who
has suffered becomes in turn the parent who has learnt the lesson.
Ruth's regeneration is bound up with the rearing of her child, so
is Sylvia's.

Part of the increasing subtlety in presentation of the effects of
upbringing must be related to Mrs. Gaskell's ability to learn from
watching the growth of her own daughters. In the brief diary in
which she recorded the early years of her own children she notes
how cast down she is by Marianne's wrong doing. This relates
to the behaviour of a two-year-old child! Her common sense and
humour quickly squashed such naïve thinking, although Dickens's
portrayal of the Murdstones and, much later, Kipling's account
of his own childhood as recorded in *Something of Myself* and
'Baa-baa Black Sheep' are a warning that such thinking was all
too common and could have scarifying results. But the fundamental seriousness with which she regarded this aspect of
family duty is never in doubt. Years later she wrote to
Charles Eliot Norton about her newly married daughter and
her son-in-law:

My only fear is literally that he should spoil Florence; he is pretty
strict and self-denying towards himself but if he could dress her in
diamonds and feed her on gold, and give her the moon to play with,
and she wished for them I don't think he would question the wisdom of
indulging her. I hope bye and bye he will lift her up into the standard
of high goodness of which she is thoroughly capable. But she is very
young for her age, and as yet requires the daily elevation of her thoughts
and aims.[20]

The training is not yet completed; the parent passes the duty on to
the husband with the new kind of affection.

Love and security, the necessary environment for passing on
and learning the moral standards and concepts of duty which enable a child to grow up and face the world; it would not be unfair
to Mrs. Gaskell to summarize briefly in such a manner her view

[20] *Letters*, p. 110.

of what the family stood for, though it would be unfair not to mention at the same time the complex permutations and subtleties of feeling and conduct which she recognizes in practice. We have already had to comment on her angry realization of how poverty can destroy family life, and it is an essential feature of Mrs. Gaskell's outlook that she is well aware of the hard knocks that the world can deliver. The emphasis placed on stability and security is itself an admission that although the family unit acts as a shock-absorber between the individual and the world at large, nevertheless the family is neither an insulated nor an isolated unit. Nor is its function necessarily restricted to the literal family. Ruth finally finds her home with the Bensons, her own child adding the element of continuity while receiving the stable background, which is particularly important as he is that most insecure and 'de-familied' of all Victorian characters—a bastard. Cynthia Kirkpatrick finds a settled home after years of being pushed off to visit relatives or be cheaply finished out of the way abroad. Lady Ludlow undertakes the creation of a 'family' as a vocation. When her poor relative Mrs. Dawson loses her husband and applies for help, she replies:

> You say you are left with nine children. I too should have had nine, if mine had all lived. I have none left but Rudolph, the present Lord Ludlow. He is married, and lives, for the most part, in London. But I entertain six young gentlewomen at my house at Connington, who are to me as daughters ... These young persons—all of condition, though out of means—are my constant companions, and I strive to do my duty as a Christian lady towards them.[21]

and her conception of the maternal duty includes marriage dowry and a legacy in her will. Margaret Dawson leaves her own mother and family but finds another. It is a natural transition from this

---

[21] *My Lady Ludlow*, p. 11. This passage provides an interesting gloss on Mrs. Gaskell's penchant for the minimal family. It is one of the very rare occasions when the large family is mentioned, and it shows how little reliability Mrs. Gaskell placed on numbers as a basis for security. In the novel she quickly reverts to what is, for all practical purposes, the one parent/one child situation. The adoption of Margaret by Lady Ludlow is also given a parallel in the adoption of Harry Greg by Mr. Horner and later by Mr. Gray. The adoption by Miss Galindo of her lover's illegitimate child introduces another familiar element.

realization of the family as something more than mere blood-relationship to the idea of the larger unit of a society composed of similar families who extend the sense of 'family' duty to other families in the neighbourhood or social group. At this stage the precepts of Christian conduct assume a more direct importance, merging into standards of behaviour to one's neighbours and so out finally to humanity at large. The various families who make up the working-class society which is the milieu of *Mary Barton* dissolve into a larger communal group. The inhabitants of Cranford rally round Miss Matty to such an extent after she loses her money that she finds her home, complete with servant, virtually unchanged until her long-vanished brother Peter can be miraculously recovered to provide a closer relationship; in terms of stability, security and affection Miss Matty's calamity is no calamity at all. But the juxtaposition of families provides the opportunity for the contrast of different standards of upbringing and conduct. In *Mary Barton* this is used in an exaggerated way to suggest a contrast of social standards; the brief account of Mr. Carson's household is a caricature to exemplify the Dives and Lazarus theme. But the contrasts between households of similar status, primarily the Wilsons, the Bartons and the Leghs (Job Legh and his granddaughter are another variation of the single parent and orphan) give us the beginnings of the analysis of a social group in terms of family constituents. This type of analysis is steadily developed.

It is inevitable that when the family is seen as the medium for passing on standards of conduct, it becomes impossible to overlook social standards. This is recognized in *North and South*, although the emphasis there is more on the difference in types of society which can be regarded as on the whole socially equal, wealth being balanced against gentility and the individual pretensions of each examined. (In *Cranford* we already have the genteel society, though on one level.) By *Wives and Daughters* the families represent also strata of society, each family training its children in the position of its own class as well as in common principles of conduct.

The acceptance of a class structure is inherent in one further aspect of the family as a unit which must be briefly mentioned. From *Cranford* onwards the family includes as an integral part the family servant; a miniature social hierachy exists. When Martha nudges Jem into marrying her so that they can take over Miss Matty's house and so arrange for Miss Matty to remain in it, Miss Matty becomes nominally 'the lodger'. In fact she remains the mistress; Martha is so aware of the real continuity of the old ways that she is afraid to announce the approaching baby in case Miss Matty might feel:

that the new claimant would require attentions from its mother that it would be faithless treason to Miss Matty to render.[22]

The family servant, very much part of the family yet very much aware of the difference in rank, becomes a main feature of Mrs. Gaskell's work; Sally in *Ruth*, Dixon in *North and South*, and Kester in *Sylvia's Lovers* and another Dixon in 'A Dark Night's Work', are examples. There is of course a long tradition of the honest and outspoken servant in literature, of whom the employer can say as Lady Capulet did to the Nurse, 'I have remembered me, thou's hear our counsel'. Such figures have an accepted function as commentators on life, society and people, as well as providing the possibility of comedy. In Mrs. Gaskell's world they also stand out as preservers of the old, stable order of things. When Dixon in *North and South* protests too much, however, she is sternly put in her place by Margaret; while it is a significant mark of the total change in Mr. Gibson's life—as well as, possibly, a sign that Mrs. Gaskell can now manage social observation without using the convention of the trusted retainer—that he agrees to dismiss Betty, or rather to accept her notice after another brush with the new Mrs. Gibson. After all, he says:

Betty has been with us sixteen years—a sort of service of the antique world. But the woman may be happier elsewhere.[23]

There is little doubt where the trouble lies, yet no doubt at all about supporting a proper order of respect.

We may notice finally in this brief account of Mrs. Gaskell's

[22] *Cranford*, p. 177.   [23] *Wives and Daughters*, p. 201.

view of the family, that her *Life of Charlotte Brontë* gives great
weight to Charlotte's background and upbringing. In many ways
the *Life* is written as a novel, it is shaped and shaded to give a curve
of interest and development that has much in common with her
other works. And it selects in particular the interplay between
character, family and background, with its subsequent springs of
action and principles of conduct that marks her fictional lives.
The affect of background, 'the peculiar forms of population and
society',[24] we shall deal with shortly. But she announces early:

I do not pretend to be able to harmonise points of character, and account
for them, and bring them all into one consistent and intelligible whole.
The family with whom I have now to do shot their roots down deeper
than I can penetrate. I cannot measure them, much less is it for me to
judge them. I have named these instances of eccentricity in the father
because I hold the knowledge of them to be necessary for a right
understanding of the life of his daughter.[25]

The biography includes considered comments on the effects of
Charlotte's mode of life on her imaginative development (p. 91),
on the results of a motherless upbringing (p. 202), and on the way
character can be perverted by being spoilt. It applies the lesson
to Branwell (p. 184) and ascribes the 'coarse' elements in Charlotte's work to the circumstances of her upbringing (pp. 599–600).
Mrs. Gaskell in her own novels has the artist's prerogative of
omniscience and selection to provide fuller consistency and intelligibility; we should not however be blind to the manner in
which her own reading of life has influenced the manner of presenting Charlotte Brontë's life. One final quotation we may use to
indicate how strongly Mrs. Gaskell held the view of the family
as the repository of all that is most important in life, emotionally
and as the guardian of essential truth. After Charlotte's marriage
she gives only the barest outline of events, she refuses to intrude
through 'the sacred doors of home'.[26]

This attitude, which affirmed the sanctity of family life, was a
commonplace of Mrs. Gaskell's time. Many reasons lie behind
it. Religion is a powerful force, marriages are made in heaven and

heaven can be deduced as having a hand in the resultant family.²⁷ But other factors—the example of Victoria's court, the sensed need for a stable unit in insecure times, the settled hierarchy of classes, the pressures of tradition—are all part of a complex growth. It is an attitude naturally reflected in the novels of the period; there are few exceptions—one thinks of Dickens's *Dombey and Son*, Anne Brontë's *The Tenant of Wildfell Hall*, George Eliot's *Scenes of Clerical Life*—to protest that heaven also implies hell, and hell may find its way into family life. Professor Kathleen Tillotson, tracing the growth of the novel concerned with 'everyday domestic and social behaviour' makes the point, ' "home is the element and trial of a Christian" . . . [home] that is, family life, parents and children, brothers and sisters, in a secure and specified setting'.²⁸ In other words, the family, as individuals, face the trials and misfortunes of life with a sense of support, of belonging by ties of affection and blood—and incidentally by being welded together by the formidable pressure of convention—to a close-knit unit which will close its ranks to help a member. At the same time, within the group there is scope for an individual's own principles to be put to the test in his conduct; he can be guided, corrected, punished or rewarded by the family; as an individual he will have to account for himself if he strays very far from the accepted view of how a member of a family behaves.

But what if the family is not 'a secure and specified setting'? We know that Mrs. Gaskell originally accepted this view of the family, as she accepted the conventional attitude to wives and mothers:

How all a woman's life, at least so it seems to me now, ought to have a reference to the period when she will be fulfilling one of her greatest and highest duties, those of a mother.²⁹

²⁷ The attitude to small children is also important. The 'Immortality Ode' view of small children as heavenly visitors lasted a long time, reinforced by the useful (to men) belief that motherhood was a divine vocation. Blake's version of the baby 'Like a fiend hid in a cloud' had to await the advent of psychology for support.
²⁸ *Tillotson*, p. 135. Her argument is that the atmosphere of religious controversy sparked off analysis of doctrines, in terms of analysis of states of mind and motive in novels. But discussion of doctrines became indelicate. The habit of analysis remained, transferred to conduct (which ought to be inspired by beliefs).
²⁹ *Diary*, p. 10.

and although she modified the balance of priorities when she
later had to fit the needs of a writer into the domestic scene, she
never altered the basic viewpoint. Yet we have seen that 'home'
for the Gaskellian heroine may answer very dubiously to the
description, such secure homes (they are never populous) being
presented as intimations or reminiscences of an ideal. They are
still the end to be wished; Mary Barton marries Jem and we last
see her in a home of her own, with husband, children and grand-
mother around, in an idealized setting. But even such idealizations,
which are also conventions of the happy ending, fade out of her
novels. The relationships remain either in the prospect of marriage, or the consolidation of the remaining family.

It has been observed that Mrs. Gaskell is to some extent reflecting a truth drawn from her own background, that all children
may not have such a stable and full background. But we have to
ask why, as a novelist, she rejects the whole area of experience
which included her own married life and that of many friends.
One reason has been suggested, that the 'diminished' family can
reflect her feelings about security or its absence. Another, how
conscious it is difficult to say, is that it enables her to twist the
emotional screw tighter. By concentrating the forces of family
feeling into, say, the single relationship between mother and
child, the emotional content is enormously heightened. Trollope
certainly knew it:

. . . there is a wife whose husband is a brute to her, who loses an only
child—his heir—and who is rebuked by her lord because the boy dies.
Her sorrow is, I think, pathetic.[30]

the writer detaching himself professionally from the emotions
which, as an individual, he shares.

There are, however, two more points which may be briefly
mentioned at this stage. One is her integrity, which prevented her
from disregarding the rather obtrusive realities near her Manchester doorstep. She remained an optimist as regards her view
of the essential goodness of the human soul, but she never allowed
this particular optimism to cloud her perception of the fact that

[30] Anthony Trollope, *Autobiography*, O.U.P. (World's Classics), 1941, p. 180. He is
discussing *The Claverings*.

life could be, and often was, harsh and cruel. She quickly stopped writing about the details of local misery, but seems to have accepted always the general view that life is hard as often as not.

More important probably is the fact that the diminished family links up with her interest in the individual and in basic standards. When the setting is not secure, when family affection and guidance are not available as a buffer between the individual and society at large, the individual is liable to be thrown on to his own resources. At the same time such periods of trial or temptation are those which most require sympathetic loyalty and above all affection to confide in. The orphan is resourceless—we think of Ruth wishing to run for help to the old family servant and afraid to try; the single parent may well be too busy, or too overwhelmed, or too selfish to care properly; the only child has no brother or sister to confide in. It is in this particular complex of test of character, minimal ties of affection, and emotional stress that Mrs. Gaskell sets her work and draws her conclusions.

There is a direct correlation between Mrs. Gaskell's treatment of this situation and the tone of her novels. Her comedies, from 'Mr. Harrison's Confessions' to *Wives and Daughters*, have as their main setting a background of security. 'Mr. Harrison's Confessions' has it is true the exceptional figure of a happy orphan as its hero, but the story is carefully set as a reminiscence in a family frame. The opening paragraph:

The fire was burning gaily. My wife had just gone upstairs to put baby to bed.[31]

sets the tone, particularly as we are told within a few lines that this domesticated husband is the hero of the comedy which follows. The darkening of the scene in *Sylvia's Lovers* occurs with the break-up of the Robson family. And in *Wives and Daughters* we notice that there is a movement away from the diminishing family. Set in the background, and representing all the power, stability and tradition of the landed aristocracy in its domain, is the Cumnor family, happy, united and numerous. The internal movement of the novel is also towards cohesion, away from dis-

[31] *My Lady Ludlow*, p. 405.

integration. Mr. Gibson marries and completes his family. Cynthia gains an affectionate parent and sister to confide in. The new Mrs. Gibson gains security and, for all her superficiality, does provide the guidance and affection within her limited capacity which the adolescent Molly has lacked. Even in the Hamley family, which follows the pattern we have learned to expect, the two brothers confide in and support each other. In this respect, as in others, the shift towards stability is marked. This view of the individual life as mirroring a movement between instability and stability sets a pattern which controls the structure of Mrs. Gaskell's novels and stories, reinforced by the urge to reconciliation which has previously been noted as fundamental to her beliefs. It links up also with her feeling for tradition, which she sees in one way as an element of continuity in a changing world, and with her gradual abandonment of the Manchester background as she escapes to scenes and circumstances where the rapidly shifting patterns of a changing society can be distanced if not ignored.

It is useful to pause at this stage for consideration of a special feature of Mrs. Gaskell's earlier work, her treatment of seduction, prostitutes and bastards. The 'fallen woman' was no novelty in fiction when she was writing, nor was there any lack of sympathy:

Hood's 'Bridge of Sighs' and Mrs. Gaskell's *Mary Barton* in the 'forties, provide familiar examples of this concern for the Fallen Woman, which recurs in many novels of the period; Mrs. Gaskell returned to the theme several times, and it was taken up by Kingsley, George Eliot, Wilkie Collins, Trollope and others, down to Hardy's defiant presentation of 'A Pure Woman' in the 1890s. All these invited the reader to regard with more understanding and forgiveness 'these tarnished and battered images of God'. Some of them indicated how the unfortunate girls might be restored to a decent place in society, usually through private rather than institutional benevolence.[32]

My reason for dealing with the matter here is that it is germane to Mrs. Gaskell's ideas on family and society (though the subject has

[32] Philip Collins, *Dickens and Crime*, Macmillan, 1962, p. 94.

wider implications); in particular it is necessary to modify a wrong emphasis that seems to have been given to critical consideration of *Ruth*.

Mrs. Gaskell deals with the problem in *Mary Barton* (1848), in 'Lizzie Leigh' (1850), twice in *Ruth* (1853), and in *My Lady Ludlow* (1858); in addition 'The Manchester Marriage' (1858) has oblique implications. In all of these except *Mary Barton* the centre of the situation is quite clearly what Miss Hopkins calls 'the problem of the unmarried mother'.[33] It will be easier therefore to deal with the case of Esther in *Mary Barton* first as she is the only one of the group who is fully conceived of as a prostitute. Qualification is still necessary, for Esther is shown to have followed the miserable pattern of the girl who is seduced and betrayed; she took to prostitution when abandoned in order to provide for her sick baby and talks wildly to Jem of her little girl, who was "like a little angel . . . 'Blessed are the pure'."[34]

Esther is not vicious, she gets no sexual pleasure from prostitution and has to dull her senses with drink to carry on. She is shown as an outcast, rejected by family and society, and is drawn in the unloveliest physical light. The 'Seed of Holiness' still survives, as her action to save Mary from a similar fate and her fears about not seeing her dead child in Heaven go to show, but nowhere is any hint of a possible reconciliation with society given. She might have been saved—the possibility is rhetorically hinted at but not developed—if Jem had been quicker when she first talked to him about Mary, but Jem's thoughts are elsewhere and it is too late when he considers that:

He had not done enough to save her. One more effort, and she might have come.[35]

but this 'saving' refers to the soul and personal life. As it is she is left literally homeless, sleeping in the streets. But if society fails to receive her living, it makes its gesture as she is dying, and she dies repentant, forgiven by the family, with a soul reverting to innocence:

[33] *Hopkins*, p. 89.   [34] *Mary Barton*, p. 186.   [35] ibid., p. 190.

She held the locket containing her child's hair still in her hand, and once or twice she kissed it with a long soft kiss.[36]

Mrs. Gaskell is quite plain about the miseries of Esther's profession, and nowhere in her work is there any suggestion that sexual passion provides pleasure or profit in itself. But even in this, her only forthright treatment of prostitution, Esther is seen as a mother manquée; it proves impossible to discuss her without coming back to this point.

'Lizzie Leigh' makes the same point even more clearly. Lizzie hovers round the house where she has abandoned her child[37] but she is luckier than Esther; her mother finds her. There is no social forgiveness, the pair retire to live in deep isolation quietly doing good, but Lizzie has been allowed to remake the closest family tie and it is implied that she is forgiven, at a distance, by her brother and his wife, the girl who had taken in the abandoned baby. The problem of the child is still avoided however, the novelist has to arrange an accidental death for it in order to side-step any real solution. And although we see the beginnings of Lizzie's public regeneration in the blessings of the remote poor to whom she dedicates her life, the embargo on the child still persists:

They dared not lay her by the stern grandfather in Milne Row churchyard, but they bore her to a lone moorland graveyard . . .[38]

A further step was needed to show that the claim to a position in society as well as to maternal love were rights that society could think about respecting.

In *Ruth* there is no question of prostitution. Ruth is a seduced innocent and is reclaimed by her adopted family, the Bensons. By now Mrs. Gaskell has come out openly in favour of the view that the fallen woman—not a prostitute—can earn reacceptance into normal life, but a powerful and hardly subsidiary theme is the right of the illegitimate child Leonard to a proper home and a place in society. By the time of Betty in *My Lady Ludlow* the

[36] *Mary Barton*, p. 456.
[37] The suggestion that Lizzie should not abandon the child completely came from Dickens, but even without the amended climax of her return the nexus of the mother-child interest is clear.　　[38] *Cranford*, p. 240.

unmarried mother is already dead; Miss Galindo adopts the daughter (Betty) and she eventually marries the reclaimed urchin Harry Gregson, who has become a respected schoolmaster and is another outcast finally accepted by society.[39]

The progression is a clear one. The interest in the child and its freedom from any taint is present from the beginning, grows stronger and finally dominates. (In 'The Manchester Marriage' where accidental bigamy is the theme—which Tennyson took up in 'Enoch Arden'—the returned castaway drowns himself after realizing that his wife has children by the second marriage.) The problem of the fallen woman is not stressed as primarily one of sin, while the pressure of poverty is seen working on maternal love for a starving child rather than on selfish interests. Where a child is concerned, the right to a family life is more important than any question of propriety.

To return to *Ruth* briefly. Mrs. Gaskell spends a good deal of time describing the effect on Leonard of the circumstances of his birth. The first stage covers his upbringing before the secret is discovered, a model upbringing by Mrs. Gaskell's standards. The household is a God-fearing yet humane one, he has affection without being spoilt, he is well educated and his character is given a solid foundation. When the secret is revealed, the effects of the discovery fall with most impact on him, and only the security of home enables him to survive the trial. The climax to his own story is when he is adopted again, after Ruth has died in an almost holy glory, by the local doctor who reveals that he too is illegitimate, yet is now married and universally respected. The addition of this artificially contrived ending as a descant on the theme is further evidence that to consider *Ruth* merely as a treatment of the 'fallen woman' is to overlook the equally important theme of the family and upbringing which encloses it. To say as much is not to deny the obvious importance placed on the declared aim of inducing the public to modify its ideas about sin as related to the 'fallen

[39] Mrs. Browning, in *Aurora Leigh*, had set a kind of precedent by making Romney Leigh propose to Marian Erle. Even if the marriage does not take place, the characters and situation are treated seriously. But it is useful to recall that Jane Austen in *Emma* had created a novel whose plot revolves round Emma's plans to make a bastard, Harriet, marry a gentleman.

woman', although as Greg pointed out in 'The False Morality of
Lady Novelists' her arguments were contradictory; if Ruth was so
pure then it was false morality to require her to die in the process
of redemption. One suspects that Mrs. Gaskell was aware of the
necessity of reconciling moral principles with the realities of
social practice:

Ruth *must needs* perish, but atoned and glorified. That is required by
man's sense of the Eternal Laws of the World's-order.[40]

I have already commented on the theme of reconciliation as a
logical consequence of the nature of Mrs. Gaskell's religious belief. Reconciliation implies some form of conflict between individuals or between social groups, or between both, and *North
and South* is an example of a novel quite deliberately structured to
engineer a complex of such conflicts. Bunsen's comment touches
on this point, that the conflict lies between 'laws' and individual
principles. It is this awareness of and sensitivity to the conflict
that is one of the elements helping to raise Mrs. Gaskell's work
above the common run. We have seen the foundations on which
the individual standards were raised; it is next necessary to examine two other aspects which are of major importance to a
right understanding of her work, her attitude to tradition and her
interest in the behaviour of individuals and communities. The
two have much in common.

[40] Letter of the Chevalier Bunsen to Susannah Winkworth quoted in Shaen, op. cit.,
p. 99. Mrs. Gaskell knew that this sort of judgement need not be correct; in the introduction to 'The Well of Pen Morfa' (1850) she relates a true story of a woman who earned
the respect of her neighbours by her care of her crippled illegitimate child. The death of
Ruth is an uneasy gesture—the melodrama and style reveal it—to public and social
convention, and was rightly attacked by discerning critics.

CHAPTER V

Tradition and Transformation

By the eighteen-sixties the wrench is past; the 'antediluvians',
the 'patriarchs', in a decreasing minority, 'mumble their old stories'
of a vanished world—of their Dorlecote Mills and their Holling-
fords, and their Dullboroughs. The two worlds are by then at least
separate and distinct . . .[1]

The 'wrench' is from the old pre-railway England to the new
post-railway era. It created a contrast of the two worlds that
was as important for the Englishman of the time as was the
existence of Disraeli's two nations:

Changes in the landscape of town and country, movements of population, changes in social habits, all were abrupt, disconcerting, immediately evident.[1]

It was a change that Arnold symbolized in 'Thyrsis' by the search
for the signal elm in a landscape which:

Hath since our day put by
The coronals of that forgotten time.
Down each green bank hath gone the ploughboy's team . . .[2]

For Mrs. Gaskell, brought up in a traditional and self-contained
community where the neighbouring railroad 'had been vehe-
mently petitioned against' as 'obnoxious',[3] then translated by
marriage to the industrial centre of England (yet only fifteen
miles away) whose society had early realized:

what great future lay concealed in that rude model of Sir Richard
Arkwright's.[4]

[1] *Tillotson*, p. 107.
[2] Matthew Arnold, *The Poetical Works*, O.U.P., 1942, p. 389.
[3] *Cranford*, p. 4.   [4] *North and South*, p. 95.

the fact of change was sharply and continuously brought home as a social and technological phenomenon. Her novels derive energy and depth from her apprehension of this situation, they reflect in many ways the desire to find a basis of stability in the shifting pattern of the age she lived in.

We have so far examined two 'stable' elements, those of religion and of the family and its affections. Both of these may be primarily regarded as individual matters; ultimately they affect society powerfully, but they are seen from the first as private concerns and confirmed at the last by private experience and judgement.[5] For Mrs. Gaskell they provide the basis on which the individual can adjust his own character to the world around him. They also reflect the importance which she attached to individual feelings, to the emotions rather than to the intellect.

But important as these feelings were to her, she was exercised equally by the idea of change in the relationships between different groups. She realized, and not simply intuitively, that the forces at work were such as to destroy the social attitudes and beliefs previously shared by all sections of society and which had provided a sense of communal unity cutting across distinctions of class and wealth. The physical change in the world around her she could take in her stride; however much she preferred the country to the new industrial town she had no sentimental feeling about old things simply because they were old (a different matter from feelings about things which carried sentimental associations or social values). She notes with obvious approval the growth of Keighley as a manufacturing centre:

Keighley is in process of transformation from a populous old-fashioned village into a still more populous and flourishing town. It is evident to the stranger that, as the gable-ended houses, which obtrude themselves corner-wise on the widening street, fall vacant, they are pulled down to allow of greater space for traffic and a more modern style of

[5] 'Not that I meerly owe this Title Christian to the Font, my Education, or the clime wherein I was born (as being bred up either to confirm those Principles my Parents instilled into my unwary Understanding, or by a general consent proceed in the Religion of my Country;) but having in my riper years and confirmed Judgement seen and examined all . . .'
Sir Thomas Browne, *Religio Medici*, Everyman, 1940, p. 3.

architecture. The quaint and narrow shop-windows of fifty years ago are giving way to large panes and plate-glass . . . nothing can be more opposed than the state of society, the modes of thinking, the standards of reference on all points of morality, manners, and even politics and religion, in such a new manufacturing place as Keighley in the north, and any stately, sleepy, picturesque, cathedral town in the south. Yet the aspect of Keighley promises well for future stateliness, if not picturesqueness.[6]

This seems very far from being the voice of the narrator of *Cranford*; it is very like the narrator of *North and South*, and it is the voice of Mrs. Gaskell 'in propria persona' commenting on the changing scene. It is also, we may note in passing, the thematic structure of *North and South* being carried over for use in the biography, a part of the shaping process to which the *Life* was subjected. Picturesqueness is put quietly in its place where the needs of progress are concerned, as well as having its inconvenience noted: 'There is no painted wood to require continual beautifying, or else present a shabby aspect', she notes in the passage from which I have quoted. The reference to the state of society in the new industrial centre is particularly illuminating. It is not made pejoratively, just noted as a key to any understanding of the area, while the manner of its insertion represents a quiet stressing of a comparison which Mrs. Gaskell makes because these matters are to her of primary significance, even though her immediate aim is introductory description.

Yet the tone of *Cranford* is one that re-emerges, modified and capable of greater range, in the final and most successful work, and is present as an undertone even in *North and South*; it is a reflection of her feeling for tradition. This is not simply a matter of realizing the importance of continuity in an age of change, nor of noting with regret the passing of manners and customs to which memory and affection cling, though both these aspects are present. There is also the sense in which tradition is the family group writ large, society as an organic growth handing down its values through the generations and ensuring that within the changing environment society retains a cohesion of manners and

[6] *Life*, pp. 1-2.

values. Yet tradition is itself liable to change, Hollingford is not
Cranford. Nor are individual traditions considered necessarily to
be good in themselves. Mrs. Gaskell inserts a telling episode into
the closing chapters of *North and South* when Margaret revisits her
old home, the pretty southern village of Helstone still remote from
the railway, and encounters the incident of a cat being roasted
alive to bring about fulfilment of a wish. Tradition which implies
squalor and ignorance is not to be cloaked under sentimental
attitudes, such as those expressed by her conservative godfather
Mr. Bell about the supposedly gentle, natural influences of home
training and Bible reading. Education is part of the change and
must be used to eliminate what is outworn or wrong:

> I own I am wrong about schooling. Anything rather than have that
> child brought up in such practical paganism.[7]

as Mr. Bell hurriedly admits, and schooling implies the influence
of society upon society to supplement and where necessary correct
the narrower range and vision of family life. It is a theme she
expanded in *My Lady Ludlow.*

In this sense 'Tradition' is a wide concept which has to be
distinguished from any wholesale respect for 'traditions', for it
embraces major issues of continuity, order and the transmission of
standards in society at large. Within this concept the values of the
present can be shown in relation to the values of the past by
using examples; Cranford is itself a symbol of moral and social
virtues and an attitude to life which is worth preserving even if
the detailed life is anachronistic. Miss Matty's shouldering of
personal responsibility for her shares in the bank which failed
gives us the contrast.

Mrs. Gaskell, in spite of her awareness of the necessity for
change, regards tradition as a value in its own right, giving
weight and a spiritual authority to those sections of life it touches.
For this is the point; certain sections of life—they can be thought
of in general terms as the ones contained in the new forms of
society—are by virtue of their newness untraditional, they are
both the agents and representatives of change. But other sections

---

[7] *North and South*, p. 467.

—largely those concerned with relationships between individuals —have a tradition based on accepted values. In conditions of change the pressure on traditional values increases because the social forms which have in the past adapted themselves to contain and transmit these values may no longer be available. We have noted how Mrs. Gaskell seizes on this issue within the narrow range of the family, dwelling on the dangers involved when the family unit is threatened. The same situation applies in the larger context of society when it has to reorganize itself to meet new demands after some of its roots with tradition are severed. This happens in *Mary Barton* and *North and South* because of industrialization; it also happens in 'Lois the Witch' when a community is transplanted and has to put down fresh roots in a changed environment. In each case there is a process of adaptation during which these beliefs and standards which Mrs. Gaskell regarded as vitally important are endangered.

In order to be able to carry the argument further we must return to show the ways in which tradition appears in her work. It will be found as widely diffused and as integral as religion, ranging from religion itself, through class distinctions and environment down to delight in the quirks and peculiarities of local customs and amateur antiquarianism. For the sake of convenience this range can be considered under a few headings, but the distinctions will necessarily be arbitrary in so far as they represent facets of one thing.

At the beginning of December 1857 Mrs. Gaskell wrote a long chronicle letter to Norton, its main theme being the delight in finally achieving her desire to see Oxford and in sharing for a few days its special life and historical associations. She exclaims, in a passage which has been often used for explaining its author:

. . . I like dearly to call up pictures,—and thoughts suggested by so utterly different a life to Manchester. I believe I *am* Mediaeval,— and *un* Manchester, and un American. I do like associations . . . I like Kings and Queens, and nightingales and mignonettes and roses.[8]

[8] *Letters*, p. 16.

and later on, deploring the possible lack of appreciation in America of all that Christmas means, she sends her greeting to the ballad historian, Child, for:

I believe he likes old things and customs enough to understand me.[9]

Her comments reveal a mind that turns naturally and with pleasure to 'old things and customs', as well as revealing a reaction against those features of modernity that Manchester and America stood for; they further indicate a romantic rather than a historical view of the past, which the emphasis on 'associations' stresses. This interest in the past is an interest in its own right, irrespective of the ideas and significances that accrete round episodes, and it crops up throughout her writing. Her earliest published work was the letter on Clopton House which she contributed when still at school to William Howitt's *Visits to Remarkable Places*, while her non-fictional work reveals her constant delight in curious customs and historical incidents, the human interest being an essential element in them. The past excites her curiosity while leading on to a consideration of human interests and behaviour.

She is not, however, as she claims under the heady influence of Oxford, 'mediaeval'; she seems to be largely unaffected by the mediaevalizing of the period and only in one episode does she perpetrate anything that seems to fall in with that particular fashion. This is the unconvincing scene in *Sylvia's Lovers* in which the sick and weary Philip temporarily becomes a Bedesman in the old charitable hospital of St. Sepulchre on his way home from war to his wife. But what does occur frequently is detail about past custom and about things to which she can attribute associations, actual or imagined. These include the customs and stories which fill *Cranford*, old Alice's knowledge of herbs in *Mary Barton*, the long digression in the *Life* about the guild of crossbow-men who once lived at the Pensionnat Héger, the frequent references to old traditions about flowers; one could extend the list indefinitely. Very rarely one comes across an almost Hardy-like leap of the imagination, as in the description of the gargoyle which symbolizes for Ruth a hope and a peace:

[9] *Letters*, p. 18.

If mortal gaze had never sought its meaning before, in the deep shadow where it had been placed long centuries ago, yet Ruth's did now.[10]

She could reconstruct the lives and manners of the past to some extent, as in *Sylvia's Lovers*, and was prepared to go to considerable pains in such a case to achieve a reasonable authenticity of background and event. But she is not a historian or a historical novelist, her interest stops short at the extension of her knowledge for sheer love of history or further insight. Her approach is indicated when she states:

I have always been interested in the conversation of any one who could tell me anything about the Huguenots; and, little by little, I have picked up many fragments of information respecting them. . . . I have now told all I know about the Huguenots. I pass the mark to some one else.[11]

These first and last sentences from her article 'Traits and Stories of the Huguenots' are, with the title itself, not unfairly representative of her historical method. Her too ready acceptance of highly coloured stories about Charlotte Brontë's father, and of the supposed affaire between Branwell and his employer's wife (Mrs. Robinson) will also be recalled.

The demonstration of this interest in 'old customs and things'— it cannot really be called an antiquarian interest—can be briefly dealt with, for we are not discussing a novelist who, like Scott, is actively appealing through detail and reference to our historical imagination. Several of her shorter stories are re-workings or embroidering of local tales or events, and a favourite way of beginning a story is by some sentence such as:

I have always been much interested by the traditions which are scattered up and down North Wales relating to Owen Glendower . . .[12]

Such stories come fluently and complete, rather too fluently and complete for the good of artistic self-control and quality. Much of this work, for example 'The Squire's Story' which retells the history of a local highwayman who set up as a gentleman, or

---

[10] *Ruth*, p. 280.   [11] *Cranford*, pp. 490 and 505.
[12] Introduction to 'The Doom of the Griffiths', *My Lady Ludlow*, p. 237.

'Morton Hall' with its elaborate three-phased historical narrative woven melodramatically round the history of a house and the theme of reconciliation, is deliberate hack-work. It came easily, and also provided an outlet for another strain in Mrs. Gaskell's nature, the not unusual combination of an interest in the supernatural with a streak of morbidity. It was a mixture which admirably suited Dickens as the editor of *Household Words* and *All the Year Round*, and Mrs. Gaskell knew that she could place such work without any great difficulty. There are signs that she was aware of the level at which these stories operated and recognized the dangers to an artist in producing for such a market. Certainly the attempt to have 'Lois the Witch' published elsewhere, and her disappointment at failing, are clear enough. Even allowing for Mrs. Gaskell's antipathy to Dickens' editorial methods, and for the strained relationship which had occurred for a period because of them, there is no getting away from the dismissive force of the epithet 'Dickensy' when she writes to Norton of her failure to place 'Lois the Witch' away from *All the Year Round*:

I *know* it is fated to go into this new Dickensy periodical and I did so hope to escape it.[13]

In fairness one must add that she was still contented to carry on using the despised journal as an outlet for pocket-money work, and that although she placed her best work of the later period with Thackeray in the *Cornhill*, she also produced some material for Thackeray (e.g. 'Curious if True') which might have made Dickens hesitate.

This use of tradition, the passing on of tales and episodes with little trouble other than that of providing a reasonable polish and some structural tightening, has small concern with the more complex question of changing values. The stories provide vehicles for the demonstration of personal standards in action, but for the most part they lack depth, which is, one assumes, why she wanted to present 'Lois the Witch' in a more substantial literary environment. They do however show her receptivity for such material,

[13] Quoted in *Hopkins*, p. 154. Only a part of this letter of 9 March 1859, is given in the *Letters*.

although if Mrs. Gaskell's reputation were to depend on them there would be little more to be said about her as a writer. But she was also able to appreciate the deeper and wider reaching significance of tradition in terms of individual and social tension; personal experience and individual sympathy providing her with a way in. This receptivity for traditional material is therefore important as marking both the existence of the sympathy and an awareness that it can be significant, just as these features are important for George Eliot and Hardy; the use made of this knowledge and insight is the measure of Mrs. Gaskell's limitations and particular excellences. She has neither the intellectual sweep, the visionary and imaginative power nor the sense of history which George Eliot and Hardy in their own ways control. Her strength lies in the quality of intimate sympathy and shrewd observation; she works with an immediacy of apprehension within her narrower range of the conduct and values of ordinary society, yet she has sufficient imaginative awareness of the tensions of insecurity as they were affecting the lower levels for her to register something more than an emotional response. She does not at any stage make the complete synthesis that, for example, Dickens produces in *Bleak House*, when with one symbolic simile he unites the local incident to a sudden universal vision:

From the village school of Chesney Wold, intact as it is this minute, to the whole framework of society: from the whole framework of society, to the aforesaid framework, receiving tremendous cracks in consequence of people (ironmasters, lead-mistresses and what not) not minding their catechism, and getting out of the station unto which they are called . . . and so obliterating the landmarks, and opening the floodgates, and all the rest of it;—this is the swift progress of the Dedlock mind.[14]

She stays within the framework, or the juxtaposition of frameworks, that she knows, making only one attempt, which will be looked at later, to handle the process of change on a more general basis, yet sensitive to the feeling of instability that permeated down to small communities and cross-sections of society and of which Sir Leicester Dedlock is the indignant spokesman.

[14] *Bleak House*, O.U.P., 1951, p. 397.

The immediate debt to local tradition and custom is often acknowledged. Many stories contain a sort of preface giving the circumstances behind their acquisition and showing Mrs. Gaskell as an amateur folk-lorist and sociologist, an aspect of her method that will also need to be considered. Other episodes similarly acquired are embedded in her novels; sometimes at the expense of a drastic straining of the structure as with the story of Clément, a sixty-five page melodrama forced into the quiet narration of *My Lady Ludlow*, sometimes woven in more skilfully as is Sally's account of her wooing which she tells to amuse Ruth. Mrs. Gaskell was one of those who find it difficult to resist a digression; to this extent her fondness for reminiscence and local tales affects the mechanics of her art as well as the tautness of her style.

What sparks Mrs. Gaskell's imagination is some aspect of the past—custom, legend, monument—which still has life or to which associations can be connected. Being of a character inclined by nature and upbringing to the traditional, she was intuitively susceptible to the enrichment and force which custom could provide. Her affection for her religion is a case in point, she was hardly moved by the niceties of doctrinal matters but emotionally stirred by the traditions of the sect to which she belonged, the antiquity of the chapels at which she worshipped and the memory of the priests who had suffered for their principles during the Great Ejectment of 1662. The Unitarians could claim common ancestry with the established church, with a touch of martyrdom to boot; they certainly felt no inferiority. It is this spirit of an independence and pride upheld by tradition which supports Thurston Benson and gives meaning to the closely detailed description of the chapel 'built about the time of Matthew and Philip Henry' of which he is minister.[15] Mr. Hale, nerving himself to renounce his membership of the Established Church and

[15] *Ruth*, p. 150. The Henrys were two of the two thousand priests who suffered under the Act of Uniformity. Matthew Henry's commentaries were a standard reference work for the Unitarians. Knutsford chapel, described in *Ruth*, was built in 1689 and was the centre of the Cheshire association of which Matthew Henry was often moderator.

One can only be astonished at the sheer bad taste of Henry James's cheap sneer in *The Portrait of a Lady*:

He at least knew now that she had no traditions! It had not been in his prevision of things that she should reveal such flatness; her sentiments were worthy of a radical

his living, tries to strengthen his resolution by thinking of the two thousand and:

trying to steal some of their bravery; but it is of no use—no use—I cannot help feeling it acutely.[16]

The pull of the two traditions leaves him irresolute, suitably so for a novel whose theme is the reconciliation of old and new (though this particular problem is shelved, as Mrs. Gaskell does not meddle with doctrine, and Mr. Hale's doubts are used to manipulate the move from South to North more than to discuss religion).

This sense of the living energy of the past complements, if it is not part of, her feeling that the present is an unknown quantity to which it is difficult to assign values; at the same time it sets an involuntary limit to the period she covers. Mrs. Gaskell mainly confines herself, as has been noted, to the immediate or not too remote past, where associations can operate from personal memory or from traditions still active and which lead out to known and secure standards of conduct. She once put her consciousness of uncertainty about the new England into words, when dealing with criticism of *Mary Barton*. Having noted that the views she attributes to working men are correct within her knowledge,—'I have personal evidence,' she says—she goes on to put the problem:

I do think that we must all acknowledge that there are duties connected with the manufacturing system not fully understood as yet, and evils existing in relation to it which may be remedied in some degree, although we as yet do not see how; but surely there is no harm in directing the attention to the existence of such evils.[17]

To set against this awareness of a new type of society still groping for the social laws which would give it cohesion and a common sense of purpose, there is the picture of the unified society which is developed in *Cranford*. It is as though Mrs. Gaskell, frightened by the analysis she had felt it her duty to

newspaper or of a Unitarian preacher . . . he despised her; she had no traditions, and the moral horizon of a Unitarian minister.
                                        Houghton Mifflin and Co., N.Y., 1891, pp. 378–9.
He knew and admired Mrs. Gaskell; he knew the New England Unitarians who included Emerson and Norton.   [16] *North and South*, p. 36.
    [17] Letter from Mrs. Gaskell to Miss Ewart, quoted in *Haldane*, p. 46.

attempt, reverted instinctively to the security of the older system which co-existed with the new. For Cranford society is quite specifically presented as a system. 'There were rules and regulations for visiting and calls.' The ladies of Cranford can cope with all contingencies—the opening paragraph lists these in all their bewildering variety from chasing geese out of gardens to running the parish—while the narrator is led to conclude that many of the consequences arising from the Cranford pattern of life 'might be introduced into many circles of society to their great improvement'. The fact that the society presented is a limited one only serves to emphasize the point that everyone moved comfortably within an accepted social framework. Individual life is not cramped by such an existence; on the contrary 'each has her own individuality, not to say eccentricity, pretty strongly developed', and these 'individualities' are used as the matter of the book. But in social relationships the individuals become 'we', ('we' and 'us' are the standard pronouns), in spite of differences of wealth 'we were all aristocrats' and had 'esprit de corps'; any peculiarity had its accepted place 'as the most natural thing in the world' and society rested on the fact that 'she knew, and we knew, and she knew that we knew, and we knew that she knew that we knew.'[18] These opening pages of *Cranford*, for all their apparent ingenuousness and simplicity, explain nevertheless why when trouble does enter the Cranford world it can be so effectively dealt with. The chapter is called, we should note, 'Our Society'. The major trouble which does arise, the closure of the bank, is a manifestation of the insecurity of the new industrial world; Miss Matty meets it as an individual by acting on personal standards, but she is then supported by a social structure which appreciates and shares those standards, understands its duties and has evolved patterns of behaviour to support the individual as a member of the community. Moreover all ranks, from servant and labourer to aristocracy, acquiesce in the structure; where change has to be faced, as when Lady Glenmire marries Mr. Hoggins, the society is able to embrace the change by an adjustment that allows for moral and individual values and yet preserves the framework.

[18] These quotations all occur in the introductory pages 1–4.

The introduction to *Ruth* shows Mrs. Gaskell still consciously trying to get to grips with the relationship between old and new conventions, and the tension arising when some particular problem places individual conduct at variance with what is normally accepted. The passage must be quoted at length; it follows an introductory paragraph which describes carefully the appearance of an old country town and conjures up a brief scene by day and night:

The traditions of those bygone times, even to the smallest social particular, enable one to understand more clearly the circumstances which contributed to the formation of character. The daily life into which people are born, and into which they are absorbed before they are well aware, forms chains which only one in a hundred has moral strength enough to despise, and to break when the right time comes— when an inward necessity for independent individual action arises, which is superior to all outward conventionalities. Therefore, it is well to know what were the chains of daily domestic habit, which were the natural leading-strings of our forefathers before they learnt to go alone.

The picturesqueness of those ancient streets has departed now. The Astleys, the Dunstans, the Waverhams—names of power in that district—go up duly to London in the season, and have sold their residences in the county town fifty years ago, or more. And when the county town lost its attraction for the Astleys, the Dunstans, the Waverhams, how could it be supposed that the Domvilles, the Bextons, and the Wildes would continue to go and winter there in their second-rate houses, and with their increased expenditure? So the grand old houses stood empty awhile; and then speculators ventured to purchase, and to turn the deserted mansions into many smaller dwellings, fitted for professional men, or even (bend your ear lower, lest the shade of Marmaduke, first Baron Waverham, hear) into shops!

Even that was not so very bad, compared with the next innovation on the old glories. The shopkeepers found out that the once fashionable street was dark, and that the dingy light did not show off their goods to advantage; the surgeon could not see to draw his patients' teeth; the lawyer had to ring for candles an hour earlier than he was accustomed to do when living in a more plebeian street. In short, by mutual consent, the whole front of one side of the street was pulled down, and rebuilt in the flat, mean, unrelieved style of George the Third.[19]

[19] *Ruth*, pp. 2–3.

The complicated relationship which is traced between tradition and conduct takes in environment, upbringing and character before pointing to the necessity of tension between tradition, in its form of convention, and moral integrity, for the expression 'when the right time comes' indicates an inherent inevitability. The fact of change is stated, as it is in the previously quoted extract from the *Life*, in terms of a description of change visibly in action in a community, although in this case the change is regarded more as a process of decline. Both in *Ruth* and in the *Life* attention is focused on the encroachment of commerce and the professions; in the former we see also a shrewd eye cast on the ecology of social classes.

But the interesting feature is that the introduction promises far more than the novel performs. *Ruth* does deal with the defiance of convention, but there is little or no attempt made in it to portray the links with the past, while the descriptive passages amplifying the theory turn out to have little function other than to serve as a rather grandiose preliminary to the setting of the milliner's workroom in which we first see Ruth.

It is almost as if the problem was felt so urgently that Mrs. Gaskell composed a preliminary justification for the position when she was not in fact ready to deal with it, not that the social problem novel was ever the genre to which she was really suited. *Ruth* narrows down to the one theme, important enough admittedly, of the conflict between 'moral strength' and 'outward conventionalities', but the vaster theme of the gradual dissolution of old traditions and the rise of new forms of society, which is adumbrated in the gradual transfiguration of the old buildings, is hardly touched on. The Bellingham family, which was presumably meant to represent the old aristocratic tradition, is diminished in importance, as far as appearance in the novel goes, to supplying stock figures for the plot; there is the haughty aristocratic mother and the weak aristocratic seducer of a son who both act according to the clichés of class privilege. The action still rests on individual values, mainly those that have been discussed in the previous sections.

The deliberate attempt to write such a novel as the first few pages of *Ruth* seem to presage was never made in fact. Mrs. Gaskell's nearest attempt to it was in *North and South*, which represents her supreme effort to write the novel of social change. It was a failure; it was bound to be one. However genuinely and rationally she could welcome the good points of the new order and of individuals who represented it, her imagination was not seized by the prospect of 'Progress' as was Dickens's or Tennyson's. She reflects a different patterning of values seen from a different angle, and as she is both an honest and a sensitive observer this is part of her importance. *North and South* reached its conclusions by a mechanical process of equating values; it fulfilled the moral duty she felt as a novelist and which, as she had confided to Miss Ewart, was part of her reason for choosing the subject matter of *Mary Barton*. She could go no further, for her inclinations and sympathies were against this approach. She turned back to examine the traditions and social order which represented the stability she knew. In doing so she paid more attention to two aspects which had always been present in her work, but which now assumed a greater prominence: the values inherent in the life of the country as opposed to the life of the town, and the acceptance of a social hierarchy. These have now to be considered.

CHAPTER VI

The World of Manchester

MRS. GASKELL is a regional novelist, but she is at home in more than one region. It is this sense of familiarity, the feeling of being 'at home', that is one of the qualities of her better work and gives some tint of naturalness even to the Penny Magazine tracts. She has been regarded as the novelist of Knutsford and Manchester. Yvonne ffrench stated in 1949 that:

For at least two decades after her death she was popularly identified as "the author of *Mary Barton*". Three generations later, by a process of readjustment, she is established for good as the author of *Cranford*.[1]

With the passage of another fifteen years the author of *Mary Barton* is still known, with *Ruth* and *North and South* also in the reckoning, while the creator of *Cranford* has had her reputation enhanced by the recognition belatedly given to *Wives and Daughters* and *Cousin Phillis*. Yet the antithesis of Knutsford and Manchester is a basic one and must be understood, although as an explanation of her work it is too simple, and makes little allowance for the range and subtlety of her observations. It tends to support by inference the view that Mrs. Gaskell is either a reminiscent or a reform novelist. At the same time it fails to make clear that her development stems from both sides, and these sides contain values which she finds elsewhere as well, although most prominently and conveniently in her two 'homes'. However, once we realize that her range of reference and experience is wider, Knutsford and Manchester are convenient symbols to use, while as areas of reference and social background they are very important.

In one sense she may be regarded as the novelist of a single region, that of North-West England in the middle of the nine-

---

[1] *Mrs. Gaskell*, Home and Van Thal, 1949, p. 43.

teenth century. The area she knows and writes of is geographically a compact one, from Denbighshire in North Wales (Ruth adopts the pseudonym of Mrs. Denbigh) to the Lake District. She can move outside it, as Hardy occasionally moved outside of Wessex, but on the whole she stays within. But whereas Hardy's Wessex is a spiritual and social as well as a geographical unit, Mrs. Gaskell's region was one of violent contrasts of every sort. For Hardy the division between town and country does not exist, as the famous description of Casterbridge makes clear:

Casterbridge was the complement of the rural life around; not its urban opposite. Bees and butterflies in the corn-fields at the top of the town, who desired to get to the meads at the bottom, took no circuitous course, but flew straight down High Street without any apparent consciousness that they were traversing strange latitudes.[2]

and in his untouched countryside man's nature is measured starkly against the long perspective of historical and evolutionary time. But for Mrs. Gaskell the town stood out as something alien to the countryside:

A low grey cloud was the first sign of Eccleston; it was the smoke of the town hanging over the plain.[3]

and the inhabitants of the town formed a society that had little in common with the countryside around it. The landmarks of Nature had been obliterated, and visible history stretched back at most a couple of hundred years, marked by a house or a chapel. Town is in contrast with country, the country on the whole preserving traditions that the town had destroyed. Their contrasts and oppositions dominate Mrs. Gaskell's work: she had made her home in each and her development involves the gradual process of choice between the standards and feelings which each invoked, together with some attempt to reconcile the good she found in each.

There are a number of stories and articles that deal with life and events outside of this area. The chief of these, the novel *Sylvia's Lovers*, can perhaps be regarded as an extension (the Whitby area

[2] Thomas Hardy, *The Mayor of Casterbridge*, Macmillan, 1920, p. 68.
[3] *Ruth*, p. 132.

of Yorkshire, where she went on holiday) of the Lancashire background, and is distinctive rather for being an historical novel, a peculiarity it shares with 'Lois the Witch' and some short stories. Another influence derives from her travels in Europe, notably from the interest she developed in France. The European experience is responsible for several stories and articles, as well as for episodes and detail such as the holiday in Rome and the misfortunes of the voyage home which occur in 'A Dark Night's Work'. In most of the articles and stories which do handle historical material one can also trace that type of interest which is not so much historical as a lively curiosity about strange, novel, or old customs and the people affected by them.

Besides *Mary Barton* there appeared in 1848 a small volume called *Life in Manchester* which contained three short stories. These were 'Libbie Marsh's Three Eras', 'The Sexton's Hero', and 'Christmas Storms and Sunshines', written and originally published in *Howitt's Journal* under the pseudonym of Cotton Mather Mills in the latter half of 1847 and the beginning of 1848. The second and third stories are moral anecdotes which have negligible reference to Manchester itself. The second, a story of quiet heroism, has a well described setting on the Lancashire coast supporting a dramatic and pathetic local story. The third is a Dickensian type of lower middle-class domestic sketch, attempted in the Dickens vein of descriptive humorous characterization and pathos. Mrs. Gaskell is not at home with lower class gentility nor with Dickens's humorous method, and she wisely does not repeat this attempt at life in the Todgers manner. But the other story, though trite and moralizing, has its interest for her development. It is the first of a series of tales and novels by Mrs. Gaskell which had Manchester as a setting and which continued until, with the appearance of *North and South* in 1855, Manchester abruptly vanished from Mrs. Gaskell's scene.[4] From these stories we may understand what Manchester stood for in her work.

In 'Libbie Marsh's Three Eras' interest as far as the story goes is

[4] 'The Manchester Marriage' (1858) has nothing to do with Manchester apart from its opening paragraphs, which are discussed later. See p. 267 for the link between 'Libbie Marsh's Three Eras' and *Mary Barton*.

focused on Libbie herself, the plain girl who finds happiness in helping a sick child and then in comforting the embittered mother when the child dies. The attitude is based firmly on conceptions of individual belief and duty, pointed by the moral (it is called that) which concludes the tale: 'She has a purpose in life; and that purpose is a holy one.'[5] But a further interest is provided by the method of narration. The construction is in three episodes which are used to sketch in aspects of working-class life as they affect two groups of characters; the careless extravagance of a family with some security and relative wealth being opposed to the struggles and misfortunes of a less prosperous one. The eye for detail based on intimate knowledge is already at work, and the background is at least as interesting as the plot, while avoiding too much sentiment. Manchester emerges out of three scenes, to which she gives the titles Valentine's Day, Whitsuntide, and Michaelmas. By choosing local holidays for the episodes she is able to include a variety of local customs and traditions as well as to provide herself with an easy device for dealing with the time element, but it is the central episode rather than the general technique that requires our attention here. It describes the customary Whitsuntide outing to the country, and in it we find Mrs. Gaskell's first presentation of Manchester as ugliness and dirt, a condition of life automatically precluding anything gracious or satisfying to the senses, an environment calculated to degrade and depress. She sees its inhabitants as nevertheless responsive to the influence of Nature when given the chance, and takes the narrator's privilege of commenting on it in a Wordsworthian and rather patronizing way. (This hint of the patronizing soon disappears from her work.)

Depend upon it, this complete sylvan repose, this accessible quiet, this lapping the soul in green images of the country, forms the most complete contrast to a town's-person, and consequently has over such the greatest power of charm.[6]

Charm is one asset Manchester never has for Mrs. Gaskell. It possesses the moral virtues, as she interpreted them, and is

[5] *Mary Barton*, p. 489.
[6] ibid., p. 474. The style is unfortunate, but this is beginner's work.

eminently an arena for their display; the story is meant to illustrate that these virtues—supported by religion—are part of the
nature of man. But Manchester was also an inescapable fact, for
her as well as for her characters; the turning away from it that
marks the later stages of her career owes a good deal to personal
antipathy, although it is never the attempt to turn back the clock
that William Morris later proposed. Nor does she make the
mistake of equating the hard life of the mill hand with inevitable
drabness and the debasement of the intelligence and the emotions.
If she shows amply enough how this could happen, and a main
purpose was to show that it did happen, she was also to show a
love of beauty and a lively intellectual curiosity as capable of co-
existing with squalor and poverty. We touch on one of the
essentials in her view of the 'Manchester' way of life when dealing
with this aspect of charm. She would have agreed in this one
respect with Morris; man does not live by bread alone, yet the
Manchester she depicts offered little to the spirit. It was 'ugly,
smoky Manchester' even though in the same breath it was also
'dear busy, earnest, noble-working Manchester',[7] and much as
she praised its virtues and recognized the individual qualities of
those who lived in it, she was temperamentally averse to living
there herself.

Mrs. Gaskell's letters and her life itself support this view. The
letters contain frequent descriptions of the countryside or of
places of interest but Manchester is hardly ever mentioned without
a groan. This desire to get away from Manchester has been
referred to already in the general context of traditions and
associations, but a positive dislike is also present. 'I should like
to be going tomorrow', she wrote to Norton about a trip she
proposed:

---

[7] *Mary Barton*, p. 477. The influence of Carlyle at this stage is obvious, but Manchester
by now had become the symbol of the new age. Disraeli, responsive as always to the feeling of the times, had expressed it in suitably dramatic terms in 1844:

  "Ah! but the Mediterranean!" exclaimed Coningsby. "What would I not give to
see Athens!"

  "I have seen it," said the stranger, slightly shrugging his shoulders, "and more
wonderful things. Phantoms and spectres. The Age of Ruins is past. Have you seen
Manchester?"

                            Coningsby, Hughenden edition, 1882, pp. 114–15.

and out of this misty foggy Manchester, which gives me a perpetual headache very hard to bear.[8]

and later she mentions:

one of my bad head aches; which I am afraid are produced by the air of Manchester, as I hardly ever have them—certainly not anything like so violently; anywhere else.[9]

It is difficult not to connect Mrs. Gaskell's bad health with a mental as well as a physical reaction to her environment, or to avoid drawing conclusions from the fact that as she earned more money from her writing she spent longer periods away from the city. The purchase of the house at Alton in Hampshire, with the purpose of inducing her husband to retire and live there, was the final effort. She died at Alton when her plans were made but before she was able to try inducing her husband to make the break. The attempt would certainly have failed for the Rev. Mr. Gaskell enjoyed his work and his surroundings. Paradoxically, domestic ties, which she held in such high regard, were themselves an obstacle to her wishes.

Manchester was not merely a depressing place to live in, it represented also a burden of duties which her character and position compelled her to accept, and we have seen that she was not at all clear what those duties ought to be. So the anxiety over the lack of a precise sense of purpose, which was a direct result of strange and changing conditions, was added to her distaste for the city itself. It influenced her later decision to concentrate as a novelist on communities and patterns of behaviour which she could interpret with a confidence derived from being fully and affectionately aware of the social forces at work.

One type of help, the duty of the Christian towards his fellow men, was plain enough, and Mrs. Gaskell grasped at this certainty while exploring the context within which the duties were supposed to operate. We must note here another important point about her 'Manchester', it is fully as limited in its social range as Cranford, and to the same purpose. The 'amazons' of Cranford represented in essence its moral core and energy; the mill-

[8] *Letters*, p. 44.   [9] ibid., p. 53.

working community symbolized for her the driving force of Manchester. Her own social world of the cultured professional and manufacturing class does not appear, neither do the important shopkeeping and professional communities. Another major omission is reference to the Irish immigrants who constituted a sizeable proportion of the population and were its dregs. One reason for this omission was undoubtedly religious, for tolerant as she was Mrs. Gaskell must have realized that any appeal to society through religion in general terms could not at that time have included Roman Catholicism, nor would her duties as a dissenting minister's wife have brought her into any close touch with it. She was aware of them as a group and as part of the complex social problem. In *Ruth* she correctly traces the origins of the cholera epidemic to 'the low Irish lodging houses' and acknowledges their priests as the first to give warning, while Thornton in *North and South* imports Irish labour as strike breakers. But a view of the city as a whole, embracing it with affectionate comprehension for all its blemishes in the manner with which Dickens treats his London, was never attempted, and was probably beyond her ability or sympathy. It was certainly beyond her purpose.

Both the range of society and the physical aspects of Manchester presented in *Mary Barton* are little less limited than in the preceding story. We are given a generalized working-class area, ranging from the worst type of slum to neat cheerfulness, but there is no naming of streets, districts and relationships. When we do get a rare detail, as in Barton's shopping along the prosperous London Road after pawning his clothes to buy food for the Davenports, the road is used as an excuse for moral apothegms. When Wilson walks to the Carsons to get Davenport an infirmary order we only know that he had:

about two miles to walk before he reached Mr. Carson's house, which was almost in the country.[10]

This is not Manchester the city but Manchester the symbol of a type of background for living. The detail enters with individual

[10] *Mary Barton*, p. 73.

homes, and in this early novel the descriptions are often set pieces. It is well done and tellingly done; we are left convinced that Manchester stands for conditions that affront the dignity of life and starve the senses. Even when wealth is shown, as at Carson's house, the same ugliness and tastelessness are observed, made comfortable and rather gross with money. Against this setting we see individuals, families, the social group which it concerns, fighting or succumbing to the external influence according to the strength of their moral natures and the integrity of the human heart.

The social range is equally limited, rarely moving beyond the world of the mills and more particularly of the mill workers. The mill owners necessarily appear in the plot because of the theme of reconciliation and understanding between masters and men, but we see them only as the local variant of Dives to the working Lazarus. The one exaggerated, almost caricatured scene of domestic life in a master's home is drawn less with an eye to reality than with the aim of shocking after the slum scene which precedes it. We get a small amount of variety in the working background; Mary herself is a seamstress and Alice a dealer in herbs. But the total effect is one of almost claustrophobic narrowness in the way of life. Mrs. Gaskell's achievement is to bring home the extent to which life was cramped and conditioned by the physical, social and mental environment of the new technologies.

It is within this narrow compass that Mrs. Gaskell begins to look at the complexity of the social problem, and her starting point is that the human being is an individual soul. The term 'soul' is imprecisely used; its connotations cluster round religion but extend in aesthetic, social and emotional directions, though she often reserves the term 'heart' for matters more exclusively dealing with emotions and affections. The earlier quotation from 'Libbie Marsh's Three Eras' gives us the inclusive use in the reference to 'this lapping the soul in green images of the country' and *Mary Barton*, with its opening scene of the same type of holiday excursion, repeats the point that these influences are normally excluded. It is notable that Alice Wilson, the gentlest and most patiently enduring character in the book, is sustained by her early memories of the countryside and by her trade as a herbalist which keeps her in touch with nature. The ending of the novel is also significant. The main characters emigrate, and Raymond Williams has suggested[11] that this is the author's way out from finding a genuine solution. There is some truth in this, but equally important is the life they have escaped to. Although Jem is an engineer he has contrived to settle in a setting of rustic simplicity. The Manchester family have emigrated spiritually as well, back to Nature:

I see a long, low, wooden house, with room enough and to spare. The old primeval trees are felled and gone for many a mile around; one alone remains to overshadow the gable-end of the cottage. There is a garden around the dwelling, and far beyond that stretches an orchard. The glory of an Indian summer is over all, making the heart leap at the sight of its gorgeous beauty.[12]

Not to wild, untamed nature, a town is nearby, but at least back within the influence of the 'charm' which Manchester lacked.

There are other outlets for the soul. Job Legh's interest in natural history and his granddaughter's love of music are examples of intellectual and artistic escape from the immediate environment. So in their own way are the bright colours and garish tastes that Mrs. Gaskell draws attention to: Barton's 'one gay red-and-yellow silk pocket-handkerchief' which he pawns;[13] the 'bright green japanned tea-tray, having a couple of scarlet lovers embracing in the middle', which 'gave a richness of colouring' to the Barton home;[14] Esther's love of tawdry finery foreshadowing her eventual flight. These things represent the imagination and the senses fighting against the negative forces of drabness and dreariness. Mrs. Gaskell shared in this experience and in the sense of frustration that had always to be mastered. She wrote to Norton in the spring of 1859:

We are always full of hope and of plans in the flower-line, just about this time of year. But the east winds and the smoke always come; only one cannot live without hoping.[15]

[11] op. cit., Part I, Chap. 5.   [12] *Mary Barton*, p. 457.   [13] ibid., p. 66.
[14] ibid., p. 13.   [15] *Letters*, p. 32.

Yet for all the drabness and rootlessness, fostered by circumstances ranging from 'honest, decent poverty' to 'grinding squalid misery'[16] she had been forced to recognize a strength and vigour, a sense of purpose in Manchester. She realized that a new power was thrusting through, and that the individual suffering that distressed her was in some way part of the inevitable change. In searching for an explanation that would enable her to reconcile her beliefs and humanity with the harsh effects of the change, it was natural that she should turn first to religion, in the manner of Job Legh's final opinion:

It's true it was a sore time for the hand-loom weavers when power-looms came in: them new-fangled things make a man's life like a lottery; and yet I'll never misdoubt that power-looms, and railways, and all such-like inventions, are the gifts of God. I have lived long enough, too, to see that it is a part of His plan to send suffering to bring out a higher good . . .[17]

He goes on to explain to Mr. Carson, in the passage that was previously quoted in part, the duty of the fortunate to help the less fortunate. But the religious answer was a palliative, and not a very successful one. If there was an appropriate answer, it had to be found in terms of the new power itself and the moral energy it generated.

Her perception of the new energy and its achievement is apparent in numerous small details. She comments on:

an acuteness and intelligence of countenance, which has often been noticed in a manufacturing population . . .[18]

and there is pride in the way she talks of the firm for whom Jem Wilson worked:

one of the great firms of engineers, who send from out their towns of workshops engines and machinery to the dominions of the Czar and the Sultan.[19]

[16] *Mary Barton*, p. 429.   [17] ibid., p. 448.   [18] ibid., p. 3.

[19] ibid., p. 29. Dickens speaks with similar pride about Daniel Doyce in *Little Dorrit*, but the Great Exhibition had by then produced public awareness of British engineering supremacy. It is ironical that Mrs. Gaskell's only account of the export of British skill covered the farcical visit of a gardener to Persia in 'The Shah's English Gardener'.

as there is also in the way she refers the reader to the life of Sir
J. E. Smith for an account of the scientific reputation earned by
working-class 'amateurs' in the industrial cities, of whom Job
Legh is a type.[20]

Such explicit comments are, however, infrequent at this stage
and can be interpreted also, though not wholly, as a salute to the
human spirit and intelligence which refused to be dominated by
its new surroundings. Her real tribute to the representatives of the
new spirit only comes after she has decided her own attitude to
these problems. In *Cousin Phillis* she is able to give the fine and
unsentimental account (based, according to Mrs. Haldane, on
James Nasmyth) of Paul Manning's father, and present him as a
worthy counterpart to the farmer-minister Holman. The attempt
to give just praise and recognition to the spirit of industrial
progress had in the meantime to be made, and is to be found in
North and South. Until that novel was written the use made of
Manchester or of factory life involves no deeper awareness, the
author concentrating on the individual predicament and individual moral duty. But before *North and South* can be fully understood
it becomes necessary to deal with two further points. The first,
which can be briefly handled, is that 'Manchester' does not stand
for town life in general as opposed to country life. The second
requires fuller treatment; it concerns the position that the Knutsford world and the country hold in relation to the ideas and the
emotions which 'Manchester' evoked.

In one obvious sense Manchester does of course stand for 'city'
as against 'country'; we have already remarked on its divorce
from Nature. (That word will itself need more definition later.
It covers the elements of country and of what is natural; and
regards love of the country as one aspect of the natural.) In other
ways it—or the manufacturing town of the particular novel or
story—is regarded in the conventional way as the place where
country people go wrong, adrift from the moral and customary
restraints of their closely knit communities. Girls are seduced
there, weak young men become criminal there. I have remarked
that in the industrial world we are always conscious of an air of

[20] *Mary Barton*, Chap. 5.

moral strenuousness and a sense of purpose activating industrial life. But the 'town', when it is the place where youth goes wrong, lacks these qualities. It is also the distant place, somewhere 'away'; we mainly see or hear of it from the vantage point of home. Edward Browne in 'The Moorland Cottage', Leonard Bradshaw in *Ruth*, and Benjamin Huntroyd in 'The Crooked Branch' are three varied and varyingly effective treatments of this theme of being cut off from family influence and control, with some comments on billiards, play-going, and undesirable companions to suggest the necessary temptations.

London is the 'city' in this sense, the centre where energy has been sapped, standards weakened, and where people concern themselves with trivialities. Mrs. Gaskell knew it well and after the success of *Mary Barton* visited it frequently, yet it occurs in her work only as a distant, fashionable and rather heartless contrast to Manchester. In 'The Manchester Marriage' she gave a detailed statement of how London appeared to a Mancunian—and to a great extent still does!:

he had an odd, shrewd contempt for the inhabitants; whom he always pictured to himself as fine, lazy people; caring nothing but for fashion and aristocracy, and lounging away their days in Bond Street and such places; ruining good English, and ready in their turn to despise him as a provincial. The hours that the men of business kept in the city scandalised him, too, accustomed as he was to the early dinners of Manchester folk and the consequently far longer evenings. Still, he was pleased to go to London; though he would not for the world have confessed it, even to himself . . . he might have been justified in taking a much larger house than the one he did, had he not thought himself bound to set an example to Londoners of how little a Manchester man of business cared for show. Inside, however, he furnished it with an unusual degree of comfort . . . Moreover, his northern sense of hospitality was such, that, if he were at home, he could hardly suffer a visitor to leave the house without forcing meat and drink upon him. Every servant in the house was well warmed, well fed, and kindly treated . . . he amused himself by following out all his accustomed habits and individual ways, in defiance of what any of his new neighbours might think.[21]

[21] *My Lady Ludlow*, p. 492–3.

London was strange in ways and looks. Manchester was large
enough and growing, but could still be regarded as relatively
compact and as a community of sorts in purpose, while London
was too vast for that, it was 'that big mass o' a place',[22] a lonely
place where neighbourliness was not the habit. It produced self-
centred characters, attracted there by ambition or brought up in
its atmosphere of snobbery and vanity. At best they are like Mr.
Kirkpatrick 'struggling on in his profession' until:

the comparative table-land of Q.C.-dom gained . . . Mr. Kirkpatrick
had leisure for family feeling . . .[23]

At worst they are like Henry Lennox in *North and South* or Ralph
Corbett in 'A Dark Night's Work', completely sacrificing affection and the honesty of their emotions to ambition. London
mocks the provincialism and poverty of the Chartist delegates, and
kills off Margaret's parents in *Mary Barton*, Job Legh leaving them:

in a big, crowded, lonely churchyard in London. I were loath to leave
them there, as I thought, when they rose again, they'd feel so strange
at first away fra' Manchester, and all old friends . . .[24]

We are given one side of London; quite deliberately, let us do
Mrs. Gaskell justice in this. In the *Life* she explains the attraction
of the capital for Branwell by describing it from his point of
view—'that mysterious London—that Babylon the great'[25] but
later on she can quote from *Villette* Charlotte's awareness of
distinctions which she herself knew just as well:

Since those days I have seen the West End, the parks, the fine
squares; but I love the City far better. The City seems so much more in
earnest; its business, its rush, its roar are such serious things, sights,
sounds. The City is getting its living—the West End but enjoying its
pleasure. At the West End you may be amused; but in the City you are
deeply excited.[26]

Now this is precisely a distinction Mrs. Gaskell wishes to make
between the Manchester and the London of her fiction, and which
she had expressed already; possibly this is the reason why the

[22] *Mary Barton*, p. 118.   [23] *Wives and Daughters*, pp. 486–7.
[24] *Mary Barton*, p. 118.   [25] *Life*, p. 136.   [26] ibid., p. 370.

quotation had stuck in her mind. When Margaret Hale has become an heiress in *North and South*, a brief chapter, No. 47, is devoted mainly to the London life in which she is going to live. It is a chapter whose tone is adapted chiefly to trivialities. The beginning of the next chapter swings back to Milton with something approaching the rhythm and fervour that Dickens used for his railway scenes in *Dombey and Son*, and possibly with a last echo of Carlyle:

Meanwhile at Milton the chimneys smoked, the ceaseless roar and mighty beat and dazzling whirl of machinery struggled and strove perpetually. Senseless and purposeless were wood and iron and steam in their endless labours; but the persistence of their monotonous work was rivalled in tireless endurance by the strong crowds, who, with sense and with purpose, were busy and restless in seeking after—What?[27]

The 'What?' is part of the total problem. That which demands our attention here is the sense of purpose and energy setting Milton-Manchester apart from the pursuit of pleasure and vanity, and from the accompanying moral enervation which unfortunate London was called on to epitomize.

[27] *North and South*, pp. 498–9.

CHAPTER VII

The World of Cranford

'EVERY schoolboy knows' that Cranford is Knutsford, the small country town where Mrs. Gaskell was brought up, and critical comments on her work all make this point. They seem to mean by this that Mrs. Gaskell draws on her knowledge of Knutsford and her memories of its inhabitants for her detail; its topography, its customs and traditions, its stories and incidents, even its characters are used. But when all is said and done Cranford is a fiction, however much its components are based on a reality. Nor is all of Knutsford represented by a long way; the details used are selected, and Henry James has reminded us that selection is a prime element of art. Cranford is an interpretation made through the medium of the art of fiction, and we have to ask what this interpretation is; what, in other words, Cranford represents as Mrs. Gaskell has described it.

Knowing also that Cranford (to use it as a generic name) reappears in her work under many guises, just as Manchester reappears as Drumble, Milton, etc., we have further to study its varying manifestations, and even to enquire whether it occupies always the same position in time and space. We shall find that it does not. For Cranford represents certain attitudes and standards in a way of life conveniently given substance by being embodied in the life of country-town society, although that society is itself subject to modification.

The best approach is probably through a study of *Cranford* itself. It will be necessary to say something first about the origin, development and general nature of the novel, and to deal with one objection which might be raised to treating Cranford as an interpretation. The objection—it is inherent in most of the not very satisfactory studies of *Cranford* that have appeared—is that it is not a novel, and is hardly to be ranked as fiction; that it is a set of reminiscences thinly disguised as fiction, something like Conrad's *The Mirror of the Sea* but carried slightly further in its method. How far it is a novel will be discussed when the development of Mrs. Gaskell's technique is examined. That it is fiction should be obvious as we follow the story line of each episode, and the gradual linking of episodes into a larger structural unity, while increasing our acquaintance with the relatively few characters round whom and through whom *Cranford* grows. Anecdotes and incidents, such as the story of the piece of antique lace swallowed by Mrs. Forrester's cat, are taken from life or local legend, but Mrs. Gaskell has no hesitation in altering facts and reshaping events to suit her purpose. An example of this is the first episode, originally written without thought of a successor. In this story (published in 1851) the climax worked up to is the death of Capt. Brown when he is run over by a train. Yet the railway did not come to Knutsford until 1862; Mrs. Gaskell invented the story, and since a railway was required for it, a railway there was.[1] But this is standard practice with most writers, and such a commonplace needs emphasizing only because of an attitude that seems to have developed towards this particular book.

    Cranford began as a self-contained story (now the first two chapters of the book) published by Dickens in *Household Words* on 13 December 1851, the story using material from the original short essay 'The Last Generation in England' which was published obscurely in *Sartain's Union Magazine* in America during 1849. It concentrates almost entirely on the social setting, which is firmly presented as feminine, middle-aged to elderly, genteel, and sharing a 'general but unacknowledged poverty'—although this poverty is interpreted in the light of maintaining the modest standards of gentility summed up in the phrase 'elegant economy'.[2] The setting once established, the story is woven round the arrival of the elderly widower, Capt. Brown, and his two daughters as

---

[1] G. A. Payne, *Mrs. Gaskell and Knutsford*, Clarkson and Griffiths, 1900 (p. 12) gives details about the railway. Mrs. Gaskell herself throws light on the invention of the whole story in a letter to Ruskin quoted by Ward (*Cranford*, p. xii) "The beginning of 'Cranford' was one paper in 'Household Words'; and I never meant to write more, so killed Captain Brown very much against my will."   [2] *Cranford*, p. 4.

newcomers to Cranford, and their reception by the 'Amazons'
who are won over by the frank and natural behaviour of the
Captain—even though he is a man. The elder daughter is ill and
finally dies; just before this happens the Captain is himself killed
by a train while saving a child. A faithful admirer returns to
marry the younger daughter.

As a story this first episode is slight, simple and unoriginal, a
mixture of pathos, mild melodrama and happy ending. Yet the
unobtrusive and undemanding nature of the story is its virtue; it is
admirably suited to permit the narrative of daily incident and custom which carries it along and provides the real interest. The central
figure is not, in fact, Captain Brown; it is Miss Deborah Jenkyns, the
rector's daughter and admitted arbitrator of Cranford manners.

The enthusiasm of Dickens and his readers prompted Mrs.
Gaskell to provide further episodes, and with these episodes she
made important changes. The dominating Miss Jenkyns has died;
her quiet and unassertive sister, Miss Matty, becomes the central
figure. It is around Miss Matty that the episodes develop until they
have finally limned her history and character in a narrative that
accumulates unity as it proceeds. And all the time the delicate
nuances of behaviour in the circumscribed society and its small
country town are being described in incidents that, whether trivial
or major within the narrative, keep proportion to the social scene.
Miss Matty's muted early love affair, the youth and disappearance of
her brother, the stir caused by the marriage of an 'aristocratic' Cran-
fordian to the local surgeon, the loss of her small income and the
return of the missing brother are the main threads which take us
back and forwards in time as the dialogue and narrative quietly
build up an acutely observed and detailed study of a way of life.[3]

[3] The sixteen chapters of the book as we now have it (excluding the much later addition
'The Cage at Cranford', 1863), were originally published as eight episodes in nine instalments at unequal intervals between 13 Dec. 1851 and 21 May 1853. They all appeared in
Household Words and were published as a book in June 1853. The eight episodes—I give present chapter numbers after each—were with minor modifications 'Our Society at Cranford'
(1–2), 'A Love Affair at Cranford' (3–4), 'Memory at Cranford' (5–6), 'Visiting at Cranford' (7–8), 'The Great Cranford Panic', in two instalments (9–11), 'Stopped Payment at
Cranford' (12–13), 'Friends in Need at Cranford' (14), and 'A Happy Return to Cranford'
(15–16). These titles show clearly the intention to describe facets of Cranford life, yet
the change from the early descriptive titles to the later story titles also marks the transition
to a more definite narrative structure.

Cranford makes its initial impression by its tone and by the sheer felicity of incident and dialogue. The narrative attitude is one of humour, a humour based on sympathy and affection laced with common sense and a nice eye (or ear) for observation. It admits that life can be serious, but the narrative viewpoint is just sufficiently detached to keep events in proportion, and to refuse to act as though a recognition of what is serious necessarily involves solemnity or joylessness. The observation is shrewd; it notes what is amusing without poking fun. Above all it is the sort of humour that is possible only in an environment in which the general run of events is pleasant, and the inhabitants are free from the continual presence of hardship and the daily evidence of man's inhumanity to man. Given such surroundings, it is possible to concentrate on the minor details of life—one's own and one's neighbours.

Cranford life is securely built on an accepted order of behaviour. When Jessie Brown insists on going to her father's funeral, Miss Jenkyns firmly pronounces:

It is not fit for you to go alone. It would be against both propriety and humanity were I to allow it.[4]

And in saying this she has mentioned the two principles—propriety and humanity—which directly control Cranford conduct. The book is a portrayal of a community where these principles govern action; there may be argument on the interpretation of propriety (never about humanity) but it is unthinkable that any other basis of conduct can exist. It is because of this that *Cranford* is in its essence, not simply in its background and detail, different from the Manchester stories, in which propriety and humanity are present but can also be conspicuously absent. Drumble, the great manufacturing town only twenty miles from Cranford, is mentioned just often enough to keep us aware that other attitudes exist. It is at Drumble that the Town and Country Bank in which Miss Matty's small savings are invested stops payment, an impersonal attitude to obligations which Miss Matty quietly refutes

[4] *Cranford*, p. 21.

by changing Farmer Dobson's now worthless note into sovereigns.[5]

It may be considered that *Cranford*, in its assumption of the un-questioned acceptance of such principles is an idealization, but we are kept aware of other attitudes. When Miss Matty is set up in business selling tea, her guilelessness never leads to loss. This is incredible to Mr. Smith, the businessman father of the narrator, Mary Smith, and we have the quiet irony of her comment from the Cranford viewpoint:

> But my father says "such simplicity might be very well in Cranford, but would never do in the world." And I fancy the world must be very bad, for with all my father's suspicion of every one with whom he has dealings, and in spite of all his many precautions, he lost upwards of a thousands pounds by roguery only last year.[6]

Cranford is not out of this world, the eager pursuit of the latest fashions by its inhabitants shows that; it merely prefers to stick to its own ways of doing things. There is even an air of modest triumph, as of having trapped a rare specimen, in the query which concludes the story of Betsy Barker's cow—'Do you ever see cows dressed in grey flannel in London?'[7] But while we are allowed to smile at the ludicrous picture, we are invited to admire the practical and humanitarian intention which can defy the ludicrous and be understood.

Drumble is the newer, commercial world; it contains the drive, energy and knowhow represented by the narrator's father, who spares a day to come and advise about Miss Matty's future. Yet how much does he really do? The old-fashioned ladies acting according to their lights have already raised a fund; the loyal maid has hustled her bewildered fiancé into marriage to provide a home; even the tea-selling scheme has been suggested by Mary.

---

[5] The bank failure incident was possibly taken from conversation with Charlotte Brontë (although such failures occurred in Manchester at that time). Its counterpart occurs in Charlotte's letters (*Life*, pp. 420-1) which describe her loss from the failure of the York and North Midland Bank, and in which the retention of the shares in deference to Emily's wish parallels Miss Matty's retention of the shares out of respect for Deborah. The episode of the old letters may also be a Brontë reminiscence. In 1850 Mr. Brontë showed Charlotte his wife's letters, which were of the same unexpectedly informal type as those of Miss Matty's mother. The occasion is related by Charlotte in a letter (ibid., p. 441).

[6] *Cranford*, p. 174.   [7] ibid., p. 6.

The implication all the time is that clear notions of duty and behaviour can achieve all that is necessary—if everybody acts by them. *Cranford* ultimately arrives at the same conclusion as *Mary Barton*, but it starts from the opposite direction.

Because of its assumptions there is no need to preach, we are given the illustration without the sermon. The third and vital principle, Religion, on which all else is based, is not discussed because it is accepted and acted on. It appears therefore only where it is natural to find it, at the death-bed of Miss Brown for example, taking its place without strain or emphasis in the dialogue of people whose Christianity is so native to them that they would be surprised, and rather shocked, at any suggestion of a need to proclaim it, let alone defend it. And being natural, it can be treated with the same humour as any other aspect of human conduct:

I thought of Miss Jenkyns, grey, withered, and wrinkled, and I wondered if her mother had known her in the courts of heaven . . .

reflects Mary, reacting spontaneously to the incongruous comparison between the elderly reality and the fond mother's early hope that she would be 'a regular beauty'. Her continuation is equally natural and logical:

and then I knew that she had, and that they stood there in angelic guise.[8]

Propriety is not offended, any more than it is by Peter's traveller's tale of shooting a cherubim by accident from the top of a mountain. In the Manchester stories religion carries implications too serious to be joked about; in Cranford security of belief permits laughter.

The impression we are encouraged to get of Cranford is of an old-fashioned place a generation ago, though clear indications—such as the reading of the current number of *The Pickwick Papers* and the passage of time after that—show that the calendar time is roughly contemporary. But the narrative threads move back to the late eighteenth century, and Cranford is shown as a con-

<hr/>

[8] *Cranford*, p. 54.

tinuity, a surviving as well as a present reality personified particularly in Miss Matty. Yet in a hundred little touches—the popularity of Dickens in spite of Miss Jenkyns's defence of Dr. Johnson is one—change is suggested. Cranford is not static, it has to accept interference from the outside world. Its whole tenor indicates for example a gradual shifting of the social balance, 'dubious' members such as Betty Barker, Mrs. Fitz-Adam and the 'vulgar' Mr. Hoggins are admitted, as their worth is accepted. The point is that the values of the traditional outlook are maintained. If one half of propriety deals with trivialities, the other half comprises fundamental and proven standards of conduct; the two aspects are so interwined that the trivial helps support the total fabric and is part of the pattern of stability. When customs and opinions wither they may be allowed to drop away, but often they are alive with the values they grew in.

It is over simple to accept *Cranford* as a nostalgic idealization, though to some extent it has this quality. Yet only to some extent; in spite of its lightness of treatment it is informed by a serious concern for known and trusted standards, and this has supplied part of its strength to survive. Nor is life itself idealized. Its characters suffer, life is unfair to them. (Ruskin felt this so strongly that the first time he tried to read Cranford he 'flew into a passion at Captain Brown's being killed and wouldn't go any further'.)[9] They have the imperfections of other people and one at least, Mrs. Jamieson, is not particularly pleasant. But in the major principles they are representatively firm. It is disconcerting to find that Mrs. Gaskell herself has anticipated this sort of misinterpretation when she makes Miss Jenkyns say:

People talk a great deal about idealising nowadays, whatever that may mean.[10]

but it is less difficult, on re-reading the book to see the qualities in it which made George Eliot—and no one has ever accused her of a lack of serious purpose or of superficiality—say 'my feeling towards Life and Art had some affinity with the feeling which had inspired *Cranford* and the earlier chapters of *Mary Barton*'.[11]

[9] *Cranford*, p. xxiv—Ward quotes the letter.   [10] ibid., pp. 54–5.
[11] Gordon S. Haight (ed.) *The George Eliot Letters*, Vol. III, 11 Nov. 1859, Yale, 1954.

It is important to remember that the story is told in the first person by Mary Smith who identifies herself with Cranford although she lives in Drumble.[12] She remarks towards the end:

For my own part, I had vibrated all my life between Drumble and Cranford . . .[13]

and in 'vibrating' she was exchanging one kind of reality for another and showing a preference. What she chose was more than a social system, it was also an environment, one moreover penetrated for Mrs. Gaskell with associations of childhood and home. Then again, it was a present reality, not some distant and now dream-like paradise lost. Cranford, I repeat, is not Knutsford, but there is a good deal of Knutsford in Cranford, and Knutsford was a neighbouring locality where friends lived and her daughters went to school. It provides a solid element of normality for imagination and memory to bite on.

Morally then, Cranford represents a set of values and beliefs resting firmly on tradition though capable of gradual change. Socially, as has been shown, it is associated with stability based on these values. Its attitudes are not rigid, but they are conservative to change. In all these aspects it is in contrast to the new industrial towns or to London, where conditions promoted a personal and social struggle for existence, with the 'cash nexus' competing against the old ties of humanity, religion and class obligation for supremacy.

We now have to consider Cranford as a place. Physically, as an environment for living, it had the charm that Manchester so conspicuously lacked, and which is a marked feature of the Cranford world. In slightly earlier dealings as an author with this world, in 'Mr. Harrison's Confessions' (Feb.-Apr. 1851), Mrs. Gaskell felt the need to express her sense of this contrast. We note the first-person narrator again, as Mr. Harrison recounts his arrival from London as a young doctor about to become junior partner to his old-fashioned uncle in Dunscombe (socially and physically a version of Cranford). On his first evening he sits in the window of

---

[12] 'Cranford' stories are marked by this narrative self-identification, which is discussed later.   [13] *Cranford*, p. 185.

his lodgings in the main street and allows the little town to make its impression on him. The description must be quoted at length:

Dunscombe calls itself a town, but I should call it a village. Really, looking from Jocelyn's, it is a very picturesque place. The houses are anything but regular; they may be mean in their details; but altogether they look well; they have not that flat unrelieved front, which many towns of far more pretensions present. Here and there a bow-window —every now and then a gable, cutting up against the sky—occasionally a projecting upper story—throws good effect of light and shadow along the street; and they have a queer fashion of their own of colouring the whitewash of some of the houses with a sort of pink blotting-paper tinge, more like the stone of which Mayence is built than anything else. It may be very bad taste, but to my mind it gives a rich warmth to the colouring. Then, here and there a dwelling-house has a court in front, with a grass-plot on each side of the flagged walk, and a large tree or two—limes or horse-chestnuts—which send their great projecting upper branches over into the street, making round dry places of shelter on the pavement in the times of summer showers.

While I was sitting in the bow-window, thinking of the contrast between this place and the lodgings in the heart of London, which I had left only twelve hours before—the window open here, and, although in the centre of the town, admitting only scents from the mignonette boxes on the sill, instead of the dust and smoke of ———— Street— the only sound heard in this, the principal street, being the voices of mothers calling their playing children home to bed, and the eight o'clock bell of the old parish church bimbomming in remembrance of the curfew: while I was sitting thus idly . . .[14]

and the story begins its affectionately easy course of shrewd and humorous observation, which includes some incidents of pathos and anxiety as a reminder that here also life is not always idyllic.

The overall impression made by this description is one of tranquillity not so much stated as conveyed by the accumulation of detail. The initial impact is through the senses, which individually find pleasure in sight, sound and smell; but the senses reveal an environment of calm, innocence and security. The references to shelter, to warmth, to children playing and church bells ringing, add up to something more than an enjoyable scene. There is no

[14] *My Lady Ludlow*, pp. 407-8.

pretence of perfection; mean detail and bad taste are admitted, just as the narrative that follows deals in faults as well as virtues. The faults underline the humanity without detracting from the general sense of pleasure and peace, they are part of the impression which proves better than that of 'towns of far more pretensions'. The comparison to bigger towns (Manchester was obviously in her mind) prepares us for the statement that gives the whole passage its inner meaning, the quietly inserted contrast to London. The contrast itself is not described; we are left with the emphatic sense of relief expressed in the new environment.

The effect is, in its modest way, similar in principle to that which Wordsworth claimed for his 'Nature', the individual could be in accord with his environment and draw moral strength from it. A quiet, small country town does not however have quite the same effect as a wild Cumberland lake or mountain. As Wordsworth, having marvelled at the Alps, still turned to his smaller mountains for inspiration and meaning, knowing the effect:

> Of custom that prepares a partial scale
> In which the little oft outweighs the great . . .[15]

so Mrs. Gaskell chose the retired little town she knew as her reference scale.

There can be little doubt also that part of the attitude derived from Mrs. Gaskell's sense of personal relaxation in connexion with Knutsford, and this too is reflected. Neither in memory nor in contemporary visits was she on duty as the minister's wife; she could relax as a member by right of a secure little group in surroundings which did not offend her senses nor nudge her moral conscience. It was a small world and a thoroughly known one. 'We know all the people here, and they know us, and all the duties of life seem so easy and simple compared to those of a great town,'[16] as she said later about another village. This freedom from the strain of moral strenuousness transferred itself to Cran-

---

[15] 'The Prelude' XII, 195–6, *The Poetical Works of Wordsworth*, O.U.P., 1926. Mrs. Gaskell shared Wordsworth's outlook sufficiently to work the last two lines of 'A slumber did my spirit seal' almost word for word into her account of Molly Gibson's shock. (*Wives and Daughters*, p. 432.)
[16] *Letters*, p. 26.

ford and its inhabitants. They display the mixture of virtues and failings which Mrs. Gaskell accepted as the common recipe for mankind, but the pressure on the individual was less. There was a more congenial soil for virtue, failings were rarely aggravated into extremes of conduct. In the earlier Cranford world particularly there is sorrow but little misery and no daily struggle to maintain common humanity or decency.

It is no more possible than it is with Manchester to define in rigid and precise terms exactly what Cranford 'stands for', but we can see the principles and feelings which govern it. It is associated with pleasant and tranquil surroundings, a sense of security and stability, a way of life guided by order, custom and a clear vision of right and wrong in great and small things, free equally from the poverty and the desire for 'progress' that occupied the nervous energy and time of the new industrial society. It is a world in which there is leisure for humanity and social obligations, and sufficient means to support them. Moreover it is not a remote ideal. Cranford as a town and a society may ignore a few awkward facts, but it represents a type that existed alongside the new materialism. It was possible to make a choice.

Two further qualities which as it were tinge the Cranford world may be referred to in rounding off this account of its essence. One has already been touched on earlier, the stability of its class structure. In *Cranford* the characters all know their place, and all accept without hesitation the general scheme of things. In practice we are hardly aware from the book of any section of Cranford except the genteel one—for the servants are part of the gentility, mirror-images reflecting views and beliefs, more conscious of the niceties of position than their mistresses, with the autocratic Mr. Mulliner representing Mrs. Jamieson's precedence. Jem Hearn, the joiner whose bachelor days are unceremoniously cut short so that he can set up house to provide a home for Martha's mistress, acquiesces with hardly a demur.[17] This is partly, it must be admitted, out of personal respect for

[17] The female of the species is more deadly than the male. A minor theme in all Mrs. Gaskell's work is the power of a woman to get things done, if necessary at the expense of a man. She was never a 'feminist' but her sketches of the discomforted male generally have a small sparkle to them.

Miss Matty; however she in turn represents the standards of Cranford at their purest. But we must recognize that this is a very circumscribed society; Mrs. Gaskell is not yet ready to deal with Cranford values in more complex social situations and general experience.

The other quality is the presence of the countryside, which is part of the physical charm of Cranford. While it is true that Cranford is a country town, the country is very much a background and barely mentioned. When it occurs, as in the journey out to Thomas Holbrook's farm, it is domesticated and humanized. 'The fragrant smell of the neighbouring hayfields came in every now and then,'[18] no more. Now Mrs. Gaskell can respond to the country: she shares Wordsworth's affection for Cumberland and its statesmen, she also knows the Lancashire coast. But in this aspect of nature, uncivilized and awe-inspiring, Cranford has no share. In fact, Mrs. Gaskell tends to rare patches of stiffness and 'purple writing' when elevating her expression towards Wordsworthian ends. 'Descriptions of nature as such', comments Ward, 'were not specially in Mrs. Gaskell's way . . .' while his conclusion could hardly be bettered:

But her "walks in the country" (to borrow Miss Mitford's phrase) had for their starting-point and goal the abodes of men and women.[19]

Before turning to the development of the Cranford theme, and the manner in which it gained ascendancy in her work, it may be useful to show the extent to which the image of Cranford established itself in her mind as a correlative to the standards and attitudes associated with it. This is clear in *Ruth*. Eccleston, the town to which the Bensons take the despairing and weary Ruth, is clearly Manchester. But the Benson's home and garden, its neighbourhood, the old chapel, the little dissenting community in which she finds first rest, then peace and security, are all described in Cranford terms. It is a flaw in the book, though compensated for by other excellences, that this account of Ruth's tranquil period is descriptively and socially out of keeping with both the smoke-ridden town described on her arrival and with

[18] *Cranford*, p. 186.   [19] ibid., p. xiii.

the populous, cholera-ridden, Irish slums she works in after her
tranquillity has been shattered. At this stage in her career Mrs.
Gaskell was still 'vibrating' between the two different types of life
with which she was associated. Something of the resulting confusion she half-realizes. The opening of the chapter 'After Five
Years' (Ch. 19) notes the quiet passage of time, and the narrator—
who is this time the author-commentator—realizes that this sort
of peace is not what we would expect to find in such a city. She
covers it by linking up with that past which had been described at
the beginning of the novel, before change and progress had set in:

[an observer] would have noted some changes which had imperceptibly come over all; but he, too, would have thought, that the life which
had brought so little of turmoil and vicissitude must have been calm
and tranquil, and in accordance with the bygone activity of the town
in which their existence passed away.[20]

During the period up to the publication of *North and South*
Mrs. Gaskell had turned frequently to the Cranford world as a
relief from the industrial society in which she lived and which she
was writing about. Much of this turning away may be regarded as
a form of escape achieved by the expression, through fiction, of
her preference. Occasionally she varies the physical milieu, making
it more specifically country, although still a Cranford type of
country. The story of 'My French Master' for example is set
vaguely on the edge of a forest, while its account of the refugee
aristocrat who quietly settles down as a language master until the
Bourbon restoration entices him home, only to further disappointment and eventual return, enables her to bring in her interest in French life and history. Sometimes, as in 'Morton Hall'—
set on the outskirts of Drumble—she gives extra rein to her interest in local tradition and legend, moving the story back to give
a perspective of event and continuity. Characteristically these
stories are not essentially happy ones; Mrs. Gaskell, as has been
pointed out, did not attempt to escape from the harsh aspects of
life itself, and the Cranford tales vary from the near farce of
'Mr. Harrison's Confessions' to the sombre shading of 'Morton

[20] *Ruth*, p. 199. The quotation should be linked with the passage quoted earlier (p. 85)
with its implied promise to deal with changing traditions and environment.

Hall'. But they all have in common a background of happiness and humour, an actual or potential pleasure seen in the physical setting and its society. So in 'My French Master' the misfortunes of M. de Chalabre and the echoes of the French Revolution are framed within the quiet and affectionate detail of the narrator's childhood. The basically tragic linked episodes of 'Morton Hall' are mediated through the narrative and background of the elderly sisters, whose idiosyncracies, emotions, speech and outlook control and give humour to the story.

'Morton Hall' has a further interest in its relation to the novel that followed. In itself it is, like so many of Mrs. Gaskell's stories that are now forgotten about, well worth the disinterring, and it could almost act as a model for the display in a short space of many of her talents and interests, though it is not one of her finest. The loosely linked episodes connect the past of the old house to the present through the vicissitudes of its owners at various periods; their particular interest is in the naïve anticipation of the theme of *North and South*. In the final episode the last descendant of the aristocratic Mortons marries the wealthy cotton-spinner Carr, himself descended from the family that dispossessed the Mortons during the Civil War. The marriage ends the ill-fortune that the narrator traces to the curse put on the family by Alice Carr, who had married a Morton at the Restoration and suffered for it.[21] By this romantic and roundabout method the world of Cranford and Manchester are united. The last we hear of the Hall is that it is being pulled down as the town overtakes it, while the social gap between landed gentry and manufacturer is bridged by the plot twist:

"His ancestors," said Ethelinda. "Has he got ancestors? That's one good point about him, at any rate. I didn't know cotton spinners had ancestors."[22]

The story was published in two parts at the end of November, 1853, in *Household Words*. It may be assumed therefore that it was written after Mrs. Gaskell had begun work on *North and*

[21] This may well have given Dickens a hint for Miss Havisham and Satis House in *Great Expectations*. Alice Carr returns to the house, locked as it was left with food served, and lives in it half-crazed with the desire for revenge.
[22] *Cranford*, p. 488.

South, the novel which was to be her full scale attempt to reconcile the virtues of the Cranford and Manchester worlds.

It should be clear that the relaxation of tenseness to be found in the daily life of this world does not imply any relaxation of moral standards, or that moral effort is not necessary. A choice between good and bad behaviour is constantly having to be made. Miss Matty's reaction to the bank failure has been quoted as an example of a moral decision which disregards personal consequences. We may note in contrast her friend Miss Pole's convenient habit of rationalizing in minor matters to assuage her vanity and curiosity, as when she ignores a previous affront to accept Mrs. Jamieson's invitation.

In 1850 Mrs. Gaskell was asked to write a Christmas book. These Christmas books were expected to edify as well as entertain; a mixture of excitement and moral uplift for family enjoyment was wanted, such as Dickens supplied in his Christmas stories. Mrs. Gaskell's response was 'The Moorland Cottage', the first of her stories to be given a Cranford setting. Some of the blame for a potentially fine tale spoilt must be placed therefore on the circumstances. The result is nevertheless instructive. The story develops from an account of Mrs. Browne and her children, Edward and Maggie, and Mrs. Browne's insistence, as widow of the late curate, on her genteel status. When the wealthy landowner Mr. Buxton decides to help the Brownes a certain intimacy develops between the children of each family, with the result that as they grow up Maggie and Frank Buxton fall in love against his father's wishes. In the meantime Edward, educated by Mr. Buxton, has developed into a weak and spoilt character who finally swindles his benefactor. By this means Edward is made an instrument for breaking off the engagement: Mr. Buxton will help him escape if Maggie gives up Frank. Her refusal, and Frank's, are moral decisions, and Mr. Buxton accepts the expedient of Maggie going to America with Edward to allow Frank time for reconsideration. A timely shipwreck in which Edward is drowned and Frank saves Maggie solves problems and brings Mr. Buxton round.

There is little of Christmas in this but plenty of the conventions of plot situation, drama and pathos. Yet it starts off in a totally different manner, with a description of the peaceful country scene preceding a humorously astringent presentation of Mrs. Browne with the detailed and naturally recounted incidents of family relationships. 'I told you', Charlotte Brontë said, 'that the book opened like a daisy.'[23] And the tone of this opening is never really lost—it preserves the tale from triteness. The ensuing melodrama is forced into this setting and tone, in fact forces itself for stretches right out of the setting (the same effect, but in reverse, of what we saw happen in *Ruth*). From time to time as well the narrator's moral elbow nudges us with edifying comment towards some particular lesson, while the dialogue takes on an artificial energy.

What has happened is, of course, an unconscious change of intention; the story as begun was not fulfilling the aim intended. Had Mrs. Gaskell finished as she began she would have written herself straight into the manner of *Wives and Daughters*[24] but the demands of Christmas Book publication ran counter to the method and attitude for Cranford. Moreover she was strongly influenced by the feeling that a writer had a duty, which she interpreted as a didactic duty. It is tantalizing, for Mrs. Gaskell was patently on the verge of following her inclinations and natural talents. Even as it is, Cranford morality and setting permeate the tale, in conflict with Edward's greed and selfishness, or the tinge of hard material morality in Mr. Buxton. 'The Moorland Cottage' is, by the standards of Mrs. Gaskell's better work, a failure, but it is the failure of a good writer distracted from her proper course. It is fair to add that Charlotte Brontë approved the direction it took. She went on to say, 'I now tell you it finished like a herb—a balsamic herb with healing in its leaves.' The medicinal infusion of morality, we need to remember, suited the nineteenth-century palate.

[23] Quoted in *Hopkins*, pp. 98–9.
[24] Much of 'The Moorland Cottage' does, in fact, anticipate *Wives and Daughters*. Mrs. Browne is a sketch for Clare, Maggie for Molly Gibson, Mr. and Mrs. Buxton for Squire and Mrs. Hamley, Frank for Roger Hamley. Mrs. Gaskell's feeling for situation and character was already pointing her to her true material, but technique, experience and maturity as a novelist were needed before she could handle it.

After *North and South* (more strictly, after the *Life*), Mrs. Gaskell turned away with almost decisive completeness from the Manchester world. She gives up with it the attempt to deal with the 'big' problems and broad issues, and paradoxically universalizes her work by restricting it to the individual problems of life in a small community. For by doing this she is able to ignore external pressures which, as the reader realizes only too well, cannot be interpreted in terms of individual behaviour other than by a process of simplification which may with some truth be labelled as a romantic idealization. The decision, whether she consciously thought of it as such or not, was undoubtedly influenced by the criticism which *Mary Barton, Ruth* and *North and South* attracted, and which while praising her ability as a writer told her bluntly that she was attempting solutions of matters beyond her experience. Once the decision had been taken she was free to regard her work solely from the point of view of the novelist; it is as a novelist and not as a moralist that she succeeds or fails in her later work; even the apparent exception of the feeble didacticism which closes *Sylvia's Lovers* is largely a novelist's failure. *My Lady Ludlow, Sylvia's Lovers, Cousin Phillis* and *Wives and Daughters* are expressions of Cranford values, stages in her progress to the final and full expression of the Cranford world in its complexity and strength, while showing it as a durable form of society capable of standing the pressure of other attitudes. There is also little doubt that living in Manchester had depressed and influenced her; her later years of greater independence, travel and the contacts which fame brought, allowed fuller vent to her natural outlook.

For the social historian who is a novelist, setting is as important as characters and incident, for these only develop meaning within their context. This is why it has been necessary to emphasize the importance of detail, whether of custom and manners or dress and buildings, as part of the very meaning of the Cranford world. But a balanced account must add more.

Cranford and the early stories which share its context all tend to look back, depicting a society set in its ways; it is a world of the middle-aged, and in more than one sense responds to the title of its original sketch, 'The Last Generation in England'. In her later work the centre of interest gradually switches to the young and to the adaptable. The Cranford ethos is not lost, nor is the setting with all that it stands for, but the small section of society whose attitudes and behaviour occupy the whole of the early book has retreated into the background of *Wives and Daughters*, represented by the Miss Brownings. Old-fashioned, slightly comic in their rigidity of outlook, bewildered by strange patterns of behaviour and thought, they are still respected for their principles and loved for their goodness. They are the hereditary custodians of manners and ethics who need to be propitiated by all sections of society, even by the modern and aristocratic Lady Harriet, and who have handed on the principles to be adopted and adapted by the next generation. The novelist now catches not merely a whole society but one in the process of change, evolving without discontinuity from its less complex predecessor.

Mrs. Gaskell insists on humanity as well as propriety, and as the context of her work broadens, her insight into human nature and feeling deepens. 'A historian', remarked Conrad, 'may be an artist too, and a novelist is a historian, the preserver, the keeper, the expounder of human experience.'[25] No novelist, however, can deal with the whole of human experience; in the end he must select from those areas of it with which he is familiar, and then make a further choice of presentation based on personal preference and values. Mrs. Gaskell made her choice when settling for the Cranford world. Her humour found its natural outlet through her examination of 'propriety' and her sensibility in the 'humanity', while her art as a novelist as well as her views as an individual found their full expression in the fusion of the two aspects.

[25] Joseph Conrad, 'Henry James', *Notes on Life & Letters*, Dent, 1949, p. 17.

CHAPTER VIII

Society and Sociology

MRS. GASKELL is a novelist whose concern is with people's behaviour and the standards on which it is based. As behaviour is a social matter, being conditioned by society as well as being manifested in it, she is therefore concerned with social groups. But she is not concerned with society in the abstract, with analysing or criticizing the remote forces which mould or alter it, although we have already seen that she is quite acute enough an observer to realize that such forces must inevitably produce change. She is in fact, especially when her fondness for traditions and old habits is taken into account, surprisingly receptive to such inevitable change, and remarkably little burdened by any narrow conservatism, although she does not disguise her personal preferences.

But a community, from Mrs. Gaskell's point of view, relies ultimately on its recognition that society is a matter of order and hierarchy, with its members mutually respecting the rank as well as the individuality of each other; once given such a framework the individual can move easily and unselfconsciously within it. One of the clearest expositions of this occurs in *Wives and Daughters*. The chapter heading, 'Molly Finds Herself Patronized', is itself a warning. Lady Harriet, exercising the privilege of the county family to cross-question the local community, has sent away the agent who interrupts her conversation with Molly:

"I cannot bear that sort of person," said Lady Harriet, almost before he was out of hearing; "giving himself airs of gallantry towards one to whom his simple respect is all his duty. I can talk to one of my father's labourers with pleasure, while with a man like that underbred fop I am all over thorns and nettles."[1]

[1] *Wives and Daughters*, p. 183.

The comment shows clearly the dual evaluation of individual and social rank, and begins an analysis whose purpose is to 'place' Molly as an individual (pretty, intelligent, spirited but not aggressive), and as a class representative (daughter of the local doctor who is respected, welcomed in the county family but free of social climbing and conscious of his own dignity). The analysis also, incidentally, places Molly in her function of 'informant', the character in the novel having access to all levels of the community. At this point she is being put on terms with Lady Harriet, who is a representative of the aristocracy; the conversation is turned so that she can shortly ask:

"Your ladyship" (the title was the first-fruits of the lesson, as Molly took it, on paying due respect)—"your ladyship keeps speaking of the sort of—the class of—people to which I belong, as if it was a kind of strange animal you were talking about . . ."

to which Lady Harriet finally replies:

Don't you see, little one, I talk after my kind, just as you talk after your kind. It's only on the surface with both of us. Why, I daresay some of your good Hollingford ladies talk of the poor people in a manner which they would consider just as impertinent in their turn, if they could hear it.

It is because Molly is 'simple and truthful', in other words because as an individual she is both natural and deserving of respect, that Lady Harriet has:

talked unconsciously to you as I would—well! now here's another piece of impertinence—as I would to my equal—in rank, I mean; for I don't set myself up in solid things as any better than my neighbours.[2]

The whole dialogue brings out clearly the elements which make a society cohere; the sense of hierarchy, its gradations, the natural attitudes, tones and styles of address which go with them, yet accompanied by a sense that individual merit in 'solid things' can be separated from rank and accepted in its own right, always provided that the conventions which stabilize society are not interfered with.

Wives and Daughters is the final and mature reflection of Mrs.

[2] *Wives and Daughters*, pp. 184–5.

Gaskell's views, The whole novel shows a subtle appreciation of the discriminations which underwrite the successful functioning of a society (I am not here concerned with its criticisms of over-rigid or insensitive attitudes and behaviour). Chapters, 2, 3, and 4 ('A Novice amongst the Great Folk', 'Molly Gibson's Childhood', 'Mr. Gibson's Neighbours') repay careful reading for their initial portrayal of the social balance in Hollingford, while the sub-plot of Osborne Hamley's unequal marriage is a special instance of the effects produced by any disturbance on a section of society which still had a legal as well as customary interest in maintaining that balance:

most of them gentlemen of property, and [who] saw the full importance of proving the marriage of an eldest son, and installing his child as the natural heir to a long-descended estate.[3]

But the same attitude (apart from the special case of landed influence), was present in *Mary Barton*, and underlines its conclusions that:

it was most desirable to have educated workers, capable of judging, not mere machines of ignorant men; and to have them bound to their employers by the ties of respect and affection, not by mere money bargains alone . . .[4]

Different social ranges existed in the new industrial cities, where the manufacturer was the chief power. We have already looked at these, and need note only that Mrs. Gaskell has taken her bearings and worked out the levels. She knows and respects the working class, but there is no nonsense about equality. When the manufacturer Thornton apologizes to the mill-hand Higgins for calling him a liar, they can talk on equal terms of manliness and human dignity, and shake hands in recognition of these qualities, but the social relationship is understood by both. Higgins thanks him, a rare concession of respect from a proud man:

"And this is a deal from me," said Mr. Thornton, giving Higgins's hand a good grip. "Now mind, you come sharp to your time," continued he, resuming the master.[5]

The urban revolution and its consequences overthrew certain previously accepted types of distinction while the geographical

[3] *Wives and Daughters*, p. 685.   [4] *Mary Barton*, p. 451.   [5] *North and South*, p. 389.

proximity of Manchester and Knutsford brought the contrast home. Mrs. Gaskell was prepared to accept these consequences within their proper framework, which is to say that she realized the stupidity of trying to classify the social strata of Manchester by the categories of London or Knutsford. Margaret Hale makes this mistake, and her first step towards a consciousness of a new type of society is when her father quickly tells her off when she describes Thornton as:

"Altogether a man who seems made for his niche, mamma; sagacious, and strong, as becomes a great tradesman."
"Don't call the Milton manufacturers tradesmen, Margaret," said her father. "They are very different."
"Are they? I apply the word to all who have something tangible to sell; but, if you think the term is not correct, papa, I won't use it."[6]

There is here still the identification of 'gentlemen' with certain ranks and professions, an identification which Dickens attacked so bitterly and brilliantly in *Great Expectations* in 1862, and which Mrs. Gaskell had already queried on the same grounds, that gentlemanliness is a quality of character rather than of birth or education. Nevertheless some of the prejudice against certain classes, such as shopkeepers, still clings, as when, in *Cranford*, Miss Pole comments:

You and I, Miss Matty, would have been ashamed to have known that our marriage was spoken of in a grocer's shop, in the hearing of shopmen![7]

In a letter to Norton about the marriage of one of his friends, Mrs. Gaskell can twit him gently on his failure to understand social niceties:

And you don't understand what are our 'aristocratical feelings' when you make a sort of apology to Marianne about his marrying a governess. That does not hurt us in the least,—it would if he married an uneducated girl, a daughter of a rich *trades*person.[8]

Behind this prejudice lies a habit of gentility too inbred to be overcome; shopkeepers, unlike brewers or iron-masters or mill-

[6] *North and South*, p. 73.   [7] *Cranford*, p. 137.   [8] *Letters*, p. 11.

owners, had not yet found a level above respectability. Nevertheless, in *Sylvia's Lovers* the hero (if the novel can be said to have
one; Philip Hepburn, like Pip, is more an anti-hero) is a shopkeeper, although the shop has the patina of local colouring in a
historical novel. Moreover we are specifically given in Molly
Corney's husband the reminder of the shopkeeper in all his solid
vulgarity, while Philip is jerked away from his counter to a
romantic career and a pathetic death.

It is not that Mrs. Gaskell is a snob, or that her characters—
except a few deliberately drawn so—are snobs in the Thackerayan
sense of judging individuals, and their own success, in terms of
social position. Mrs. Gaskell positions herself, as authoress, carefully and yet quite naturally according to the lessons and habits
of her own upbringing and experience. She stays on the whole in
the professional, middle-class, social range, a narrow and well-
defined range within which she can explore the human character
on a secure basis. Jane Austen had done the same before her;
Virginia Woolf was to do it after her; a novelist, quite apart from
personal beliefs, can write with ease and assurance when within
her social group. Her attitude is not at all that caricatured by
Dickens in 'The Chimes':

> Oh, let us love our occupations,
> Bless the squire and his relations,
> Live upon our daily rations,
> And always know our proper stations.[9]

She shares in her attitude a general movement of the period,
which Professor Burn has summarized as a shift in writing, from:

> novels in which the basic structure of society was discussed in terms
> of bitter satire and deep passion to those in which personal problems
> were discussed against the background of a society whose structure was
> assumed to be sufficiently stable.[10]

Her concern for stability was always near the surface, something
not to be overlooked.

A glance at her work will show how much Mrs. Gaskell was

---

[9] *Christmas Books*, O.U.P., 1954, p. 107. Lady Bowley has this set to music for her
evening employment classes.
[10] Quoted in Asa Briggs, *Victorian People*, Odhams, 1954, p. 31.

filled with the spirit of the amateur sociologist. She has a genuine curiosity which is independent of any ulterior motive, she likes receiving and giving information. So does the village gossip; the satirically slanted dialogues from *Cranford* to *Wives and Daughters* reveal that she was familiar with gossip and found amusement in it, though realizing how harmful it can be. She is fond of speculation about things as well as people, a lively curiosity about life around her is very clear in her occasional essays and articles. And it is useful to remind ourselves that to call an author a regional novelist does not imply that he never moves about, or is an innocent abroad. Mrs. Gaskell knew the world at large; she was often and gladly away from Manchester; in London or France or Germany, or visiting friends in the country as well as receiving from all over the world visitors coming to see the famous novelist. She had the education and intelligence to understand and weigh much of what she saw. The mere fact of travel does not imply a broadened outlook, but we must realize that Mrs. Gaskell, when she turned back to her local scene, did not do so naïvely. It would be equally wrong to make any extensive claim for her as an intellectual cosmopolite: she was an intelligent educated woman, worldly-wise without being worldly. Tolerant and informed enough to be an inquirer rather than a judge in new situations, she carried her own map of human nature with her on which to plot them.

So far we have considered only the two main areas of experience and the effect of their juxtaposition. She found another type of social grouping, still within her 'region', in the Lake District and the West Riding, and to some extent in North Wales. Perhaps 'grouping' is hardly the best term for a way of life she describes in 'Half a Lifetime Ago' as:

just, independent, upright; not given to much speaking; kind-hearted, but not demonstrative; disliking change, and new ways, and new people; sensible and shrewd; each household self-contained, and its members having little curiosity as to their neighbours . . .[11]

[11] *My Lady Ludlow*, p. 280. This is a second example of an early work ('Martha Preston') published in *Sartain's Union Magazine* (1851) and revised for later publication. The decision to revise the story, which appeared in Oct. 1855 in *Household Words*, may have been stimulated by the work she had begun that June on Charlotte Brontë.

The 'statesmen' of the fells interested her as people and as a community, and the introductory pages of this very powerful story form a comprehensive little essay on them. This story and others dealing with the area are important also as they show that in appreciating this social background she was already prepared for her task as the biographer of Charlotte Brontë.

Her visits to France produced a small crop of essays as well as material for stories. When she writes about French life it is nearly always to give an account of how people live, or to explain some interesting or bizarre fact of history. The scene may be contemporary, as in the journal which she published as 'French Life'—although this also dives off into byways of history—or historical as in 'Traits and Stories of the Huguenots' or 'An Accursed Race', the story of the persecuted Cagots in the Middle Ages.

She reads an out-of-the-way French book and can 'imagine some account of it may not be displeasing to the readers of *Household Words*'[12] who are then given, in 'Modern Greek Songs' a rambling account of some traditional Greek customs. Later readers of *All the Year Round* were told, in 'An Italian Institution' about the power of the Camorra. And the same curious eye for the social scene can be turned on England, as in 'Cumberland Sheep Shearers', or when she considers the new social phenomenon of the detective in 'Disappearances'. All these are occasional articles, pocket-money work; they represent items which took her interest and which she could write about easily.

In all of them she starts from a particular locality and particular types of people. Just as we have seen that in dealing with the Cranford country her focus is always people and their behaviour, so with other countries and times it is the human interest which lies behind the description or anecdote. Her approach is the one she attributes to Ruth when the girl sits in the window on Sunday looking out at the strange city and its buildings:

she saw one or two figures loiter along on the sunny side of the street, in all the enjoyment of their fine clothes and Sunday leisure; and she imagined histories for them, and tried to picture to herself their homes and their daily doings.[13]

12 *Ruth*, p. 471.   13 ibid., p. 34.

She begins from reality, from the individual in his setting. For the human interest—whether in contemporary or historical account—has been in evidence in all that has been said. And this interest can be linked directly with what has already been said about her feeling for associations. A locality or social custom is nothing without its associations, as Margaret Hale found when she had to move to Milton. All her ties and memories were with the village she had left, her appreciation of Milton began only when she had made her first personal contact there:

From that day Milton became a brighter place to her. It was not the long, bleak sunny days of spring, nor yet was it that time was reconciling her to the town of her habitation. It was that in it she had found a human interest.[14]

Mrs. Gaskell finds in natural feeling the common experience which links humanity in spite of its variety of societies and classes; in that and in religion, for she stays within the Christian world of Western Europe. So she contrasts societies as she observes them and notes how much people in Cumberland or London or France have in common with the inhabitants of Lancashire. This note of comparison begins 'An Accursed Race'; 'We have', she says, 'our prejudices in England', and clinches the argument for the brotherhood of man by ending an article on medieval France with an epitaph remembered from her schooldays in Stratford-on-Avon:

The moral of the history of the accursed race may, perhaps, be best conveyed in the words of an epitaph on Mrs. Mary Hand, who lies buried in the churchyard of Stratford-on-Avon—

> What faults you saw in me,
> Pray strive to shun;
> And look at home; there's
> Something to be done.[15]

The scene at a Greek death-bed reminds her of an anecdote from Lancashire, while one of her delightful essays, 'Company Manners' is a detailed study of French and English attitudes to social functions.

[14] *North and South*, p. 84.   [15] *My Lady Ludlow*, pp. 218 and 235.

Before Mrs. Gaskell opted for the Cranford world—and in so doing withdrew from any direct evaluation of the contemporary scene—she made a major effort to compare the traditional pattern of society with the new societies that were obviously beginning to dominate the English scene, and to find the common elements which could unite them. *North and South* was the final effort to combine her novel-writing with a direct gesture to her sense of moral duty, and it is not surprising in view of the principles she held that it should attempt a reconciliation. It does achieve one, rather artificially, at the level of feelings and affections; any claim to achieve it at the social level must be denied. *North and South* is altogether a crucial book in Mrs. Gaskell's development as a novelist, for its theme and for the complexity of technique which it inspired, and it must be considered in detail.

CHAPTER IX

The Attempt at Reconciliation: 'North and South'

I T is impossible to arrive at a fair judgement of *North and South*, and at the same time to relate it to her other work, without some reference to the circumstances of its creation. It is not the novel it might have been if the method of publication and the consequent pressures on the author had been different; the influence of these circumstances must be allowed for. In addition its links with previous work need to be understood if we are to see why it is of peculiar importance in Mrs. Gaskell's development.

It was the first novel that Mrs. Gaskell wrote as a regular serial, and although much of it was finished in advance of publication, the demands of writing to suit the form of the weekly instalment irked her in the extreme. She had begun to write it in 1853, and in May of that year Dickens was urging her to let him have it for *Household Words*: 'The subject is certainly *not* too serious, so sensibly treated. I have no doubt you may do a great deal of good by pursuing it in *Household Words* . . . Send the papers as you write them to me. Meanwhile I will think of a name for them, and bring it to bear upon yours if I think it improvable.'[1] and a year later he is urging the title of *North and South* on her as he wishes to announce publication.[2]

The result of her agreement to let the story appear as a serial may have affected the book as we have it. The rather curt, if polite, preface added when it was printed in book form, apolo-

[1] 3 May 1853—Letters from Dickens to Mrs. Gaskell in the John Rylands Library.
[2] 26 July 1854—The announcement appeared a few days later; publication began on 2 Sept.

gizing for defects in construction due to the pressure of serial writing, conceals a history of growing annoyance on both sides. Dickens as editor tried to make Mrs. Gaskell understand that a serial was more than arbitrarily chopped-up sequences of a book; Mrs. Gaskell as author obstinately and evasively resisted the demand to tailor her story to the requirements of space, episode interest and chapter sections. Much of the story of this fascinating tussle between two famous authors—for Dickens had an author's as well as an editor's eye on faults in the novel—may be read elsewhere.[3] Mrs. Gaskell cannot however be excused a certain evasiveness in her recollections of what happened, and of having used hindsight in blaming Dickens completely for attempting to make her modify the MSS. against her will. There is a letter extant which, although it has the impersonal salutation of 'My Dear Sir' can only be addressed to him, and from its references to the nearly finished MS. can be dated at the end of 1854 or the first few days of 1855. The paragraphs dealing with *North and South* are quoted in full in order to include the tongue in cheek reference to the number of deaths. Perhaps Dickens's acid comments on her propensity to kill off characters had come to her ears:

My Dear Sir,

    I was very much gratified by your note the other day; *very* much indeed. I dare say I shall like my story, when I am a little farther from it; at present I can only feel depressed about it, I meant it to have been so much better. I send what I am afraid you will think too large a batch of it by this post. What Mr. Wills has got already *fills up* the No. for January 13, leaving me only two more numbers, Janry 20, & Janry 27th. So what I send today is meant to be crammed & stuffed into Janry 20th; & I'm afraid I've nearly as much more for Janry 27.

    It is 33 pages of my writing that I send today. I have tried to shorten & compress it, both because it was a dull piece, & to get it into reasonable length, but there were a whole catalogue of events to be got over: and what I want to tell you now is this,—Mr. Gaskell has looked this

    [3] See A. B. Hopkins, 'Dickens and Mrs. Gaskell', *Huntington Library Quarterly*, Vol. 9, No. 4, 1946, for a discussion of the artistic aspect, also her *Elizabeth Gaskell*. Details of misjudgements on the editorial and printing side can be found in the letters edited by R. C. Lehmann as *Charles Dickens as Editor*, Smith, Elder, 1912.

piece well over. So I don't think there will be any carelessnesses left in it, & so there ought not to be any misprints; therefore I never wish to see its face again; but, *if you will keep the MS for me, & shorten it as you think best for H.W.* I shall be very glad. Shortened I see it must be.

I think a better title than N. & S. would have been 'Death and Variations'. There are 5 deaths, each beautifully suited to the character of the individual. . . .[4]

We need to note for the present purpose that Mrs. Gaskell may have been obliged, in spite of a reluctance to modify her natural, rather leisurely method of handling narrative, to huddle events towards a solution. The construction of *North and South* towards the end is forced, the conclusion almost ludicrous in its suddenness, but this is not entirely Mrs. Gaskell's fault.

As far as the theme is concerned, the title is apt enough, but it is not Mrs. Gaskell's own. She had provisionally thought of 'Margaret Hale', a lack-lustre suggestion that Dickens was right to alter; his own suggestion had more point and punch. Nevertheless, Mrs. Gaskell's colourless title does imply that the centre of interest is in the character of Margaret and her personal life. This is true; 'the social problem at the heart of the story is never allowed to swamp the human conflict',[5] whereas Dickens's alternative emphasizes the social aspect, and not all of that.

The theme itself must be linked to *Mary Barton*. When W. R. Greg complained of her first novel that it was one-sided and unfair to the masters (he was not alone in this) the criticism went home. Mrs. Gaskell wrote to his sister-in-law:

I regretted the disapprobation . . . because I knew that such a feeling would be conscientiously and thoughtfully entertained by men who are acquainted by long experience with the life, a portion of which I had endeavoured to represent; and whose actions during a long course of years have proved that the interests of their work-people are as dear to them as their own. Such disapproval . . . would be given if I had misrepresented, or so represented, a part as the whole, as that people

---

[4] Letters of Mrs. Gaskell in the library of the University of California, Los Angeles, Cat. 100/bx 38, No. 9. The italics are Mrs. Gaskell's.
[5] Yvonne ffrench, op. cit., p. 59.

at a distance should be misled and prejudiced against the masters, and that class be estranged from class.[6]

North and South is partly then an attempt to redress the balance. But more is involved than this. The point of view shifts, as Cazamian points out, to the middle-class, a shift already fore-shadowed in *Ruth*, where the social milieu of Mr. Bradshaw the wealthy merchant and Mr. Benson the poor but gentlemanly minister parallels that of the industrialist Mr. Thornton and the ex-vicar Mr. Hale. Mrs. Gaskell had moved her narrative centre to the class to which she belonged and into which she had most insight, and there it was to remain.

The plot of *North and South* is basically a simple one. Margaret Hale is a well-bred and cultured girl from the South of England who is suddenly pitch-forked with little money or status into the drab, harsh world of a major northern manufacturing town. Its leading figure is the strong-willed, brusque and self-made manu-facturer John Thornton, who falls in love with her. They finally learn to understand each other and in the process to appreciate the qualities of the social and environmental world which each had despised in the other.

Even this reduction to the simplest terms—a process which can make the subtlest novel seem stupid—shows that the plot is matched with a theme of contrast suggestive of the method by which the novel is to develop. And the novel is very far from being simple in its development. Nevertheless it is right to begin by drawing attention to the fundamental 'boy meets girl' basis on which the theme is built. Mrs. Gaskell's concern for people, their feelings and behaviour is never allowed to become subordinate to an intellectual conception. If there is a tug between theme and characters, it will be the characters who win; that is inherent in Mrs. Gaskell's outlook. But the strain may be felt.

The novel develops by stages, and in each stage fresh themes are introduced which involve their own sub-plots and motivation

---

[6] Quoted by Ward, *Mary Barton*, pp. lxii–lxiii. The letter is in draft, and may possibly not have been sent. It goes on to explain how the novel grew, and to admit that while it aimed at showing the effect of suffering on a particular type of man, she accepted the force of Greg's comments.

as well as an elaboration of the central plot and main theme. The first stage is set in the South. We see Margaret among the wealthy relatives in London with whom she was brought up; then in the picturesque vicarage of Helstone in Hampshire where her parents live. This little shelter of elegant economy and minor troubles— it has the makings of a Cranford corner—is demolished by the religious conscience of Mr. Hale. He resigns his living because of doctrinal doubts, but not before an ambitious young barrister from the London circle (Henry Lennox) has proposed to Margaret and been refused. The conscientious and scholarly vicar, the consciously genteel wife, the class-conscious and lady-like daughter and the snobbish family maid move with all their prejudices to grimy, competitive and energetic Milton.

Milton has been suggested by Mr. Bell, a college friend of Mr. Hale having property and influence there. If Mr. Hale hopes to make a living as a private tutor, then Milton is full of rich industrial families with children to be improved. They have an introduction to Thornton, and Mr. Hale has enough sense and tolerance to recognize character and brains. But the prejudices of his family are strong, matched only by the pride of Thornton's mother in his achievement and Milton's power.

In the meantime Margaret has got to know Bessy Higgins, a feverishly religious consumptive mill-girl, and her agnostic father Nicholas who is a union leader. While Thornton in the drawing-room states the case of the masters, Higgins in his kitchen states that of the workers as the threatened strike materializes and the two industrial worlds of masters and men clash. Thornton's mill becomes a target for attack as hot-heads move the strike into the violence which Higgins has steadily opposed.

Meanwhile Mrs. Hale has become dangerously ill. Margaret has to visit the Thorntons' house, which is in the mill yard, and is caught up in the riot. After urging Thornton to face the mob, she is injured in trying to shield him from it. But she cannot bear the idea of being thought of as setting her cap at the wealthy manufacturer, and when Thornton pushes aside his own doubts and prejudices to propose, he is rejected with a brusqueness that Margaret realizes afterwards was insulting.

The relationship with Thornton is complicated by a further personal twist. The dying Mrs. Hale wishes to see her son Frederick, till now a shadowy figure. Frederick is a naval officer who led a mutiny against his captain's inhumanity and is now an exile liable to death if he returns, and whose existence is never mentioned. He comes, and Margaret meets the brother she has hardly known. After Mrs. Hale's death Frederick hopes to get away unnoticed from a local station. But Mr. Thornton happens to see him with Margaret, while the long arm of coincidence also brings recognition by an old enemy, an ex-sailor turned porter. There is a scuffle, resulting in the later death of the porter. Margaret, to protect her brother, has to lie to the police and to Thornton, who assumes that Frederick is a secret lover.

The complicated plot on its several levels now moves towards solution and reconciliation. Thornton takes the unemployed Higgins on after the strike, partly owing to Margaret's manœuvres. Mr. Hale dies and Mr. Bell adopts Margaret, who soon inherits his property and wealth. Now Margaret's fortunes rise as Thornton's, affected by the strike and trade conditions, fall, while his threatened ruin incidentally threatens the experiments in co-operation between master and men that he has introduced. Margaret is back once more in the South, in London with her relatives, with Lennox courting her again. But she and Thornton are brought together over business and she is now his landlord. The final reconciliation is marriage and partnership; the North wins.

The obvious major theme, worked out chiefly in the relationship between Margaret Hale and John Thornton, is the reconciliation of the attitudes and social values of North and South, with the acceptance of the valuable qualities in both and the recognition of faults and prejudices on both sides. But it is doubtful whether this is really the controlling idea of the novel. To begin with, the basic contrast is only one of a number, not always represented by the North–South opposition. The beauty of Helstone, for example, is contrasted to the ugliness of Milton, but the values of both are contrasted to the idle luxury of London. The importance of religion is common to both sides of the conflict and has its own theme of conscience and dissent. The conflict between masters and men is purely a Milton affair, although northern independence is set against southern paternalism.

What we have in fact is a plea for a better understanding of the merits of the new industrial power which has emerged. In order to make this plea the South, as a way of life, is presented as fostering a rather pointless type of existence in its cities and a brutalized spiritless type of worker in its country. It has charm but lack of purpose. It does, however, inherit the knowledge and practice of the arts and graces of life which make life enjoyable, and the human respect for personal feelings and general humanity which can make harsh conditions tolerable. But these qualities are seen as belonging to the past by the North, which has vitality and command of the future. Thornton defends his lack of reverence for the past by stressing that:

to men groping in new circumstances, it would be finer if the words of experience could direct us how to act in what concerns us most intimately and immediately; which is full of difficulties that must be encountered; and upon the mode in which they are met and con-quered—not merely pushed aside for the time—depends our future.[7]

and he 'laughs outright' at Mr. Bell's suggestion that Oxford might be able to help. This is a North concerned with material and practical ends, in too much of a hurry and too beset by immediate problems to appreciate other values. Mrs. Gaskell endeavours to hold the balance between the two attitudes—the improved relationships in Thornton's mill after the strike are put forward as a material gain arising from the practical application of 'southern' principles—but the attempt is skimped because it gets merged in another aim, to present a balanced interpretation of the social conflict within the North. The major part of the book deals with Milton and presents a detailed and lively description of employer and employee. The South is barely sketched in, apart from the introduction and the brief section of the return visit to Helstone and final stay in London it exists mainly as an Aunt Sally in argument. There is nothing to match the life and vigour

[7] *North and South*, pp. 398–9.

of the Milton scenes. The novel is a piece of special pleading on behalf of the North as far as the contrast is concerned. Margaret Hale is a projection of the attitudes which Mrs. Gaskell felt she ought to take; she attempts to defeat her prejudices by dealing with them in fiction, making the novel a fantasy substitute for a failure in reality.

The result is that the 'South' is at best a muted and sometimes a distorted version of the Cranford world, and for the purposes of making it as complete a foil as possible she includes London in its orbit, although we have seen that in other ways London is itself contrasted to the Cranford world. Certain aspects are retained, the most obvious being the attraction of the countryside itself, exemplified in Helstone. Yet even here Margaret is made to point out that:

our skies are not always as deep a blue as they are now. We have rain, and our leaves do fall, and get sodden . . .[8]

and when she returns to Helstone—an account preluded by a glowing description of a peaceful country scene, she finds eventually that change has occurred here as well. Although she sighs over the 'old picturesqueness' and can answer 'Nothing' when Mr. Bell asks her what is wrong, she is forced to accept the idea of change; not only in households and places, but in herself and in life:

Nothing had been the same; and this slight, all-pervading instability, had given her greater pain than if all had been too entirely changed for her to recognise it.[9]

But she finally accepts that a static world 'would retrograde and become corrupt . . .':

Looking out of myself, and my own painful sense of change, the progress of all around me is right and necessary . . .[10]

The element of continuity is provided by the feelings and moral principles which have previously been discussed; these are applied to Milton as they were to Manchester in *Mary Barton*.

[8] *North and South*, p. 29.   [9] ibid., p. 478.   [10] ibid., p. 479.

Other elements of the old stable order are seen from the dark side. Instead of the pleasant traditions of Cranford we have the brutal superstition of roasting a live cat, the elegant economy of Miss Matty is replaced by the peevish complaints and exaggerated gentility of Mrs. Hale. And whereas in *Mary Barton* the country life is held up as a wholesome contrast to industrialization, now when Higgins tells Margaret of his intention to become a farm-worker she warns him against it by a hair-raising account of the misery and degradation it would entail. The rose-coloured spectacles have been discarded with a vengeance in her eagerness to praise the benefits of industrial life. One is left wondering how on earth Margaret could ever have enjoyed living in the gloomy scene she paints.

London in this context represents the appeal of the superficial:

the eventless ease in which no struggle or endeavour was required.

It has taste, refinement of manners, an easy sociability, but its feelings and affections are shallow. Its wealth is not earned, and is consequently valued only for the luxuries it provides, while human relationships between the different classes are non-existent:

There might be toilers and moilers there in London, but she never saw them; the very servants lived in an undergound world of their own, of which she knew neither the hopes nor the fears . . .[11]

At least, in Helstone, people were treated as individuals. The maid Dixon has a recognized position in the family; the village families may have been objects of philanthropy but their hopes and fears were shared. In this respect London shares its fault with the Milton that Margaret finds, and which in the person of Thornton she sets out to reform. Taste and refinement are seen as qualities to be desired although in London the pursuit of them occupies too much time and becomes a sort of hedonism. The Hales' drawing-room in Milton, in spite of their relative poverty, conforms to the standards of:

plainness and simplicity which are of themselves the framework of elegance.[12]

[11] *North and South*, p. 445.   [12] ibid., p. 69.

Both their own home and that of Margaret's aunt in London are places intended for living and enjoyment; the antithesis of Mrs. Thornton's drawing-room with its ostentation and 'effect of icy, snowy discomfort'.[13] But this is something that education and habit in the use of wealth can remedy, while none of London's superficial graces can make up for the lack of moral strenuousness and sense of purpose for which it stands condemned.

This South, which is not the Cranford world, is also the starting point for the discovery of the North; once the Hales are in Milton the novel develops as a study of Milton life, and it is a North that is glamourized in balance with the de-glamourizing of the South, although the glamourizing process is kept, with one important exception, to matters of moral and practical energy. The South has been allotted the attractions of beauty, sensibility and inherited culture; the North is allowed spiritual energy, mental drive and the claim to the future. But Mrs. Gaskell's personal dislike of the Manchester setting does not permit her to deny its ugliness. Milton has the drabness, the dirt, the depressing atmosphere of its world, and Mrs. Hale may truly be said to die of Manchester.

The ugly and uncouth setting reflects unfairly the sound spirit and purposeful activity:

People thronged the footpaths, most of them well-dressed as regarded the material, but with a slovenly looseness which struck Margaret as different from the shabby, threadbare smartness of a similar class in London.[14]

This note of solid worth not yet refined, of the rough diamond needing polish, is struck at the beginning and maintained through the characters of Thornton the master and Higgins the worker. Nevertheless some concessions about the surroundings have been made; this is not the Manchester of *Mary Barton* with its slums, its filth, its desperate poverty. The very grime is seen as an adjunct of industrial progress. The change is partly due to the need to present the city in not too bad a light, partly it is a reaction from the emotional attitudes of the early novel. Mrs. Gaskell now wishes to justify Manchester and to present a balanced picture,

[13] *North and South*, p. 131.   [14] ibid., p. 67.

extremes are therefore out. We are offered the solid but sober dignity of the Thorntons' house, the rough but sufficient comfort of the Higgins household, the threat only of hunger and hardship as against the exaggerated luxury of the Carsons' house, the oozing squalor of the Davenports' basement, the children dying of starvation.

Much more important than this selective omission is the impact of the positive romanticizing of the new power. Whether it is the steam-hammer 'recalling to Mr. Hale some of the wonderful stories of subservient genii in the Arabian Nights'[15] or Thornton's rhapsodic view of creative energy bursting out into new inventions and market conquests, this sense of glory behind the smoke and ugliness is kept before us, often transmuted into the romantic terms of battle:

"And this imagination of power, this practical realisation of a gigantic thought, came out of one man's brain in our good town. That very man has it within him to mount, step by step, on each wonder he achieves to higher marvels still. And I'll be bound to say, we have many among us who, if he were gone, could spring into the breach, and carry on the war which compels, and shall compel, all material power to yield to science."

"Your boast reminds me of the old lines—
    'I've a hundred captains in England,' he said
    'As good as ever was he'."

At her father's quotation Margaret looked suddenly up, with inquiring wonder in her eyes. How in the world had they got from cogwheels to Chevy Chase?

"It is no boast of mine," replied Mr. Thornton; "it is plain matter-of-fact. I won't deny that I am proud of belonging to a town—or perhaps I should rather say a district—the necessities of which give birth to such grandeur of conception. I would rather be a man toiling, suffering—nay, failing and successless—here, than lead a dull prosperous life in the old worn grooves of what you call more aristocratic society down in the South, with their slow days of careless ease. One may be clogged with honey and unable to rise and fly."[16]

---

[15] *North and South*, p. 92.

[16] ibid., p. 93. Mrs. Gaskell knew and genuinely admired the genius of the northern engineers. James Nasmyth, inventor of the steam-hammer, was a friend; his business partner was a relative of Mr. Gaskell.

Thornton's speech and Mr. Hale's reaction sum up the spirit in which the North is presented, as a 'grandeur of conception' to which niceties of taste and manners are secondary, refinements which it is hinted will be absorbed from the South when there is time.

Not least significant is Mr. Hale's quotation: cogwheels *are* connected with Chevy Chase, for Mrs. Gaskell is suggesting the idea of continuity, the traditional energy and genius of England being handed down to fresh blood in the challenge to the future. The eventual marriage of Margaret to Thornton symbolizes the continuity of the old in the new. In this way Mrs. Gaskell attempts the reconciliation of old culture and new energy without losing her faith in the power of tradition. Similarly the toughness, independence and intelligence of the ordinary man is presented as preserved by the new breed of working man; (we can recall that in *Mary Barton* they were shown as still immigrants from the country).

Thornton and Higgins are both, for all the realism of their background, portrayed as romantic, larger than life figures. Thornton wins Margaret by methods which are ultimately the same as those which won Desdemona for Othello. He begins with the account of his early life, although in addition to the poverty-to-riches story the novel has as its matter the experience of further struggles, so that Margaret, like Desdemona, ends by seeing his:

> visage in his mind,
> And to his honours, and his valiant parts
> Did I my soul and fortunes consecrate.

This romanticizing is a pointer to one of the book's weaknesses, the attempt to idealize something that Mrs. Gaskell does not regard as ideal. It stems from the attempt she is making, against the grain, to do justice to a way of life in which she finds qualities to admire without being in sympathy with it as a whole. She tries to come to terms with the Manchester ethos but the resolution is artificial. The failure shows in two ways, in her treatment of particular aspects and in the novel's structure.

Mrs. Gaskell is by nature an honest observer. She is also, as we have seen, an optimist inclined to take a favourable view of human nature. When, as in the Cranford world, she is dealing with a reality she loves, and couples this with her optimism, the result is a description that while not avoiding the everyday accidents and catastrophes of life cannot help suggesting that this is probably as good a type of life as is available. With the best of wills she cannot feel this about the Manchester world. She cannot, as an observer, describe it as other than depressing, with its 'long, straight, hopeless streets',[17] nor is it ever suggested that Margaret will enjoy living there even though she marries Thornton. At one stage Mrs. Gaskell even toyed with the idea of manipulating the plot so that Margaret would escape the full consequences of her choice:

"What do you think," [she wrote to Catherine Winkworth,] "of a fire burning down Mr. Thornton's mills and houses as a *help* to failure? Then Margaret could rebuild them larger and better, and need not go to live there when she's married."[18]

The constant references to beauty, refinement and gentle manners in contrast with dirt, crudity and harshness denote a basic discord; the marriage may be presented as a union of southern culture and northern energy but it carries disharmony with it. Margaret's moral sense and desire to be useful may find pleasure in the Manchester world, but not the whole woman.

Even so, the picture of Manchester has been softened from that in *Mary Barton*. The dirt has become honest dirt, and it is hinted that by law, or more probably by the practical realization that 'it repays me in the saving of coal'[19] much of it will be controlled. Factory reform is shown to be hindered by the conservatism of the workers as much as by the materialism of the masters[20] and the general picture is one of prosperity, in spite of the strike.

Mrs. Gaskell appears also to have been undecided about the type of book she was writing. In one sense she was following up the

[17] *North and South*, p. 66. The adjective 'hopeless' is a giveaway.
[18] Haldane, pp. 103–4.   [19] *North and South*, p. 94.
[20] The example given is ventilation. Bessy Higgins dies from constantly swallowing particles of fluff at work.

way opened by *Mary Barton* and *Ruth* of the novel with serious
intent and a plain social purpose; describing conditions of which
most people were ignorant while attempting to deal a blow at
facile judgements and conventional prejudices. But the way in
which the book is written shows that her natural bent for dealing
with personal relationships in a closely observed social setting is
taking command.

The treatment of religion is an example of the confusion. The
long account of Mr. Hale's crisis of belief at the beginning would
seem to point to an extended treatment of the religious conscience
and belief, but this fails to materialize, possibly because Mrs.
Gaskell was unwilling to join in the bitter controversies of the
time with yet another religious novel. Having served as a plot
device to pluck the Hales out of Helstone, religion reappears feebly
after the fashion of *Mary Barton*, as an element of personal
stability and humanity. But Mrs. Gaskell is no longer interested
as a novelist in this type of didacticism, and the religious element
appears only rarely, almost as a sop to duty, in dealing with
Higgins's character, or most unconvincingly when Thornton
breaks down after his ruin and weeps on his mother's neck:

If you would say the old good words, it would make me feel something of the pious simplicity of my childhood.[21]

This is neither the behaviour nor the speech of the man we have
got to know. We feel the artificiality; as we do with Bessy
Higgins's exaggerated religiosity which becomes sentimentalized
and melodramatic, almost a caricature of itself. And we may
note here a point that will be discussed later, that Mrs. Gaskell
lets herself in for scenes of high emotion and passion which she
cannot handle. Nor is she at ease with political and economic
argument, which the deliberate patterning of the novel calls for.
The result is that the melodramatic and the argumentative sections, even though well assimilated into her easy style, are alien
to the central, personal interest. And her humour, one of her
essential gifts, is damped down by the serious intent and the
passages of factual discussion.

[21] *North and South*, p. 507.

On the other hand her interest in personal and social relationships has become more prominent. Not only is there less moralizing than in previous work but much of what there is is carried within the dialogue and behaviour of the characters instead of being inserted as authorial comment, although there are inevitably flat spots in their portrayal as a result. We sympathize with and remember the characters as individuals, rather than as representative types; the relationship between Margaret, Thornton and Higgins which is the heart of the book quickly develops as a personal one to which their representative attitudes and prejudices are complementary. As Margaret reflects to herself, the beginnings of a brighter life were owing to the meeting with the Higgins, when 'she had found a human interest',[22] and it is this interest which gives the novel its vitality, as it is the descriptive and social detail which gives it its solidity. There is nothing artificial for example about the growth of Margaret's or Thornton's personalities. Indeed, the failures in respect of character are when they are too obviously creatures of imposed argument or demonstration, as is largely the case with Boucher the discontented and struggling mill-hand, and with Bessy Higgins; to a lesser extent with Mr. Hale and Mrs. Thornton. This is most noticeable with those characters who have more to do with stringing the plot along than with the general setting, such as Frederick Hale or the crudely melodramatic porter Leonards.

The artificiality and indecision is reflected chiefly in the elaborate construction, which has to carry the working out of the North–South balance, the conflict between masters and men, and the personal relationship between Margaret and Thornton. There is no doubt that Mrs. Gaskell learnt a lot from the handling of this complex action. She enjoyed the process of resolving its complications in the seclusion of Lea Hurst, the country home of Florence Nightingale's parents where she had been invited to work on the novel in peace. But the sense of contrivance and manipulation is too plain.[23] Some of the blame may be attributed

---

[22] *North and South*, p. 84.
[23] Ward, in his introduction (p. xxiv) claims that it must 'be rightly described as faultless'. It certainly deserves praise, but he ignores the effect on credibility.

to the demands of serialization, but there is little indication, for example, that the resolution of the Margaret–Thornton story— which carries with it the resolution of the opposed attitudes— could be other than contrived. At one stage of the writing she was actually considering adding a major sub-plot to achieve an even more elaborate balance.[24] The introduction of Frederick is pure plot-spinning (her facility in creating episodes was never fully brought under control, except perhaps in *Cousin Phillis*), while four deaths (those of Mrs. and Mr. Hale, Leonard and Mr. Bell) as well as a sudden commercial crisis are required to swing Margaret up and Thornton down on fortune's wheel. The too obvious drawing of parallels and placing of discussions have already been dealt with. Nor is there the initial inspiration of anger and passionate sympathy which makes *Mary Barton*, although a more clumsily written book, more powerful and unified in feeling.

North and South can be seen as a crucial stage in the development of Mrs. Gaskell's attitudes and her technique. Long before it was written she had noted of herself that she was not one 'me' but several:

One of my mes is, I do believe, a true Christian—(only people call her socialist and communist), another of my mes is a wife and mother . . . Now that's my "social" self I suppose. Then again I've another self with a full taste for beauty and convenience wh. is pleased on its own account. How am I to reconcile all these warring members?[25]

and later, commenting on the clash of duties between daily life and writing, she complained that:

the difficulty is where and when to make one set of duties subserve and give place to the other.[26]

This was her last full attempt at forcing her creative work to emphasize the sense of duty which was prodded by her religious

[24] 'Mrs. Thornton, the mother, to have taken as a sort of humble companion & young housekeeper the orphan daughter of an old friend in humble, retired country life on the borders of Lancashire— & this girl to be in love with Mr. Thornton in a kind of passionate despairing way—but both jealous of Margaret . . .' (quoted in *Haldane*, p. 152). She goes on to sketch the character, her imagination had already begun to give it substance.
[25] Letter to Tottie Fox, quoted in *Haldane*, p. 238. The terms 'socialist and communist' do not carry their present political or idealogical content.   [26] *Haldane*, p. 249.

and social conscience—the Christian or socialist 'me'. At the same time it was an attempt, through fiction, to achieve some form of compromise between the new industrial world and an antipathy to its ways. But her sympathies were against it; although she admired its achievement she was sensitive to the human problem involved. *Mary Barton, Ruth*, other stories and finally *North and South* had been used to carry her protests and describe realities; incidentally they had released and developed her powers to handle the long novel. After this she was to reserve the expression of her sense of public duty for daily life, and allow that side of her 'which is pleased on its own account' to have its range. The values of the Cranford world dominated; through them she was able to find a stable basis for facing a changing world, and expression for a humorous and sensitive appreciation of human feeling and social behaviour.

CHAPTER X

Manchester Abandoned:
'The Life of Charlotte Brontë'
'My Lady Ludlow'

MRS. GASKELL had been writing for eight years, from 1847 to 1855, when *North and South* was published. Her remaining fiction was written in another eight-year period from 1858 to 1865, when the best of her work with the exception of *Cranford* was produced. It was a period when her writing carried steadily fewer traces of being written with a sense of obligation towards ideals of moral or public duty, and this freedom to write to suit herself is reflected in the range and tone of what she produced. The industrial world, with which she had never been really in sympathy, disappears from her work, and with it a good deal of the earnestness which had accompanied it; a disappearance reflected technically by the way in which the amount of direct comment lessens as well as in the nature of the authorial comment that remains. She can still be serious enough, but humour and pleasantness preponderate at the end, a reflection of the more relaxed attitude and the congenial world she treats of as she returns once again to describe the manners and idiosyncrasies of Cranford, or of a way of life closely related to its traditions and principles. There is an evident relish of delight as she observes the behaviour of her characters and their individual responses to convention within the social setting in which she was happiest, that of the small country community. Three of the important stories of this period, *My Lady Ludlow*, *Cousin Phillis* and *Wives and Daughters*, have both the humour and the setting. But the serious side of her nature, with its awareness of a darker side to life, finds expression in two others, 'Lois the Witch' and *Sylvia's Lovers*, and in them, something of the old earnestness of the moral sense demands attention. With the disappearance of the social description of the industrial contemporary scene her interest in historical and old-fashioned social life also becomes more apparent. These five tales, varying in length from the 'nouvelle' to the full-blown Victorian novel, and displaying between them a considerable range of tone, treatment and subject matter, stand out as major achievements.

They have in common also an ease of construction which obviously is derived from experience. But it may also have been helped by a change of publisher, for she escaped from the exacting demands of Dickens and his weekly periodicals, letting him have only her less important work. *My Lady Ludlow* and 'Lois the Witch' did, it is true, go to Dickens, but both were completed before publication and the latter was meant to appear elsewhere, being surrendered unwillingly. *Sylvia's Lovers* was published directly as a novel, and her final achievement in *Cousin Phillis* and *Wives and Daughters* found a congenial home in the sympathetic and unrestricted pages of the *Cornhill*. This was admittedly serial publication, but monthly, and with the author's tastes and methods catered for on behalf of a more cultivated class of reader. George Smith, the publisher, had been Charlotte Brontë's publisher and friend, and she had urged Mrs. Gaskell to change to him.[1] Smith, Elder and Co. had published the *Life of Charlotte Brontë* and a warm friendship had developed between author and publisher. Although Mrs. Gaskell continued to write for Dickens she began to wish for a freer hand and finished by reserving her good work for Smith. She had acquired a technique to support her creative imagination and was free to write how she wished as well as what she wished, allowing her stories their proper length and development.

She concentrates on exploring with the full insight of her sensibility and experience the motives and feelings of her charac-

---

[1] All Mrs. Gaskell's work for periodicals, with negligible exceptions, had gone to Dickens. Her books had been published by Chapman and Hall. The problems of serialization will be dealt with when structure is discussed.

ters. While she remains the social historian of the small community, these novels and stories develop, without the pressure of
ulterior issues, that interest in personal relationships which is at
the heart of all her work; it is round the natural interplay of these
relationships, unhampered by artificial manipulations of plot to
suit a thesis, that they unfold. The underlying values and standards
of conduct are still there but more and more assimilated within
the behaviour and speech of the characters; *Cousin Phillis* and
Wives and Daughters are surely two of the most convincingly
natural novels in the English language.

The change of publisher has been mentioned as an incidental
benefit arising from the publication of the *Life*; before this second
period of Mrs. Gaskell's work can be dealt with it is essential to
take note of the biography itself, which occupied the period between *North and South* and *My Lady Ludlow*. It is too important a
work to be overlooked, although any comment on it as a biography would be out of place in this study of her fiction. Nevertheless like all great biographies it must be considered as an
imaginative reconstruction as well as a factual work, and its place
in Mrs. Gaskell's development as a writer is important.

Two points of general interest stand out. The first is that she did
not write a critical biography. She describes accurately and in
detail the circumstances in which the poems and novels of the
Brontës were written and published, and surveys the reception
they received. She recognizes the importance of the juvenilia and
duly describes them as part of their extraordinary upbringing and
imaginative development. But there is virtually no literary
criticism at all, no investigation of the psychology of the genius
or creative imagination of Charlotte, or of her sisters, save what
appears in the quoted letters and reviews. Mrs. Gaskell considers
Charlotte as an individual, the fact that she wrote great novels is
seen as part of the pattern of her life, no less but no more important than any other part. It is Charlotte the woman who is Mrs.
Gaskell's concern.

This second point, that she was preparing to write her friend's
life in some form or other before she was officially asked to do so,

is connected with this non-literary approach. She wrote to George Smith telling him that she had it in mind to write sooner or later a memoir that would:

make the world (if I am but strong enough in expression) honour the woman as much as they admired the writer.[2]

and the distinction between woman and writer was made even more clearly shortly afterwards as Mrs. Gaskell stated her conviction that:

the more she was known, the more people would honour her as a woman, separate from her character as an authoress.[3]

This approach is important. When Charlotte's father, the Rev. Patrick Brontë, and her husband the Rev. A. B. Nicholls, asked Mrs. Gaskell to undertake an official biography, they did so because she was an established author as well as a friend, and therefore uniquely able to produce something that would at one and the same time do the dead woman justice and carry authority to counter the rush of hasty and ill-informed articles that had appeared after Charlotte Brontë's death. But Mrs. Gaskell, though herself famous as a novelist, showed no interest in presenting her own evaluation of the novels, her interest was all in the woman. What had already attracted her sufficiently to make her wish to write the *Life* was Charlotte's:

wild sad life, and the beautiful character that grew out of it . . .[4]

the attraction, in other words, of handling character in setting that provided the creative impulse behind all of Mrs. Gaskell's work.

The particular attraction in this case is hardly surprising, for the romantic setting and complex characters contained most of the types of theme and relationship which Mrs. Gaskell considered to be important and which she delighted to handle. Charlotte Brontë was the perfect example of the influence of upbringing and background. She made an intelligent, affectionate and independent

[2] Letter dated 31 May, 1855, quoted in *Hopkins*, p. 160.
[3] Letter dated 4 June, 1855, ibid., p. 161.   [4]id.

central figure, yet one placing affection and duty before independence. Her religion was a vital part of her life, sustaining her and providing guidance for conduct when needed. Her sense of duty and fitness in all things supported both her perseverance and her quiet acceptance of suffering and set-back. Her principles and strength of character as well as her creative talent lifted her above the conventional norm; there was conflict between life and ambition, between conduct and convention. All in all this was such a character as Mrs. Gaskell might have wished to imagine for herself as the heroine of a novel, but with the authenticity of life and of greatness. There was the background, the self-contained and psychologically fascinating family life set against the Yorkshire moors and Yorkshire ways and customs. The drama supplied itself, in the incidents of Charlotte's life, and to hold it all together was a story of struggle and success, with behind it Mr. Nicholls' faithful love for Charlotte, nicely offset by the various proposals she received and her own unconscious and then suppressed love for Mr. Nicholls. The last few months of Charlotte's life, in its brief happiness as a wife, were seen quite naturally as a culmination overshadowing her fame as an author, and provides as fine an example of reconciliation as any of Mrs. Gaskell's own novels. The patient love of Mr. Nicholls is rewarded, while the proud and once indignant father accepts his new son-in-law as his permanent curate and companion. The other characters in the story, down to a faithful and testy old servant (Tabby) far more idiosyncratic than those she had created in *Ruth* and *North and South*, were all there.

I have said that the ingredients lay to Mrs. Gaskell's hand. It must equally be said that the shaping hand of the author brings them out in the pattern of the biography. The story of Charlotte Brontë's life was a sombre and absorbing one; as a heroine in Mrs. Gaskell's sense Charlotte needed only the slightest touch to be perfectly adapted to this interpretation. The biography, in spite of all the research that was necessary (she not only carried on a vast correspondence but travelled as far as Brussels in checking the authenticity and background) and in spite of the mass of primary documentation used, developed with the speed and assurance of a novel. From beginning to end, including all the work involved in accumulating information, took eighteen months, an incredible creative and analytical achievement. The authenticity of the portrait has never been challenged save in certain details, some of which are touched on in the following pages. There was no forcing or selection of the evidence to produce a desired result. It was Mrs. Gaskell's view of life which gathered the material of the biography and shaped it into the interpretation.

In preparing the biography Mrs. Gaskell was led into analysing character, relationships and background in great detail. Her affections were engaged, and she had the advantage of beginning with knowledge, sympathy and Charlotte's own account in conversation. The knowledge extended to the general setting of the Brontë country as well as the immediate background, to which she added her own research into the general social background; in this respect her method was an extension of her approach to her earlier novels. The necessity of weighing the effect of every action and detail in personal and social relationships, and all the time of allowing the steady accumulation of detail and incident to speak for itself, must undoubtedly have taught her a great deal. Moreover, although in many ways Charlotte's life was a tragic one, there are no major melodramatic incidents or adventures. Death and misfortune follow quietly and inevitably through its course, even the happiness at the end is muted. Melodrama and excitement is replaced by sustained psychological interest, a pattern that *Cousin Phillis* and *Wives and Daughters* follow.

There was also the necessity of effacing herself as far as possible so that the characters could speak and act for themselves, a withdrawal which involved the imaginative effort of identifying herself with the story she was unfolding, although towards the end she was able to introduce herself as the narrator who is also a character, as she had done with the character of Mary Smith in *Cranford*. The leisurely development through incident and detail of story and setting in a work so seemingly different in its nature as *Wives and Daughters* must owe a lot to the earlier experience of writing the biography, as must the increasing subtlety and natural development of feeling and motivation, though no-one could complain that her earlier work lacks understanding of human conduct. The long and sustained enquiry into the life of Charlotte Brontë and her family sharpened her ability to deal with the psychology of character.

This leads to the question of realism. Realism may be factual, the aim of presenting through detail a credible picture of settings or of daily life and conduct. There is also a realism of imaginative perception, influenced by how the writer sees humanity and human nature. Characters may be completely 'real' to the author, and presented against a solidly factual background, yet be more or less unreal to general acceptance because the writer's view of human nature is coloured or distorted by some preconception. Distortion through the mental eye may not be immediately noticeable, as a reader tends to be convinced by the reality of the scene presented, but the underlying conceptions about human nature will be clear, as in the very different worlds of say Walter Pater and Thackeray or, to take a painstakingly realistic novelist, that of George Gissing. It may happen that the logic of the factual reality clashes with the attitude taken to characters who ought to match the reality, as for example the benevolence of Dickens's benevolent characters is often untrue to the general view of human nature he presents, so that their unreality is obvious.

One can point to this fault in Mrs. Gaskell's earlier novels. Within the realism of the accounts of the Manchester world the optimistic and somewhat idealized view of human nature is slightly out of key, the hopefulness does not match our reading of the general scene. One way of correcting this incompatibility is to colour the reality presented, or to select details, so that it matches the conception of human nature which is seen in the characters, and this was virtually what Mrs. Gaskell did to achieve the unity of *Cranford*.

In dealing with the life of her friend, Mrs. Gaskell was presented at the outset with the background and the conduct of her characters as facts. It is a mark of her integrity that she accepted both— the extensive use of documents, letters and opinions of other people is ample evidence of this—and in the process of turning the two into a unity she largely refrained from drawing conclusions or pointing morals. Yet some shaping of interpretation is there, as I have said. In addition there is the occasional deliberate selection of detail to conform with the image of Charlotte which she wished to present, as well as with certain contemporary conventions of biography, even though for the period it is an outstandingly frank and honest book.[5] But on the whole the portrait presented is real in every sense, and it is noticeable that in later novels Mrs. Gaskell, while retaining her essential viewpoint, is perceptibly more objective about the present state and possible progress of human nature.

This increased objectivity is a facet of her reaction from didactic and social intent; it would have been impossible to apply the experience obtained in writing the *Life* if she had still felt that she ought to be pointing morals. But the importance of the experience of writing a biography should not be underestimated. Tolerance and sympathy, always present in her approach to other people, had kept her from easily passing judgement on others, especially when judgement would be from the standpoint of conventional attitudes, and *Ruth* is a sustained plea for understanding in place of bigotry. At the conclusion of the *Life* she sums up her own attitude in words that could certainly not have been applied to some of her earlier works:

I cannot measure or judge of such a character as hers. I cannot map out vices, and virtues, and debatable land.[6]

---

[5] There is little, but what there is is significant. A good example of the omission of detail is found on p. 470, when she quotes her own letter describing her impressions of Charlotte Brontë at their first meeting. This has been edited to omit one or two unflattering items of description such as 'a reddish face' and 'many teeth gone' which might jar on our mental image of the 'heroine' of her work. (The original is quoted in *Haldane*, p. 124.) The most outstanding feature is the way she stepped round Charlotte's passion for Paul Héger; it is generally accepted that she must have seen the full letters from which she quotes only extracts illustrating Charlotte's general attitude to life in the Pensionnat. But contemporary ideas of respect for private lives and feelings would have made it impossible to publish the whole episode. '[What is offensive] is the point on which we differ; *not* on the duty of a biographer to omit whatever can reasonably be expected to be offensive, &c. I acknowledge that duty . . .' (Mrs. Gaskell to J. S. Mill. Quoted in *Haldane*, p. 270.) Mrs. Gaskell's MS. is much more corrected than usual during this episode.

[6] *Life*, p. 642.

and this approach is scrupulously adhered to in the best of her later work. The readers are left to make their own judgement, Mrs. Gaskell having done her best to provide the full picture so that they should not:

judge harshly because they have only seen superficially and not thought deeply.[7]

One result of *The Life of Charlotte Brontë* was that Mrs. Gaskell found herself caught up once again in public and bitter controversy. For some of this she had only herself to blame, where she had failed to check her sources properly as when she accepted Branwell's (and Charlotte's) account of his relations with Mrs. Robinson. But she also accepted the risk of dealing with living people, some of whom were implicitly or directly criticized in the letters and reminiscences she quotes. They naturally defended themselves, some privately like G. H. Lewes, some publicly and angrily like Carus Wilson. There was also sharply divided critical opinion on the success of the *Life* itself, and on the propriety of writing a biography, warts and all. She disliked controversy, and the type of criticism which attacked her not as a writer but because of her opinions; it depressed her and made her physically ill.[8] She had taken some time to recover from the rough handling she had received over *Ruth*; *North and South* had been carefully balanced to avoid censure. Now she was under attack again. Reasons have already been suggested for making her glad to give up any further attempt to comment directly on the contemporary scene in her novels; to these we might add the painful aftermath of the biography.

It would be a mistake to imagine that the writing of the biography produced any drastic change in Mrs. Gaskell's art, yet

---

[7] *Life*, p. 643.

[8] In a letter to George Smith she reveals her fears: 'I look forward also with a feeling of dread to the expressions of opinion, both public & private, which will cut me two ways on the appearance of the book, and am extremely anxious to be out of the country at the time of its publication.' (*Hopkins*, p. 218.) She goes on to explain her precautions taken to make sure that the book would not be permitted to appear until she was able to get away.

its effect was considerable.[9] It served to consolidate and give depth to qualities that were already present, and to confirm her in concentrating on those aspects of character and social history and background which she found congenial. She finished her task exhausted, but potentially a better novelist.

Mrs. Gaskell's retreat from contemporary themes was thorough and permanent; the remaining stories and novels to be considered are set in the past, two of them being very definitely historical. Yet the idea of change and the concern for stability and continuity still remained with her. She concentrated now on the individual and the small community, giving full rein at last to her interest in the psychology of character and conduct, and noting, generally with quiet satire, the inconsistencies and self-deceptions which people bring to the business of living, as well as their oddities of behaviour. Social change and stability are considered first from their effect on the individual. But because they still occupy her, the past she deals with gradually moves towards the present again, while the social range extends until contrasts between sections and broad classes become as important as those between individuals and types. So it is that much of the work of this period has for its setting a more or a less immediate past, in which the transition from an older generation through the fictional 'present' can be explored in terms of social comedy, with the conclusion looking forward to a future which was in fact Mrs. Gaskell's own present.

My Lady Ludlow appeared in 1858.[10] At first sight it would appear to be a reversion to the method of *Cranford*, and in certain important ways she had picked up the threads of the earlier work. But a consistent theme runs through the story as well as a planned

[9] I can see little influence on Mrs. Gaskell of Charlotte Brontë the novelist. Mrs. Gaskell had admired her work from the outset; they met in 1850, but each followed her own course as a writer. But see the comments on *Sylvia's Lovers*. An interesting minor detail of residual influence is that Molly Gibson's governess in *Wives and Daughters* is called Miss Eyre.

[10] It was first published serially in *Household Words*. It appeared in book form as the main item in *Round the Sofa*, a collection of stories which had all been previously published in periodicals and were now loosely linked together in a chain narrative. I shall consider *My Lady Ludlow* without the slight links provided for the book.

development which, in spite of the episodic structure, is not just the set of reminiscences suggested by the apologetic remark of the narrator that:

It is no story: it has, as I said, neither beginning, middle, nor end.[11]

The theme is explicitly that of change, the gradual acceptance of new ideas and attitudes as circumstances change, but one catastrophic lapse of judgement makes the essential unity of theme and tone difficult to realize. For whatever reason, possibly led astray by her own return to a more episodic structure, she introduces as an episode a 'tale within the tale' which has only the barest factitious link to the main narrative and yet occupies nearly one third of it. This is digression on the grand eighteenth-century scale. To make matters worse, the tale introduced is a melodramatically tragic one of romantic adventure, love and death in the terrors of the French Revolution; in tone and content completely out of key with the quietly humorous treatment and serious undercurrent of the daily life, joys and sorrows of the self-contained country community she is describing. The episode has perhaps some point for the period it deals with, inasmuch as the horrors of the French Revolution reinforced the resistance to social change of any description which was an essential feature of the early nineteenth century England being described, and Lady Ludlow recounts the story (it touches on friends of the family) to emphasize the dangers of meddling with the accepted treatment of the lower classes. But the whole episode would be better out of the way; if it were cut out—and this could easily be done[12]—we would be left with a small gem; not so good as *Cranford* or

[11] *My Lady Ludlow*, p. 9.
[12] If there were a cut at p. 61, after ' "I am distressed," continued she, with a break in her ideas, "about that boy." ' and the story continued again on p. 126 with 'People seldom arrive at my age without having watched the beginning, middle and end of many lives and fortunes,' the surgery would be hardly noticeable, the gain would be immeasurable. The episode itself concerns Clément de Créquy, a young French émigré friend of the Ludlows, who returns to France to rescue his cousin Virginie, with whom he is in love. After many adventures he is about to succeed when unwittingly betrayed. Pierre, the young son of an old retainer in whose home Virginie is hiding, and who was taught to read by Clément, reads the final message concealed in a nosegay and innocently reveals it to a jealous revolutionary who is in love with Virginie. They are captured and executed. The tale allows Mrs. Gaskell to digress into her interest in France and French life.

Cousin Phillis in their different ways but of a quality too good to be ignored. I shall discuss *My Lady Ludlow* as though the story of the de Créquys were not there, in order to bring out the essential qualities of the book and do justice to them. Even with this digression omitted there are still weaknesses in the construction to be noticed, for Mrs. Gaskell wrote the story rather hurriedly and relied too much on her facility for episode and anecdote.[13]

The story is one of the gradual conquest of certain prejudices without the loss of the fine qualities which balanced them. Lady Ludlow is the last of the old-fashioned Hanburys of Hanbury Court. She is widowed, all her children but one are dead, and he dies in the course of the book. Her life is devoted to ruling and caring for the dependants of her estate, and preserving the traditions, customs and details of life that she had been brought up to. She is innately conservative, and convinced that the conditions of life of all ranks should not change; peace, stability and the preservation of sound morals and principles she sees as lying in respect for the authority and wisdom of rank and breeding:

a sort of tribute to her Order, which she had no individual right to remit, or, indeed, not to exact . . .[14]

while the lower orders have:

the duties to which they are called by God; of submission to those placed in authority over them; of contentment with the state of life to which it has pleased God to call them . . .[15]

It is not a one-sided contract; the duties and obligations of the ruling class are seen by Lady Ludlow as being just as binding and of the greatest importance, the preservation of society resting on their ability to maintain the *status quo*. Every tradition, every detail of behaviour, when seen in this light, is part of the fabric of a way of life that has changed little for many years. And Lady Ludlow, its representative, is essentially a gracious and lovable though reserved woman.

[13] She wrote to Norton on 9 March 1859 admitting that she wrote the story to cover the expenses of a trip to Germany (*Letters*, p. 30).
[14] *My Lady Ludlow*, p. 160.   [15] ibid., p. 149.

Change inevitably comes, in the person of the new young clergyman, the Rev. Mr. Gray, as selfless, as warm-hearted, and as obstinate and convinced of the correctness of his opinions as Lady Ludlow. He sees what she does not, the stagnation of the poor and the brutalizing effect of ignorance on them; just as Thornton and Carson had wished for educated and intelligent hands, so he wishes for intelligent and educated labourers to cope with changing conditions. He denies Lady Ludlow's authority on matters which his religion gives him a duty to speak on; the achievement of a school is the main thread of the narrative. But change is also at work inside the small society. The management of the Hanbury estates by old-fashioned methods is inefficient; the old steward Mr. Horner has bowed reluctantly to Lady Ludlow's wishes, yet even he has secretly been educating a local lad, Harry Gregson, the son of the poacher, to become his assistant. On Mr. Horner's death a new steward brings in new ideas, and is not ashamed to seek advice from a retired Dissenting baker whose farm is prosperous and efficient, though Dissenters are regarded as outside the pale of respectable society by the orthodox aristocrat. Then there is Miss Galindo, a sharp-tongued and kind-hearted spinster who loves and honours Lady Ludlow, and is herself well-born, though now poor. She takes into her home the illegitimate daughter of her former lover, though Lady Ludlow:

neither saw nor heard, nor was in any way cognisant of the existence of those who had no legal right to exist at all.[16]

The development of the story, necessarily episodic, is controlled by the fact that each character stands in a well-defined social and personal relationship to Lady Ludlow, and also to the others within the structure of local society. The process of adjustment is carried through on the same personal basis. Harry Gregson, crippled in an accident, gets his education and finally becomes the schoolmaster. The Rev. Mr. Gray marries Miss Galindo's adopted daughter, the new steward marries the daughter of the Dissenting baker, and Lady Ludlow, whose respect for individual merit is never blinded once she has had a chance to recognize it,

16 *My Lady Ludlow*, p. 196.

accepts the changes and finally gives a formal tea-party to characters who, at the beginning of the narrative, would not have been recognized as possible visitors to a Hanbury of Hanbury Court.

Nevertheless the change is an adjustment of social values, not a social upheaval, while the result is a vindication of moral values and standards which are in the long run common to all. Lady Ludlow still holds her position by virtue of innate goodness and personality as well as rank, the society is still a stable and well-ordered one with its gradations of rank, duties and obedience clearly understood. But it has moved itself out of the eighteenth century and is preparing to carry on in the nineteenth century while preserving its continuity with the best qualities of its past.

The qualities which distinguish *My Lady Ludlow* are founded on those which gave *Cranford* its distinction, the story comes from 'the self . . . which is pleased on its own account'. There is the same pervading sympathy for natural affections and undramatic goodness; feelings and emotions are responded to without on the whole being sentimentalized. There is the same quietly detailed and enjoyed account of traditions and manners which provides the setting and background reality, the feeling of an older, more gracious world. There is the latent sense of its minor absurdities revealed by the irony of the narrator's account; for once again we have, in Margaret Dawson, the narrator who is within but to one side of the scene, sympathetic but objective. The humour springs from the comedy of human relationships and individual idiosyncracy; enhanced this time by the creation of Miss Galindo as a recruit to the ranks of 'elegant economists'. Like Falstaff she is witty in herself and the cause of wit in others—her encounter with the mischievous and intruding duck which has been named 'Miss Galindo' is notable. She invades the second half of the book, injecting a vitality and comedy not in the more placid and ironic earlier section, as though Mrs. Gaskell realized that another view-point was needed to support the too-quiet Margaret. Miss Galindo's character has two sides, that of the sensitive well-bred lady who keeps her private troubles to herself and that of the bustling, practical and intelligent woman whose helping hand and shrewd comments come together. Her remark that:

when common-sense goes against us, I don't think we value it quite so much as we ought to do.[17]

reflects the unsentimental appreciation of human nature which is one aspect of the book.

Yet both in content and in treatment *My Lady Ludlow* is influenced by her previous work. It has its serious note; although Mrs. Gaskell has turned her back on the didactic novel and on the problems of industrial society she retains her concern with the principles and beliefs she had been dealing with. Nor are the motives behind conduct trivial—such as Miss Galindo's break with Lady Ludlow over the illegitimate Bessy or the concern for the poor and ignorant which partly causes Mr. Gray's collapse—in spite of their being contained in the framework of comedy. The village world, while still a relatively small community, has widened. It covers several classes instead of the one class of *Cranford*; Lady Ludlow the aristocrat and Job Gregson the poacher mark the extremes of a scale which has its gentlefolk, farmers, bakers, clergymen. The 'beauty and convenience' of the surroundings is still dominant but the squalor talked of as existing round Helstone in *North and South* is present in Hareman's Common, with its 'yellow pools of stagnant water' and 'cluster of rude mud houses'.[18] The characters are more varied and the main ones more complex, the world they live in is harsher and more exposed to pain and suffering. The Cranford world has been enlarged to include much that was originally reserved for the drearier Manchester world, and although the setting has been pushed more specifically into the past than that of *Cranford*, its characters are more modern in essence. Within this setting Mrs. Gaskell's interest is now centred on personal life; the problem of change is seen through the mind and emotions of Lady Ludlow and against the life of Hanbury Court, which is an extension of her personality. As with *Ruth*, Mrs. Gaskell has chosen to call the story by the name of the central character, and *My Lady Ludlow* is

[17] *My Lady Ludlow*, p. 197.   [18] ibid., p. 35.

in fact a portrait with background; a study of temperament and character delicately and objectively presented; within its limits the maturest she had achieved.[19]

Problems which had been dealt with in earlier work re-appear now as personal problems. For example, the question of illegitimacy is raised with Bessy, Miss Galindo's daughter. Whereas in *Ruth* the problem was given general significance, it is now treated as a personal affair and reflects a facet of Lady Ludlow's character. Problems of Orthodoxy and Dissent, and even of irreligion, are now viewed as individual ones and come within the compass of personal prejudice, the narrator setting the tone with her naïve comment on Dissenters:

I looked upon them almost as if they were rhinoceroses. I wanted to see a live Dissenter, I believe, and yet I wished it were over.[20]

Yet the personal problems involve social ones. The tinge of earnestness is still present; we can suspect that Mr. Gray will one day write a strongly didactic novel and regard Charles Kingsley as his model. When Mr. Gray accuses Lady Ludlow of being 'all-powerful as far as material power goes'[21] he is acknowledging the social hierarchy, and his struggle is against the pervasive authority of rank, with the accompanying social powers of:

those ceremonies and forms which are, I suppose, the etiquette of your ladyship's rank of life . . .[22]

The fact that Mr. Gray gets his school is a triumph for social conscience as well as religious duty.

The treatment of religion shows an interesting change. It is no longer being pushed as a panacea, for all concerned are religious; what do come under discussion are the nature of religion and the social and conventional forms it takes. Its treatment is part of the rejection of broad social issues in favour of personal ones; in working towards a closer and deeper analysis of the individual

---

[19] The titles of Mrs. Gaskell's novels are evidence of her primary interest in individuals, especially if we remember that *North and South* was originally called 'Margaret Hale'. (*Mary Barton* was a shift from 'John Barton', which made more sense.) *Cranford* and *Wives and Daughters* are revealing as titles by this reckoning.

[20] *My Lady Ludlow*, p. 141.   [21] ibid., p. 147.   [22] ibid., p. 147.

mind and heart Mrs. Gaskell looks at the religion of individuals. In this case, where it is part of a study of prejudice and change, it is seen within the comic viewpoint; while religion is not made fun of, religious attitudes are.

She ranges widely in her study of religious types. Lady Ludlow is the old-fashioned, orthodox and sincere Christian whose religion is a matter of personal practice and public example. The enthusiasm and emotional colouring of Mr. Gray's equally sincere Christianity and new-fangled ideas are distasteful and alarming to her. She sees clergymen and religion as part of the social pattern: we meet the servile family parson of her grandfather's time and the kindly but lazy and worldly country-gentleman parson in Mr. Gray's predecessor, Mr. Mountford, who refrains from giving a sermon if Lady Ludlow does not want one. This is kindness and Christianity, but unexercised; as Margaret Dawson says:

I think a good run would not have come amiss, even from a moral point of view, to Mr. Mountford.[23]

Mr. Gray's Christianity is evangelical, taking precedence over material or social authority when his duty and conscience demand. He does not dispute the need for such authority; his argument is the one he opposes to Lady Ludlow's comments on 'the duties to which [the lower orders] are called by God'[24]:

I do not think of character: I think of souls.[25]

And this distinction in its way epitomizes the two aspects of religion which Mrs. Gaskell sees, the personal faith which is necessary for individual salvation and the guidance to conduct which forms character and influences personal and social relationships. It is Miss Galindo who voices the common-sense view of the compromise between the two, when she skilfully outmanœuvres her maid's attempts to be a meditative Mary rather than a practical Martha:

Now, Sally, to-morrow we'll try to hash that beef well, and to remember the butter, and work out our salvation all at the same time, for I don't see why it can't all be done, as God has set us to do it all.[26]

[23] *My Lady Ludlow*, p. 23.   [24] ibid., p. 147.   [25] ibid., p. 150.
[26] ibid., p. 145.

The acceptance of Dissenters as being somewhat less than heretics and outcasts has been mentioned. It is all part of an attitude which had been present in Mrs. Gaskell's work from the beginning, the recognition and acceptance of individual merit.

It has been necessary to discuss *My Lady Ludlow* at some length, not only because it merits it but in order to understand more clearly the apparently erratic course she followed in her succeeding work. She has shifted from the problems of new classes and divisions in society to the more congenial ground of individual adjustment; these are two sides of the one coin and she moves back into the historical past to get perspective, just as she narrows down to individual lives to examine motive, before returning once more to the roughly contemporary and treating the two together. As Lady Ludlow says of Harry Gregson:

Of course, if a lad is taught to read and write . . . his duties become complicated, and his temptations much greater, while, at the same time, he has no hereditary principles and honourable training to serve as safeguards.[27]

Mrs. Gaskell had achieved a clear view of her theme as a novelist.

[27] *My Lady Ludlow*, p. 61.

CHAPTER XI

'Lois the Witch' and 'Sylvia's Lovers'

THE two major works which followed *My Lady Ludlow*
(the short novel 'Lois the Witch' and the long novel
Sylvia's Lovers)[1] might seem to be new departures for Mrs.
Gaskell. They are avowedly historical, using documentary
material and incorporating actual incidents, instead of being contemporary or near-contemporary. The regional novelist has
turned to America and the north-east coast of Yorkshire. The note
is almost wholly serious, the outlook tragic; in 'Lois the Witch'
the almost complete absence of humour is striking while in
Sylvia's Lovers an initial sparkle becomes submerged in shadow.
A strong interest in morbid psychology is revealed, associated
with superstition. We are far from the Manchester or the Cranford worlds it would seem; different as these stories are from
each other they have in common their distinction in setting and
tone. Nevertheless, the distinction can be seen as a re-shuffling of
interests to achieve a different balance rather than a new departure.

The historical novel was by this time a respectable genre that
had been given status by Scott and raised further in esteem by
Dickens, Thackeray, Reade and Kingsley among others. It was
quite natural that an established novelist should try her hand at a
fashionable genre. But Mrs. Gaskell was already accustomed to the
use of historical event and documentary material; the writing of
Charlotte Brontë's biography was obviously the most recent as
well as the most thorough example. Blue books, articles and news-

[1] 'Lois the Witch' appeared in 1859 (8–22 Oct.) in *All the Year Round*. *Sylvia's Lovers*
was published by Smith, Elder early in 1863. One other publication in this period might
seem to claim attention. This is the short novel 'A Dark Night's Work' (*AYR*, 24 Jan.–
21 Feb., 1863) which appears instead of 'Lois the Witch' in Miss Hopkins's list of principal
writings for the period (*Hopkins*, p. 245). Miss Hopkins however later calls it 'a competent
tale but by no means out of the ordinary' (p. 259), and it is certainly not a major work.

paper accounts as well as personal experience lie behind *Mary Barton* and *North and South*. Her ability to reshape historical material into interesting narrative is seen more clearly in the articles she wrote from time to time—'Traits and Stories of the Huguenots', 'Modern Greek Songs' and 'An Accursed Race' are examples already mentioned. They illustrate also that given the necessary stimulus she could move outside of her 'region' and replace personal knowledge by acquired knowledge for background, particularly as such a stimulus would excite her antiquarian and sociological interests in old customs, unusual events, and strange societies.

Morbid psychology can also be found in earlier work. It is not handled much in the major novels, though the study of John Barton's deterioration has elements of it, but the minor stories contain many examples, while 'The Old Nurse's Story' (1852) and 'The Poor Clare' (1856) are also better than average studies in the supernatural.[2] There is an obvious link between her love of tradition and legend and her delight in ghost stories and morbidly tinged tales, which are a staple of any local mythology (she was herself an excellent raconteuse of such tales). During this period when she had begun writing largely to suit herself she produced a number of minor stories in which superstition, local legend and history are blended, often to include a study in the abnormal. 'The Grey Woman' is a good example of her facility with such material.[3]

The sombre note and tragic circumstances are a natural constituent of many of these stories; that side of Mrs. Gaskell's nature which was attracted to the pathetic and to the harrowing detail responded to such themes rather too easily. It is a response readily recognized as common to the mind of the Victorian writer and the reading public; in this respect the parallel between

---

[2] 'The Old Nurse's Story' may have influenced Henry James's *The Turn of the Screw*. He knew and admired Mrs. Gaskell's work.

[3] It is the story of the inexperienced girl who marries the handsome stranger. He turns out to be a bandit chief, head of the notorious 'chauffeurs'. Mrs. Gaskell would have learned about the 'chauffeurs' on her German holidays, which provided material for several stories. Ward discusses its possible literary sources (*Cousin Phillis*, pp. xxviii–xxxi). The story is little more than a skilful exercise in dressing up an exciting piece of local history and adding the necessary ingredients for a successful magazine piece.

Mrs. Gaskell and Dickens is close, though even Dickens felt at times that death and its halo of pathos were rather too frequent in her work.

More difficult to account for is the lack of humour. There is nothing in her biography to suggest that this was a particularly gloomy period of her life; very shortly after writing 'Lois the Witch' she was complaining to Norton about two young men, paragons of all the virtues, who, nevertheless:

I am afraid . . . had a want to me in their composition,—a want of the sense of humour, and that Dr. Arnold had too. But it *is* a *want*.[4]

Yet her imaginative work definitely reveals a response to a more complex view of good and evil, to a more tragic view of life. Earlier work had depicted misery, it is true, but the end had always been in happiness, while the presence of misery or sorrow as a necessary ingredient for her purposes was rarely allowed to subdue a touch of humour or a sense of the ridiculous. Man, from her point of view, when given half a chance was a basically cheerful, or at least optimistic, being. It is as though, with her greater objectivity and experience, she felt it necessary to face the dark side of life and human nature, to acknowledge a world in which even the ultimate influences of religion and affection could be perverted to evil and tragedy, before she turned back towards her normal world with still further depth and insight. For in spite of the careful historical treatment the stories continue the handling of a theme important in all Mrs. Gaskell's work, the behaviour of the individual or of the community under conditions in which the normal stabilizing influences are removed or placed under stress. 'Lois the Witch' is not just a fictional reconstruction of the Salem persecution, nor is *Sylvia's Lovers* merely a description of the effect of press-gangs on an area of England; the situations serve to contain studies of character and conduct as did *My Lady Ludlow*, and to explore more fully the nature of emotion and belief.

Lois the Witch

'Lois the Witch' is a tale of the Salem witch trials which took place in New England in 1692. It tells how Lois Barclay, the

[4] *Letters*, 9 March 1859, p. 34.

orphan of an orthodox English clergyman, came to America to join her relatives, failed to fit in with the gloomy, puritanical attitude of the area or the stern, moody family she found, and was finally caught in the witch-hunting hysteria that swept through New England, accused by her cousins of witchcraft, and hanged. The story as it develops is more than this however. It is an account of the perversion of good principles, of affection gone sour or become jealous, of religion turned fanatical and cruel, of a community become unstable. It presents a world where values have been twisted out of perspective.

The New England community is shown as an insecure one; two or three anecdotes told during Lois's first dinner in the country quickly sketch in a picture of settlements constantly threatened by Indians in the forest and pirates on the shore, with Puritan ministers urging their flock to see Satan in every enemy and each disaster. The absence of humour is an essential element of this background. With the departure of the ship's captain who brought her, the last link with England, this gloom becomes emphatically part of the oppressive background. The seriousness of her subject matter would not normally induce Mrs. Gaskell to abandon the saving grace of humour and common sense; that she does so here is an indication of a gravely disordered world. One of the most poignant features of the novel is the suppression of natural gaiety in Lois herself.

Her change of home is also a change from tranquillity and affection to sternness and unfamiliar habits. The family she has come to is admittedly a strange one, for Mrs. Gaskell makes it a microcosm of the fanaticism and incipient lack of balance which lay behind the outbreak. The eldest cousin, Manasseh, a man on the edge of madness, falls in love with her and translates his desire into a divinely inspired command to marry.[5] Another cousin,

[5] '*Lois the Witch*' seems to draw heavily on Crabbe's '*Ruth*' as does *Sylvia's Lovers* (see p. 176). The persecution of Lois by Manasseh parallels that of Ruth by the teacher and lay preacher:

> He talks of heaven, and let him if he will,
> But he has earthly purpose to fulfil . . .
>
> Doom'd the chance mercy of the world to trust,
> Or to wed grossness and conceal disgust.

> *Crabbe's Poetical Works*, John Murray, 1823, Vol. 6, pp. 93 and 95.

Faith, secretly in love with one of the ministers, allows herself to become morbidly jealous of Lois. The third cousin, Prudence, is a vain child with a vicious nature who accuses Lois in a fit of induced hysteria in order to attract attention. The uncle, the only kindly one in the family, dies shortly after Lois's arrival, leaving her aunt, Grace Hickson, to rule the house and find excuses for Manasseh's behaviour. In such a home a girl who was:

loving herself, delighted in being loved, and felt a jar run through her at every sign of want of love in others.[6]

was more out of place than a Cranford inhabitant would have been in a Manchester industrialist's home. The growing distrust and jealousy of the stranger cousin and her natural brightness are carefully traced, for as always Mrs. Gaskell is concerned with individuals and their feelings. The depiction of this environment of inhumanity, of the suppression of natural affection and love in the name of duty and religion, together with the growing dislike it produces, occupies the major part of the book, for it is Mrs. Gaskell's purpose to show that the death of Lois must ultimately be traced to this perversion of normal feelings and belief. In *My Lady Ludlow* prejudice could be treated sympathetically in the manner of comedy because the characters were fundamentally good and their background secure; once the restraints of firm traditions and sound principles are removed, prejudice turns to something deadly.

In such a community, shadowed by violence and isolated from gentle influences, superstition flourishes as the dark side of tradition, and Mrs. Gaskell is well aware of dealing with forces that are always latent in the human mind. She draws back briefly from her story to make the point:

We can afford to smile at them now; but our English ancestors entertained superstitions of much the same character at the same period, and with less excuse, as the circumstances surrounding them were better known, and consequently more explicable by common sense, than the real mysteries of the deep, untrodden forests of New England.[7]

[6] *Cousin Phillis*, p. 137.   [7] ibid., p. 135.

Her setting only throws into relief instincts and fears which are universal and which flourish when circumstances permit. The treatment of religion is one of the most striking features of the story. As always with Mrs. Gaskell religion is to be judged by the conduct it produces, not by the professions it makes, and we have seen that she had reached the stage as a writer when she could regard it objectively, as she did other beliefs and emotions. In this sense 'Lois the Witch' is a novel about religion without being a religious novel, although at the end she makes her own standards clear. It poses no problems, it examines with clarity and pity. She had once created a study of an individual for whom the world was an enemy, and whose faith was built on a God of wrath and revenge,[8] and had been sufficiently attracted by an account of religious persecution to write an article on it.[9] *Ruth* had portrayed intolerance in the name of religion, but the emphasis had been heavily on Christian virtues. 'Lois the Witch' carries on from *My Lady Ludlow* the study of religion in practice, whatever its denomination, and the wider social effects of the attitudes it fosters. Mrs. Gaskell faces, and reflects, the harsh un-loving world of Puritanism with which her own Unitarianism had a common ancestry. She sees it as a perversion of true Christianity in its rejection of mercy and love. It has got out of balance with life, and is therefore no longer a fit guide. Moreover, it interferes with the ordinary business of living. As Capt. Holdernesse says:

They are rare chaps for praying; down on their knees at every turn of their life. Folk are none so busy in a new country, else they would have to pray like me, with a 'Yo-hoy!' on each side of my prayer, and a rope cutting like fire through my hand.[10]

The remark can be set alongside Miss Galindo's rebuke to her would-be meditative Mary of a maid, and the attitude was to be triumphantly justified in *Cousin Phillis*. A narrow, intolerant creed and narrow intolerant emotions support each other, and life suffers for it.

---

[8] 'The Heart of John Middleton'. See Chap. 3.
[9] 'An Accursed Race.'   [10] *Cousin Phillis*, p. 114.

The events in Salem were exceptional, but Mrs. Gaskell sees them as the extreme example of an inevitable process, for the qualities she regarded as essential to a sane and stable society were missing. Yet it was not in her to present a picture of blank hopelessness. Individuals are found in the blackest period to stand out against inhumanity. Cotton Mather's own father is one, while Pastor Nolan, whom Faith loved and then hated, dies in protest:

> How much of malice—distinct, unmistakable, personal malice—was mixed up with these accusations, [comments Mrs. Gaskell as narrator] no one can now tell.[11]

But Lois's tragedy is revealed as one of personal relationships. She is the contrast to those around her, the decent person who is perplexed, frightened, but whose faith and upbringing are strong enough to resist the taint. She cries out, when Grace offers a chance of pardon if she will remove the 'spell' she is supposed to have cast on Manasseh:

> I cannot do it; I never did you or yours any wrong. How can I undo it? How can I?[12]

but common sense and normal behaviour have been lost sight of. She dies supporting the old Indian woman Nattee who has been a natural victim of the hysteria, still firm in her belief in a religion that promises love.

The strength and power of 'Lois the Witch' lies in its sober realism. The background and the historical events are presented without flourish, and with the minimum of direct explanation. She introduces few historical characters, only those such as Cotton Mather[13] and Justice Sewall who are necessary to provide authenticity, and they are incidental to the story. She invents little or nothing for them, relying on the historical record, nor does she attempt to enter their minds and feelings beyond the general conditions of the time. She avoids the mistake made in *My Lady*

---

[11] *Cousin Phillis*, p. 200.   [12] ibid., p. 203.

[13] Her early work was published under the pseudonym of Cotton Mather Mills. The canting reference to cotton mills is obvious, but the acquaintance with the early stages of Puritanism is also there. Her husband's library contained a number of works which detailed the early history of Dissent, including some on the American scene.

Ludlow of letting her weakness for episode lead into digression. The slow beginning, essential to her method of creating characters in their setting before the action develops, justifies itself in this short novel by the concentrated speed of the climax. The author stands back and allows events to produce their own effect, the moral is inherent in the behaviour of her characters.

The historical Salem episode ended with a recantation twenty years later by those who had accused and judged. 'Lois the Witch' ends quietly with this fact, the solemn declaration of regret is quoted and the story of Justice Sewall's repentance briefly included. Ralph Lucy, the English sweetheart who arrives too late to save her, repeats three times the bitter comment on such belated repentance:

All this will not bring my Lois to life again, or give me back the hope of my youth.[14]

but his final words, which end the tale, are for prayers to blot out the sin from remembrance.

For in the Salem witch hunt Mrs. Gaskell had found an episode which could exemplify her view of life and stimulate her imagination. She had drawn, in the Manchester of her earlier work, a picture of a society whose classes were self-confident and narrow-minded but which was unstable as a society because it lacked the cohesion and comfort of mutual understanding. Now she presented the same picture, shorn of reference to current controversy and concentrating on the effect on individuals. It is an indictment of intolerance and unchristian 'Christianity', more remarkable in that the author was a Dissenter whose heroine is an orthodox Anglican and whose wrongdoers—they are not villains—are Dissenters.

It is also a study in the negation of pleasant and human life. Lois comes from the Cranford world; from a little Warwickshire village which is barely mentioned but stays in her memory and has moulded her character. Salem shares with Manchester the dubious distinction of having turned its back on beauty and pleasantness, of having a pharisaical religion; it is a place where toler-

[14] *Cousin Phillis*, p. 208.

ance and humanity have been repressed. The effectiveness of the portrait of Salem lies in the hints of the other way of life which Lois knew:

There they had loved her; there she had gone about singing and re-joicing, all the day long, in the pleasant meadows by the Avon side.[15]

Sylvia's Lovers

Sylvia's Lovers marks the final phase of a period in which the emphasis had been on suffering and gloom; it was to be followed first by the pastoral elegy of *Cousin Phillis* and finally by the warmth and confidence of *Wives and Daughters*. But at this time Mrs. Gaskell seems excessively aware of the 'wearisome condition of humanity', she sees sorrow round every corner:

as, in fact, it is approaching all of us at this very time; you, reader, I, writer, have each our great sorrow bearing down upon us.[16]

and it is undeniable that the work produced between *My Lady Ludlow* and *Sylvia's Lovers* shows a concentration on gloom and morbidity.[17]

It was admittedly a time of physical strain for her. We know that she was leading a rushed life; she travelled a lot, her growing daughters and Manchester relief work were a drain on time and energy. She was run down, frequently ill. In addition the after-math of the Crimean war (Philip Hepburn is surely a memory of an ex-soldier) followed by the cotton famine and destitution arising from the American Civil War, which itself had been a threat to peace in Britain, may well have depressed her. It is only fair to add that most of the stories she wrote at this time were for

[15] *Cousin Phillis*, p. 196. Mrs. Gaskell's own schooldays had been spent, very happily, at Stratford-on-Avon.   [16] 'A Dark Night's Work', ibid., p. 434.
[17] Detailed examination is impossible here. The stories are, in order of publication and with the titles they now have: 'The Doom of the Griffiths', 'The Half Brothers', 'Right at Last', 'The Manchester Marriage' (1858); 'The Crooked Branch' (1859); 'The Grey Woman' (1861); 'Six Weeks at Heppenheim' (1862); 'A Dark Night's Work' (1863). Infanticide, parricide, filial hatred, murder, bigamy, suicide, unfaithfulness are the in-gredients; misery the pervading tone. Virtue finally triumphs in the pattern, but the triumph is usually a dreary or consolation-prize happiness. In nearly all the stories, family feeling and natural affection are perverted or disrupted. The only other work of this period was a brief fantasy ('Curious if True', 1860) and an article ('An Italian Institution', 1862) on the Camorra in her historico-sociological vein.

pin money, to offset holiday expenses or to raise money for charity, and she turned, as she usually did when her imagination or interest were not fully engaged, to local stories and incidents as an easy way of finding material for a magazine story. Such stories tend to the morbidly melodramatic. But there is no overlooking the mediocrity of much of her work in these years.

The possibility of some deeper emotional disturbance cannot be discounted. The concentration on disruption and hatred within families is significant, and she would have been passing through the 'change of life' at this period, with its accompanying restlessness. Moreover she had something to be restless about. She was looking back to a brief escape into a golden world (I use her own adjective) whose glow made the grey drabness of Manchester life more dreary by contrast. The growth of the friendship with Charles Eliot Norton which grew out of that escape throws an additional light on the feelings of the forty-six-year-old authoress.

Mrs. Gaskell had fled to Rome in 1857 on the invitation of some American friends, the Storys. She fled from the publication of *The Life of Charlotte Brontë*, though she could not be aware of the particular storm that was going to break. She had never been to Italy, she looked forward to the visit with the excitement of achieving a dream, and she arrived at carnival time. It was in this heightened emotional state of escape and fulfilment, in the actual whirl of the carnival, that she met Norton.[18] The impact of Rome and the liberation of spirit that it gave was a typically Jamesian situation, and it is proper to turn to James for insight on the episode:

To the happy conditions of the pilgrimage when it at last took place we have her testimony, from the "cold dim grey Manchester," in the following September. "It was in those charming Roman days that my life, at any rate, culminated. I shall never be so happy again. I don't think I was ever so happy before. My eyes fill with tears when I think of those days, and it is the same with all of us. They were the tip-top

[18] To be strictly accurate he had been formally introduced to her at a social evening in 1850 as a young American visiting Europe for the first time. He wrote to her in 1855 praising her books and telling how his dying father had liked to have *Cranford* read to him. But the Rome meeting, when Norton was thirty, was the effective beginning of their friendship.

point of our lives. The girls may see happier ones—I never shall."
She read all poetry into almost any friendship, and she now looked back
at the Roman felicity across an interval that had bristled with disagree-
able things. She had gone forth in the joy of having finished her vivid
Biography, but the book, though in the highest degree "successful,"
had sown her, at the same time, a crop of dragon's teeth . . . which had
bravely to be gathered in. . . . What it had, at any rate, especially done
was to embitter the aftertaste of the pleasure she had taken, in Rome,
with so good a conscience. Still, the aftertaste was to recur irrepres-
sibly. "Oh, I so long for Italy and Albano that it makes me ill!" she
sighs in another letter . . . We must let it go, however, on a couple of
the inevitable notes of home-sickness.

and he quotes a letter describing:

the amber sunlight streaming on the gold-grey Roman roofs and the
Sabine hills . . .

with her feeling that:

I would almost rather never have been there than have this ache of
yearning for the great witch who sits with you upon her seven hills.[19]

She found not only Rome but also, in Norton a sympathetic
nature that shared the same feelings and admired her as an artist;
it gave her an expansion of spirit that found little sustenance on
her return home. To the end of her life her memory reverted with
longing to the Roman holiday.

Miss Hopkins says of the friendship that:

It was love, but there was no passion in it. The feeling generated was
that between mother and son where there is complete congeniality and
understanding . . .[20]

This I think is a misinterpretation. There was affection, and there
was an aura of romance about it that grew from the meeting in the
carnival. Six years later, when she used the episode in 'A Dark
Night's Work', she drew on the details of her own experience to
describe the heroine looking down into the carnival throng to find
her long-absent friend gazing up at her. In the story they finally

[19] Henry James, *William Wetmore Story and His Friends*, Thames & Hudson, n.d. Vol. 1,
pp. 355–8. First published in 1903. The letters refer to the Storys.   [20] *Hopkins*, p. 227.

marry. There is no point, as Miss Hopkins says, in thinking of the friendship as other than an innocent one, but there seems little doubt that the whole episode developed an undercurrent of sentiment for Mrs. Gaskell in which the surrounding circumstances of holiday feeling, of Rome itself, of companionship were the major elements, in which the happy accident of Norton's presence was inextricably mixed. It left her with a feeling of dissatisfaction, a sense of anticlimax which James seized on as the essential feature.

Her letters of this period reveal, however, nothing more than tiredness, though there is a comment to Norton which seems to indicate a determination to be cheerful in spite of the times:

We are all sad here,—most people believe that we are going to war with you . . . and we are all very sad about that—then again our poor Queen's sorrow fills all our hearts. We ourselves, just we Gaskells are happy (I am thankful to say) and well.[21]

Whatever the reasons for the gloom of this period, *Sylvia's Lovers* is a product of them. But it is not a part of the hack-work or mediocrity, though tinged by them.

Unexpectedly, and in her quiet way she was constantly doing the unexpected, Mrs. Gaskell shows new depth and power. The interim period after the *Life* allowed her, consciously or not, to attempt to disentangle the sense of useful purpose from her creative imagination, a process helped by the occasional retreat into the historical or the remote. Moreover the short stories of this period, uninspired though many of them are, were concerned with individuals and feelings. *Sylvia's Lovers* shows the gain, but the disentangling process was not complete, the remnants of purpose finally clog the psychological machinery. *Sylvia's Lovers* falls short of being a great novel, though it contains a large proportion of fine things, some of the finest she achieved.

Sylvia's Lovers was published in February 1863. It was begun in 1859, when a visit to Whitby on the north-east coast of Yorkshire provided her with the germ of a story, together with accompanying detail, that would meet George Smith's offer of a thousand pounds for a three-volume novel to be published by Smith, Elder.

[21] *Letters*, 31 Dec. 1861, p. 95.

Whitby had been a whaling port, and Mrs. Gaskell heard there the story of an attack on the press-gang by the angry townsfolk in 1793 which culminated in the execution of an old man who had been one of the ring-leaders. She developed the incident, creating the characters and circumstances that could have led up to it. But the central idea, into which this incident was cleverly dovetailed, she drew from one of Crabbe's *Tales of the Hall*. 'Ruth' is a tale of the press-gang containing the elements of the abducted lover, the abandoned girl and the persistent religious wooer. Mrs. Gaskell does not follow the plot in detail, (Ruth, for example, was left pregnant) but she found to her hand the key relationships and incidents, in particular the essential relationship on which the second half of her story—the marriage between the previously rejected suitor and the girl whose lover has been taken—is based:

> He came and reason'd, and she seemed to feel
> The pains he took—her griefs began to heal.[22]

The treatment is her own, as is the plot she constructed by fusing the two sources into a unity, though she shares Crabbe's attitude to the tyranny of the press-gang and his sympathy with ordinary people.

The care she took over the novel must be stressed. By her own account she took more pains with it than with any other of her novels; even the sentiment and melodrama that tie the story up cannot be attributed to haste—though we may suspect artistic desperation. She used the experience gained from writing the *Life* to make detailed enquiries from authoritative sources, in order to provide a historically accurate basis for the events she describes. The attack on the rendezvous, for example, was checked with Admiralty records. As for the construction, we have her comments to show that desperate as the contrivance of the ending may seem, it was planned from the beginning. Writing to Forster for his comments on the completed first two volumes, she adds a sketch of the third:

to make you see how everything in the first two 'works up' to the events and crisis in that . . .

[22] op. cit., p. 90.

and seeking encouragement she adds:

I cannot help liking it myself, but that may be firstly because I have taken great pains with it, and secondly I know the end . . .[23]

But pains were no substitute for a psychologically credible ending.

I have already given a part summary of the plot in showing how the novel reflects Mrs. Gaskell's views on home and upbringing. A fuller summary reveals the shape of plot and theme. Sylvia Robson is the only daughter of a good-natured but irresponsible sailor-turned-farmer, Daniel, and his wife Bell, and she grows up to be attractive, loyal and affectionate but self-willed. Philip Hepburn, the cousin who loves her, is serious, religious and rather dull, the unromantic assistant to the leading merchant in nearby Monkshaven and later the part owner of the store. He lives with the widow Alice Rose and her meek daughter Hester. When a press-gang attack on a home-bound whaler is defied, its specksioneer (leading harpooner) Charlie Kinraid is gravely wounded, and becomes the local hero when he is carried to the funeral of a sailor who died in the scuffle. Sylvia falls in love with him and they become secretly engaged. But Kinraid is kidnapped by the press-gang on his way to rejoin his ship, an incident of which Philip by coincidence is the only witness. Philip himself is too weedy to be taken. Philip has heard rumours about Kinraid as a libertine, and while on his journey after the incident he hears more. The plot turns on his decision, triggered off by a series of trivial but cumulative circumstances acting on his passion for Sylvia, not to carry out his promise to tell her what had happened when he finds out that Kinraid is thought to have been drowned. Later the press-gang makes a sweep into Monkshaven itself; there is a riot urged on by Daniel, who instigates the burning of the press-gang's 'randyvowse'. He is arrested and later hanged. Philip is now prospering and respected, he takes care of the Robsons while Daniel is waiting trial, arranges for his defence, and is generally the prop of the women. Bell becomes half-witted, Haytersbank Farm is to be sold, and Sylvia finally agrees to marry Philip. She is a dutiful wife and in time there is also a baby daughter, but

[23] Letter from Mrs. Gaskell to John Forster, n.d.; *Brotherton*, 15 q.

Sylvia cannot forget Kinraid, who returns as a naval lieutenant to claim her and reveal Philip's duplicity. Sylvia's vow after she has refused to run away with Kinraid that:

I'll never forgive yon man, nor live with him as his wife again.[24]

provides the second turn of the plot.

It is at this stage—a late one—that the novel turns almost completely to melodrama and sentiment as events are forced to a conclusion. Philip enlists as a soldier and vanishes, later saving Kinraid's life during the siege of Acre and vanishing again, (he has adopted the name of Freeman, rather surprisingly apt as Mrs. Gaskell has normally no idea of the use of significant names). He is wounded and disfigured in an explosion, and finally returns home unrecognized to be near his wife and daughter, not daring to reveal his identity. Sylvia in the meantime has matured with responsibility and suffering, has developed a sense of religion and its standards, and has slowly realized that Philip's love was deeper and more serious than Kinraid's, who has made a useful marriage. The reconciliation is achieved when Philip saves his daughter from being drowned: he is fatally injured but dies forgiven.

Such a synopsis, moving from highlight to highlight, distorts the balance and emphasis of the novel, though it illustrates its complexity—to which must be added a series of subsidiary relationships and characters, and themes such as Hester's love for Philip. It also shows where the 'joins' of the novel occur, the author's hand pushing events along is occasionally obvious. But *Sylvia's Lovers* is not primarily a novel of incident. Nearly half of it is taken up with the gradual unfolding of Sylvia's character against the detail of daily life, it is above all a study of feelings, relationships and behaviour in their social and family setting.

Two possible influences need to be considered briefly before we examine the novel more closely. That of Charlotte Brontë has been canvassed before now. It is possibly there; certainly Sylvia is nearer to being a Brontë-ish heroine than any other in Mrs.

[24] *Sylvia's Lovers*, p. 404. The 'returned sailor' theme was already in Mrs. Gaskell's mind in 1858, when she used it for 'The Manchester Marriage', a story which may have suggested 'Enoch Arden' to Tennyson.

Gaskell's work, while the setting of farm and countryside has a similarity. But the character of Sylvia is equally to be seen as a development from heroines of the earlier novels which was to continue to Molly Gibson in *Wives and Daughters*, while the countryside was one she knew, nor is its wildness stressed. More important perhaps is the feeling that comes through the narrative, that love is more—or less—than a pure passion; certainly there is a force of sexual passion hinted at. Perhaps something may have been derived from the Brontë world, especially after Mrs. Gaskell's immersion in it for the biography, but it is hardly more than an encouragement of ideas and attitudes that were already present.

More important I suggest was the influence of George Eliot. Mrs. Gaskell had commented with rueful despair, shortly after *Adam Bede* was published, that:

I think I have a feeling that it is not worth while trying to write; while there are such books as Adam Bede & Scenes from Clerical Life . . .[25]

and her admiration never abated; the broad-minded minister's wife reluctantly accepting the sinful state of affairs between Miss Evans and Mr. Lewes. Both of the books she mentions mix humour with sadness, and follow her own method of using the detailed observation and humour of village and working life as a basis for serious observation; but they carry it to a more profound level in their analysis of emotions and actions. George Eliot had written, in *Adam Bede*, one of the first true psychological novels, and we shall see that Mrs. Gaskell is consciously doing the same thing. The two women novelists had much in common, and it has already been noted that Mrs. Gaskell had influenced George Eliot. *Adam Bede* was a historical novel set in the not very distant past, treating domestic life seriously and investing it with tragic possibilities; it mingled domestic comedy and tragedy with the serious treatment of religion. Its success might well have tempted Mrs. Gaskell to a major work in the same field. It was not a case of imitation, since these were all themes in which Mrs. Gaskell had already shown an interest. George Eliot, having learned from Mrs. Gaskell, showed her in turn new possibilities inherent in the

[25] *Letters*, 25 Oct. 1859, p. 39.

method. And though Sylvia is an individual creation, Hetty Sorrel is the wilful, attractive type of girl, seduced by a romantic infatuation, that Sylvia could have become, just as Dinah is the type of girl guided by her religion and duty that Sylvia to some extent does become. *Sylvia's Lovers* surely owes something to its nature and new depth to George Eliot.

George Eliot herself thought highly of *Sylvia's Lovers*. She wrote to George Smith, shortly after it was published:

I hope "Sylvia's Lovers" is finding a just appreciation. It seems to me of a high quality both in feeling and execution—so far as I have read.[26]

It may be as well that we have not got her comments on the final section.

Mrs. Gaskell's subsidiary interests are, as might be expected, vigorously present. The delight in traditions and old ways breathes through the book, whether in details of dress or farming or daily life, or in scenes such as the New Year party at the Corneys. All the keenness of the amateur sociologist and historian lies behind the descriptions, given life by the interest in the people who move through them. Sometimes the secondary interest obtrudes, the researcher detaching herself from the novelist to quote an Act of Parliament in detail, or to digress like another Melville on the treatment of dead whales, or in the description of the medieval almshouses of St. Sepulchre. The almshouse episode, when Philip is making his lagging way back to reconciliation and heroic death —and an evasion of the problem set by Sylvia's vow—is in the weak final section which includes the account of the seige of Acre; it is a piece of conscious medievalizing, as though she had turned to the pages of Disraeli or to the paintings of the Pre-Raphaelites, and it recalls the history of the Pensionnat Héger given in the *Life*. Yet it has its purpose, in its presentation of the peace and stability to be found as a bedesman among the old traditions and buildings of St. Sepulchre. It is this artificially isolated stability which Philip rejects after a trial; such a rejection of the past, however pleasant, in favour of the present and future, however painful, is part of Mrs. Gaskell's theme. Unfortunately it is not only the life in the

[26] *The George Eliot Letters*, Vol. 4, p. 79, 10 Mar. 1863.

almshouse that is unreal; her handling of the episode, her elaboration of it, and its diversionary effect results in a pseudo-historical digression that blurs while it romanticizes the intended contrast between a superficial and an inner stability.

For *Sylvia's Lovers* carries a stage further the examination of the uprooted individual which had already been so brilliantly sketched in 'Lois the Witch', but whereas Lois's faith had held her firm in a neurotic society, either the characters in the later work are without this rock beneath their sand, or the force of emotion is temporarily stronger than their version of religion. Nor can they fall back on the strength of family support. Philip is an orphan, while behind Sylvia's tragedy, as I have previously pointed out, lies a failure in upbringing.

We have now a full study of relationships and attitudes whose development, chiefly through the characters of Sylvia and Philip, is traced and charted to the almost complete exclusion of social change in any real sense. An awareness of shifting social patterns still frets the edges of Mrs. Gaskell's thought; there is an early digression on the conflict between the old landed gentry and the new manufacturing class in which she comments:

I have noted in other places similarly situated . . . there is a sort of latent ill-will on the part of the squires to the tradesman . . .[27]

it is a digression that looks forward to Squire Hamley in *Wives and Daughters*. The customary life of Monkshaven is itself unsettled by the demands of the press-gang, but apart from the incident of the riot we are not concerned with the town.

It is the private world that collapses. For Philip this is brought about by the intrusion of Kinraid which shatters his hopes. For Sylvia it is the collapse of her world of family security on top of the disappearance of Kinraid. Others, such as Kester the farm-servant and Hester Rose with her hopeless love for Philip, have the values of faith, tradition or upbringing to hold them steady. Mrs. Gaskell is concentrating on the individual in the stress of personal relationships, and reaching out through the individual to a view of human nature:

[27] *Sylvia's Lovers*, pp. 8–9.

to wonder if the lives of one generation were but a repetition of the lives of those who had gone before, with no variation but from the internal cause that some had greater capacity for suffering than others.[28]

Interest is focused directly on the way people behave and the feelings that govern them. She turns aside at one point to comment on this, as though she were struck by the discovery:

In the agricultural counties . . . there is little analysis of motive or comparison of characters and actions, even at this present day of enlightenment. Sixty or seventy years ago there was still less . . . taken as a general rule, it may be said that few knew what manner of men they were, compared to the numbers now who are fully conscious of their virtues, qualities, failings, and weaknesses, and who go about comparing others with themselves—not in a spirit of Pharisaism and arrogance, but with a vivid self-consciousness that more than anything else deprives characters of freshness and originality.[29]

Mrs. Gaskell was aware of being on the threshold of the age of psychology. But she was not able to accept the conclusions that her art and her analysis would lead to; she was not a tragic writer by temperament or by belief, and having created the situation of tragedy she shied away from complete acceptance of it.

This is partly because she still saw the emotional struggle in the same general terms as she had seen the social conflict of the earlier novels, as a battle between action based on principles and action based on selfishness. Ultimately, as will be seen, it becomes a microcosm of:

the discord between the laws of man and the laws of Christ . . .[30]

It is this aspect that creates the major flaw in the novel, that is prepared for, commented on and finally compels the artificial solution. When Mrs. Gaskell is dealing with how her characters feel and act, few writers can show subtler insight or sensitivity; her limitations here are those of the natures of the characters themselves, who stay within the range of the ordinary. All of the first half of the novel would provide examples, we can take one that shows not only Mrs. Gaskell's sensitivity to the feelings of her

[28] *Sylvia's Lovers*, pp. 254–5.   [29] ibid., p. 78.   [30] ibid., p. 71.

characters but also the psychological insight which shows itself in almost modern terms. Kester, the farm servant and privileged friend, argues with Sylvia when she says she will marry Philip, and tells her not to marry a man she does not love. Sylvia, bewildered by sudden disaster and grief, explains that Philip will provide a home and shelter for her mother and herself, and then bursts out with a confession of how she still thinks of Kinraid:

I've niver forgotten Charley. I think on him, I see him ivery night lying drowned, at t' bottom o' t' sea. Forgetten him! Man! it's easy talking![31]

As the chapter closes on Sylvia's misery in her decision, we see Philip leaning over a gate into the field, like a spider on the edge of his web, and even the somewhat turgid language that Mrs. Gaskell is apt to use when passionate feeling is involved cannot obscure the rightness of this picture of him:

gazing into the field with passionate eyes, devouring the fair face and figure of her, his future wife.[32]

In the next chapter we get Philip's anger when he discovers that Sylvia is still thinking of Kinraid, mixed with his tenderness for her and the longing to be able to comfort her:

But the very longing, having to be repressed, only made him more beside himself with guilt, anxiety, and rage.[33]

Such a comment anticipates modern terminology in the search for exact description of feeling and reaction. It is because of such touches, which are continually present, that we refuse to accept the later behaviour of the characters.

Love and religion are the two forces that Mrs. Gaskell works with to embody the opposing elements in man's nature, a Victorian emendation of Pope's observation that:

Two Principles in human nature reign;
Self-love, to urge, and Reason, to restrain . . .[34]

She was well enough aware of what she regarded as the darker

[31] *Sylvia's Lovers*, p. 343.   [32] ibid., p. 345.   [33] ibid., p. 347.
[34] 'Essay on Man', Epistle 2, lines 53–4 (Globe Edition, 1897, p. 202).

side of love, although she shelters behind the language of the Bible to make the point that Philip had asked God:

to grant him the desire of his eyes and the lust of his heart.[35]

But the vitality of the novel springs first of all from her description of the awakening of a young girl's heart to romantic love. It was the first time that she had made love the central issue of a major novel (for *North and South* uses it to serve the purpose of dealing with social change) and she was still unwilling to make it the central theme. In following the course of Sylvia's feelings for Philip she brings forward another view of love, more sober and more lasting, a view of:

the faithful, patient nature that still works on, striving to gain love, and capable itself of steady love all the while, [which] is a gift not given to all.[36]

This deeper feeling is associated, as we might expect, with Christianity, and Sylvia is led to an understanding of it through suffering. The want of education has been made clear, notably in one of the most humorous and effective scenes Mrs. Gaskell wrote, when Philip endeavours to teach the reluctant girl to read; it is her inability to read that leads her later to ask Alice Rose to teach her so that she can go to the Bible for comfort and help. The later sections of the novel lead away from the theme of love to that of religion and its standards, and ultimately to a reconciliation of the two which is symbolized in Philip's reconciliation with Sylvia.

The didactic emphasis on religion in the novels had been diminishing rapidly, although religion had kept its place as an essential part of life. In 'Lois the Witch' it enters naturally with history, but it need have had no essential part in the story of *Sylvia's Lovers*. It owes its existence partly to the need for a counter-balance to self-will. Mrs. Gaskell was never very comfortable with the direct treatment of love—even in *Sylvia's Lovers* the emphasis is on Sylvia's feelings rather than directly on the affair with Kinraid— nor was she at ease with the handling of any violent passion for that matter, an aspect of her work that will be discussed more

[35] *Sylvia's Lovers*, p. 187.   [36] ibid., p. 363.

fully when her style is examined. Its existence could not be ignored however. She had skated round the problem in *Ruth*, it had edged into her treatment of Thornton in *North and South*, and it is plainly to be read in the madness of Manasseh Hickson. In one story, 'The Poor Clare' (1858) she uses the idea of the doppelganger, the demonic double, to suggest latent sexuality. The spirit that shadows Lucy as the result of a curse has:

a loathsome demon soul looking out of the grey eyes, that were in turns mocking and voluptuous.[37]

The 'demon soul' and Philip's 'lust of the heart' are plainly two aspects of the same thing, an unholy part of human nature but still a part. Now she dealt with it directly as far as her nature allowed, and religion is called in to control and finally tame it, as well as to reassert itself as the highest value in its own right.

Mrs. Gaskell's reservations should not be put down to timidity or to lack of knowledge. A minister's wife in mid-nineteenth-century Manchester would have come into contact with brutal facts of life that an emancipated twentieth-century reader will know of, it is to be hoped, only in theory. Frankness about such matters was of course controlled by social taboos as far as public reference was concerned, (though it is a nice point whether the conventions of speech did not control the way people thought, since thought is largely conditioned by the existence of the expressions available to actualize it). There was further a generally accepted middle-class ideal of a rather spiritualized love which was strengthened by conventions of behaviour and speech. Whether the occasional hints of a stronger feeling which move, though rarely, below the surface of her work are evidence of repression is a matter for psychologists to argue about. A less hectic, more spiritualized view of love is certainly the one with which she is most at ease and which she handles best. Still, it could be argued, correctly I believe, that the fact of having dealt fairly fully even if obliquely with the power of desire in *Sylvia's Lovers* gave her greater depth and certainty for the portraits of Phillis Holman and Molly Gibson that were to follow.

[37] *My Lady Ludlow*, p. 362.

That the religious emphasis is imposed as part of the original conception is obvious enough. Although the first half of the novel is one in which the chief characters, including Philip himself for all his orphan upbringing in a strictly religious household, act and speak almost solely from their feelings, there is a steady current of authorial intervention to keep us alive to what is missing. A major theme, important for any understanding of Mrs. Gaskell's approach, is that:

one of the greatest signs of the real progress we have made since those times seems to be that our daily concerns of buying and selling, eating and drinking, whatsoever we do, are more tested by the real, practical standard of our religion than they were in the days of our grandfathers.[38]

and she weaves in the benevolent Forster brothers as examples of how this standard can be applied. The point is made directly relevant to the novel when she says of Philip that:

He was like too many of us: he did not place his future life in the hands of God, and only ask for grace to do His will in whatever circumstances might arise . . .[39]

Elsewhere she shows that the more objective, satirical attitude to feeble or worldly religion is still with her, as in the account of the vicar's hazy funeral sermon which dribbles away its meaningless platitudes in his desire to avoid offending either authority or the parishioners who suffered under it; or in the added touch to Philip's character given by the brief description of the vanity of dignity which made him into a regular church-goer.

The novel owes its quality to the fact that her imagination was fired as she created the characters and the life in and around Haytersbank Farm. It fails because the fate of the characters had been decided before-hand and they had to be bent back to the feelings appropriate to it. The rapidity with which genuine religious feeling is acquired is handled, in the circumstances, with considerable skill, but our interest wanes. After the changes of heart and the imposition of conventional attitudes we can be concerned only with the way the plot is wound up. Mrs. Gaskell, in order to

[38] *Sylvia's Lovers,* p. 104.   [39] ibid., p. 187.

achieve a conclusion in terms of her convictions, reverts to the sentimental fervour and piety which marks the ending of *Ruth*. The question arises why, at this stage in her career as a novelist, she should revert to this emotionally emphasized religious feeling. Part of the explanation at least may be that she was one of the many who reacted to the publication of *The Origin of Species* in November 1859, and there are indications which point this way. She would have had a personal interest in the controversy; Darwin was a relative by marriage and a defaulting member of the closely linked group of influential Unitarian families to which she belonged. (Her daughter Meta went on a continental holiday with one of Darwin's sisters in 1860.) She could hardly have been unaware, living as she did in an intellectual as well as a religious society, of the discussion that had been growing for a good many years, and had found its way into fiction and poetry.[40] But Darwin methodized the evidence that could be used for an attack on the idea of a purposeful and beneficent God, and on accepted views of an after-life. The belief in progress, which was part of contemporary thinking and is fundamental to Mrs. Gaskell's social views, was also threatened by the Darwinism that was formed from Darwin's scientific observations.

She also knew Tennyson's *In Memoriam* which posed the problems of faith, purpose and a life to come against a display of evolutionary knowledge. *Sylvia's Lovers* is dedicated to her husband, and the dedication is accompanied by an epigraph from the central, evolutionary section of *In Memoriam*. It is a peculiar epigraph if its application is meant to apply to the Rev. Mr. Gaskell, though it makes sense when considered in relation to the novel's theme:

> Oh for Thy voice to soothe and bless!
> What hope of answer, or redress?
> Behind the veil! Behind the veil![41]

---

[40] The British Association met in Manchester in 1861, and her house was full of visitors; the echoes of her hectic housekeeping sound in her letters. Huxley was one of the guests asked, though he declined. See *Rylands*, p. 50, note 2, and *Letters*, p. 94.

[41] Section 56. The punctuation is given as quoted on the title page.

The peculiarity becomes more significant when the omitted first line of the verse is considered:

O life as futile, then, as frail!

Mrs. Gaskell knew her Tennyson well, it is inconceivable that she chose her epigraph without being aware of the significance of its context. It is equally certain that many of her readers would have picked up the allusion. And the oppositions in the book, of instinct to reason, passion to duty, present satisfaction to future consequences, are gathered together in the supreme opposition of irreligion to religion. The conclusion is an emotional affirmation of faith and purpose as a guide to life. Although Mrs. Gaskell was no longer crusading publicly, she could handle the problem by setting the action in the past. It seems more than probable that when *Sylvia's Lovers* was being written it was influenced by the threat, as it seemed, to the very foundations of human conduct and human purpose.

This attitude was not to last. The emotional reaction remained a public force for many years, but it was fairly soon replaced, among more thoughtful and less rigid sections of the community, by an assimilation of the new ideas into existing ones without any harm to faith or morality. The process was perhaps easier for Unitarians, whose religion stressed an ethical rather than a fundamentalist attitude to the Bible, and who had a long tradition of respect for truth and scientific enquiry. By the time Mrs. Gaskell began to write *Wives and Daughters* she could take as her hero a character modelled partly on the young Darwin.

She had once considered calling her novel 'The Specksioneer' and then had hit on 'Philip's Idol' as she searched for an appropriate title. The suggestions show the change of emphasis that was occurring as the planned story developed. For Kinraid emerges finally as a shadowy figure for all his importance in the plot. He is not credible as a libertine, we feel that his vices and superficiality are summarily thrust upon him; we learn of them by hearsay, and at those lucky times when a spur to motivation or to plot is required. This is a further flaw in the novel, although a minor one as the interest is now on Sylvia, and, to a lesser extent, on Philip. 'Philip's Idol' does throw light on important aspects of the book. Mrs. Gaskell held on to the idea and Philip uses the expression as he reflects on his past when he lies dying. Even *Sylvia's Lovers* is not completely satisfactory as a title, for the lovers are secondary to Sylvia herself. She dominates the novel. That is why, perhaps, when we recall it, it is an impression of freshness and vitality that stays in the mind rather than one of gloom or moral demonstration. We remember Sylvia, and we remember her in her setting at Haytersbank Farm. The Cranford world is making a reappearance.

Since *My Lady Ludlow* Mrs. Gaskell had been writing about scenes outside of the world she knew best. Now it begins to impose itself again. The character of Sylvia is a fine achievement, fine by any standards, but the setting is a part of it. The finest portions of the novel are those in which the characters and background are closest to the country world and its incidents with which she is at home. The first half of the novel is not so remote from the Cranford world in either detail or conduct. It is then that Mrs. Gaskell's humour and her relish of the quirks of human behaviour appear, as when Alice makes her will[42] or when Daniel is manoeuvred out of bad temper by his wife and the tailor Donkin. As long as she is immersed in the daily life of the little community the novel is alive and fresh. But the world around it is still a dark one. It was only by an effort that the standards she valued were imposed. Yet in grappling with this world fully, which seems to reflect in spirit the cares and drabness of the Manchester she lived in, she seems to have begun to conquer the depression that weighed on her. She moved back with greater insight for her final and finest work to the world of Cranford.

[42] This is a fresh use of an incident which provides one of the best scenes in *Ruth*, when Sally makes her will.

CHAPTER XII

The Final Synthesis: I
'Cousin Phillis'

THE quality of Mrs. Gaskell's final work has a significant relation to the way it was published, in *All the Year Round* or in the *Cornhill*. Dickens, in spite of his exasperation over her obstinate refusal to obey the mechanics of serial writing, was anxious to have her work; she was one of the established writers and would attract readers. He managed to get a short novel 'A Dark Night's Work', for *All the Year Round* early in 1863, and with it a renewal of his irritation as she over-ran her space and ignored his suggestions, although Dickens had seen the completed MS and must have known that as it stood, with its slow development, it would be an awkward fit for the pro-crustean bed of weekly issues. The nature of the plot (murder, concealment, false arrest, last-minute pardon) suggests that Mrs. Gaskell was at least trying in her own way to provide something suitable, but there was nothing exceptional about the story that cost Dickens so much editorial pain. It has however a place in the final development that will be noted.

There is little to be said for the final contribution to *All the Year Round*, 'Crowley Castle', which was part of the chain story of 'Mrs. Lirriper's Lodgings' in the Christmas number for 1863 and which is remarkable only for being one of the worst things she wrote.[1] Though the first story is very much better than the second, both show signs of writing down carelessly to an audience that wanted excitement and strong feelings. A third story, how-ever, is unexpected and totally different in nature; after ten years

[1] The full title in the chain story was 'How the First Floor Went to Crowley Castle'; it had the few lines of introduction necessary to fit it into the chain.

a continuation of *Cranford* with 'The Cage at Cranford', which appeared at the end of 1863. While these stories for Dickens were being got out of the way her final and finest work, *Cousin Phillis* and then *Wives and Daughters*, began to appear in the congenial pages of the *Cornhill*.

Her writing culminated in a reaffirmation of the Cranford world, but it was a world tempered by experience, more comprehensive in its social range and looking to the future rather than back to the past. It is a world that has achieved continuity with its past and is therefore sure of its roots as it grows; above all it is a stable and secure world which stands firm when the private world collapses. Mrs. Gaskell gave to its creation, or re-creation, all the sympathy and art she had; *Wives and Daughters* is her artistic and temperamental homecoming.

A word may be said about the place of 'A Dark Night's Work' in relation to Mrs. Gaskell's later work. Mrs. Chadwick states that it was written during a holiday Mrs. Gaskell took in 1862, after a breakdown brought on by the strain of relief work in Manchester. It is in the short novel length that she liked (or one-volume as against the standard three-volume novel), using the mystery and discovery element that she was fond of; allowing for 'longeurs' it has a well developed plot. But it is muddled in conception. The plot concerns the self-sacrificing daughter whose father has committed murder and buried the body, but a quarter of the book is taken up by an account of the family history which is on the theme of false pride and upbringing, a theme incorporated into a subsidiary line of the plot with a calculating lover who deserts the girl and the unselfish lover who remains true.[2] It is typical of Mrs. Gaskell that what was conceived as an exciting story developed into a study of moral decisions and their outcome, with its centre in the character of the young Ellinor.

Its interest for us lies in the indications of a change of direction. First of these is the return, in terms of setting, to the Cranford world. The opening lines:

[2] Mrs. Gaskell drew two portraits of the calculating lover who backs down for fear that his career may be harmed: Henry Lennox in *North and South* and Ralph Corbett in 'A Dark Night's Work'. One is a lawyer, one a barrister. Cynthia in *Wives and Daughters* dispassionately marries a cool lawyer. What did Mrs. Gaskell have against the profession?

In the county town of a certain shire there lived (about forty years ago) one Mr. Wilkins, a conveyancing attorney of considerable standing.[3]

bring us back to Cranford (and to the reminiscent tone as well) but no longer to the limited society of the Amazons, while the softened distance of a generation or two vanishes as the story follows the history of Mr. Wilkins's son into the contemporary world. The historical viewpoint and perspective have been discarded. It is furthermore the world of the middle-class professional man, the society Mrs. Gaskell knew best and which was to be her point of observation for *Wives and Daughters*. Religion enters because the suitor who finally gains Ellinor's 'thin white hand' is a clergyman, Canon Livingstone, but the novel has no religious axe to grind. In this it anticipates *Cousin Phillis*. The return to the Cranford world and the objective, sympathetic irony that goes with it is still tentative. This is marked by the varied setting, for Ellinor leaves her home with its unquiet grave to stay in a distant cathedral town, and later to escape to Rome. There is in fact a division of interests, as though Mrs. Gaskell was casting round for a way of breaking back to the contemporary scene and the Cranford world and was undecided in her approach, while the morbidity of the central incident and the muted ending shows that she was still in the shadows.

The publication dates of the work in this final period help to explain what was happening. 'A Dark Night's Work' appeared in January–February 1863, and it was probably written in 1862 before *Sylvia's Lovers* was published in February 1863. There is therefore a gap of nearly a year, from approximately the end of 1862 to the end of 1863, when little creative work was done.[4] *Cousin Phillis* began in the *Cornhill* in November 1863 and ran to February 1864. *Wives and Daughters* ran from August 1864 to her death. 'The Cage at Cranford' appeared on 28 November 1863. Briefly, we have a fallow period at the end of which the Cranford world is once again fully established with *Cousin Phillis*.

---

[3] *Cousin Phillis*, p. 404. The central incident of the murder was true, a piece of Knutsford history she modified. Some of the descriptions are also from Knutsford.

[4] She wrote one short article in this period, 'An Italian Institution', which was published in *A.Y.R.* on 21 March.

('Crowley Castle' which appeared at Christmas is so obviously a piece of hack work that it can be ruled out of any serious discussion of imaginative effort; Mrs. Chadwick reports it as a re-hash of a story heard on holiday at Brighton.)

The unheralded appearance of another Cranford episode is not quite so startling in this context. There is no evidence of why Mrs. Gaskell should have written it; Dickens wanted contributions and may have urged her to reopen a profitable and popular seam but she could presumably have churned out something in her other vein had she wanted to earn money with a pot-boiler. The indications point to her having reached the stage of turning once again to the familiar setting, and of writing the episode either as an essay in re-entering it directly or as an attempt to prove to herself that she had finally re-established the appropriate frame of mind and imagination. It was the wrong way to set about it; she could not re-enter the Cranford world at the point at which she had left it, nor was this unnecessary coda needed for a work which, though episodic in origin, had been rounded to a unity. Mrs. Gaskell herself never thought very highly of it while her daughters persuaded Ward to ignore it when editing the Knutsford edition as the standard collection of her work. It was a wise decision. Yet nothing could show more clearly than the existence of this story the decisive move away from the mood and subjects that had occupied her since *My Lady Ludlow*, just as nothing is more effective than a comparison with *Cousin Phillis* to reveal the extent to which both her power as a writer and her conception of the Cranford world had developed.[5]

It was a help that at this time life was becoming easier for her. She was able to take frequent holidays away from Manchester, which she still disliked and which depressed her, travelling to the South of England, to France and even to her beloved Rome once again. There is also the point, made earlier, that she no longer had to write the sort of story that fitted the policy of *All the Year Round*, for the *Cornhill* was open to her. It was owned by George

---

[5] 'A Cage at Cranford' tells how Miss Pole was sent a 'cage' from Paris. It is the word used for the new fashion of petticoat hoops, but Cranford society is ignorant of it. The little circle assumes that it must be a new type of parrot cage and it is adapted for Miss Pole's parrot until the disconcerting truth is revealed.

Smith, her publisher and her friend, she could write to suit herself and be paid far more than she could earn by a series of stories for Dickens. This is not an attempt to make Dickens out to be a villain of the editorial sweat-shop; he was a competent and generous editor. But Smith and the *Cornhill* initiated a new policy of liberal payment and monthly production, and put up the money to attract the best contributors. Dickens offered Mrs. Gaskell £400 in 1860 for a full-length novel for *All the Year Round*, whereas Smith had offered £1,000 for the direct publication of *Sylvia's Lovers* and £2,000 for the serial and publication rights of the new novel that turned out to be *Wives and Daughters*. Moreover *The Cornhill* required only monthly parts spread over eighteen months while *All the Year Round* required weekly parts over eight months. For someone like Mrs. Gaskell, whose novels developed slowly and depended on depth of detail and observation rather than dramatic incident, the long monthly parts and the extra year allowed for completion were infinitely preferable.[6]

The world which Mrs. Gaskell creates in *Cousin Phillis* and *Wives and Daughters* is essentially that of *Cranford*, but it is a world that has changed with time and experience. It takes up at a point beyond that where *Cranford* left off; although physically it has the same setting inspired by Knutsford and its surroundings. We can date the shift if we wish, thanks to Mrs. Gaskell's habit of social observation and historical reference. The card from Holdsworth that shatters Phillis's hopes and health arrives through the local post-office which was set up after the recent penny post reform (of 1840) and this puts the main part of the story in the late eighteen-thirties. *Wives and Daughters* presents an interesting problem. It is dated by the statement that:

Five-and-forty years ago, children's pleasures in a country town were very simple . . .[7]

which would put the action approximately in the eighteen-twenties. But Roger Hamley's career has parallels to that of

---

[6] For the dealings with Dickens see *Hopkins*, Chap. 8. Gettman, *A Victorian Publisher*, C.U.P., 1960, gives a full picture of contemporary publishing, see especially p. 147 for the launching of *The Cornhill*. When she needed money she drew an advance from Smith.

[7] *Wives and Daughters*, p. 2.

Darwin, whose voyage in the 'Beagle' which began in 1831 became well known after he had published his journal. Furthermore there is a statement that Lady Cumnor takes her daughter to:

the railway station on this new line between Birmingham and London . . .[8]

The London–Birmingham line was opened in 1838.[9] It would seem that although Mrs. Gaskell was concerned to present an accurately detailed picture of her country town in the eighteen-twenties, her imagination as I shall show was occupied with the problem of social change at a later date, and that the odd reference creeps in unconsciously to betray this. The important point is that although her 'dating' references seem to give an incidental reality to the setting, this type of dating is less important than the general impression which Mrs. Gaskell conveys that we are in a society in which the world of technology or science is naturally present. *Cranford*, like the two final novels, could be called near-contemporary in dating: after all it mentions Dickens and has a railway. But it is about an old-fashioned society whose members are middle-aged; the delightful Amazons live back towards their past. The near contemporary world of the later work is a young world, the sons and daughters treading on the heels of their parents and reaching towards the future. The *Cranford* generation is still to be seen, admirable, worthy of respect and love, but old-fashioned and slightly absurd. There are very few outstanding novelists whose final work can be confidently claimed as the best, fewer whose final novels are as fresh, and younger, than the early ones.

The social world has also expanded. This had begun to happen with *My Lady Ludlow*, whose society ranged from aristocrat to farmer. But both *Cranford* and *My Lady Ludlow* were dominated by a 'genteel' or 'superior' class; in *Cousin Phillis* and *Wives and Daughters* we have middle-class—though equally interesting—people in command. Moreover, with the interest moving towards the present there is less detail of traditions and customs,

---

[8] *Wives and Daughters*, p. 705.
[9] E. L. Woodward, *The Age of Reform*, Clarendon Press, 1954, p. 44.

more concern with the emotions and behaviour of the characters. Mrs. Gaskell chopped and changed in her normal way over the title of *Wives and Daughters* but she never altered the sub-title— 'An Every-Day Story'.

We are back in a basically good and optimistic world which is on the whole in harmony with the pleasantness of the setting, while the setting itself is the mellow and serene one of the Cranford world. Yet it is a more serious world. Earlier stories of the Cranford world, not the least *Cranford* itself, had accepted the presence of suffering and unhappiness, but *Cousin Phillis* and *Wives and Daughters* bring experience and maturity to bear on it; the human sympathy with the characters she creates is deeper and more comprehensive.

She wrote from the centre of a world and a set of values which were part of her own nature. For this reason she no longer has to prove anything or bring any particular standard, such as that of religion, forward; she needs only to demonstrate. *Wives and Daughters* does not present an ideal world but it suggests how much better an inherently imperfect world could be if certain ideals of conduct were attempted. Moreover, because of this symbiosis of Mrs. Gaskell and the Cranford world, she could at the same time—it is a mark of her dealing with it—step away. The narrator is once again the observer; a bit more ironic, with more bite in her observation of character to match new insight and power as a novelist.

Above all it is a stable, assured world. In *Cranford* there is the sense of something fragile, something passing; change will occur but it is resisted and pushed as far as possible out of sight. In her final work Mrs. Gaskell accepts change, individual and social, as one of the essentials in the world she depicts. It may cause individual pain, but the world she sees is securely based. Because of this there is once again room for humour. From 'Lois the Witch' to *Sylvia's Lovers* seriousness had implied gloom. There was the occasional sparkle, for Mrs. Gaskell's acute sense of the ridiculous and her fundamental optimism could not be constantly repressed, but we have seen the tally of stories she produced. Now the strain of morbidity and depression is past, and though 'the eternal note of sadness' is carried over into *Cousin Phillis*, no one, by any stretch of the imagination, could call it a gloomy book. Humour reasserts itself with the Cranford world.

Cousin Phillis

The story of Cousin Phillis is simple enough; it amounts to little more than an episode. Paul Manning tells it, a young lad away from home for the first time as assistant to the supervising engineer of a new branch railway line. To please his parents he visits, with little hope of pleasure, a distant relative—Mr. Holman, the dissenting minister–farmer of Hope Farm—and so enters the pastoral world inhabited by his cousin Phillis. After a time his chief, Edward Holdsworth, is invited to the farm. Holdsworth is travelled, sophisticated, cultured; but he is fascinated by the way of life of the farm and by the mixture of beauty and intelligence in Phillis, while Phillis in turn is attracted by his qualities. Nothing happens outwardly, but an unspoken love grows between them, and when Holdsworth is suddenly called away to Canada Phillis becomes depressed and languid. Paul in his inexperience cheers her by revealing that Holdsworth had confided in him an intention of returning one day to marry her, and she is happy for a time until news arrives that Holdsworth has married. This second blow after the false spring of confidence is too much; Phillis falls ill and nearly dies.

The story avoids the dramatic and avoids incident, and in doing so also avoids the need for rather obvious plot-making that Mrs. Gaskell sometimes reverted to. The only weak point is in fact when she has to provide the turn in what little plot there is; Holdsworth vanishing with an urgency that betrays, though not too obviously, a push from the author. Apart from this, the story is simply the round of life at the farm and the stages in the growth and despair of a young girl's love; owing its density of texture to the wealth of its descriptive detail and to the sensitive and subtle observation of the emotions of Phillis, her father and Paul as they move in and along with the life of Hope Farm. Sympathy for individual suffering, affectionate observation of a way of life she loved, each called out narrative qualities that Mrs. Gaskell excelled in; they were never fused more completely than in *Cousin Phillis*. In showing in detail how it emerges as a development from her previous work it will be possible also to pay proper attention to the complexity that underlies its surface simplicity.

Mrs. Gaskell draws strength from a return to the memories of her youth, and *Cousin Phillis* is among other things a salute to memory. Hope Farm, with its imposing entrance flanked by pillars topped with stone balls, is Sandlebridge near Knutsford where her Holland relatives lived; Ebenezer Holman may have touches of the grandfather she barely remembered.[10] More important is the countryside whose beauty and peace pervades the story. In returning to the scenes of her youth she is also revisiting the source of her attitudes and beliefs, but this is no mere return to the past. Her values were associated most vividly and pleasantly with it, and are revitalized by contact with it, but she is no longer lingering affectionately in an outmoded way of life. Cranford and the modern world are moving together; life at Hope Farm is as practical and purposeful as life in Manchester.

The setting has the tranquillity and loveliness of the Cranford world, more so than in *Cranford* itself which concentrates on the little town and its society. It is pervasive, working directly on the senses, so that Paul:

fancied that [his] Sunday coat was scented for days afterwards by the bushes of sweetbriar and the fraxinella that perfumed the air.[11]

Even time is marked by colours and scents, as are the activities of

---

[10] She would of course have heard anecdotes about him. Nevertheless Holman, magnificently individual as he is, has traits in common with other Dissenting patriarchs. Margaret Shaen, one of the three talented Winkworth sisters, whose grandfather Dickenson and his brother were disinherited for following Whitefield, describes the way they ran their households:
    Besides the regular family worship, always conducted extempore by the head of the house, nothing special was undertaken without prayer, and the Scripture injunction, "if any be merry let him sing psalms," was literally followed, hymn singing being the constant recreation when the work of the day was over.   op. cit., p. 5.
Mr. Gaskell gave the sisters lessons (in History, Composition, Chemistry and Greek) and they became friends of the family. Some such reminiscence may well be one of the sources for the character of Holman. But Mrs. Gaskell did not need to look further than the personality and polymathian mind of her own husband for other traits.
[11] *Cousin Phillis*, p. 12.

the seasons. It is not, however, a world cut off from progress, or for that matter from suffering, nor are the Manchester virtues of energy and practicality excluded. The meeting of the two is symbolized in the arrival of Paul's father, the self-made engineer, to visit Mr. Holman:

It was odd and yet pleasant to me to perceive how these two men, each having led up to this point such totally dissimilar lives, seemed to come together by instinct, after one quiet straight look into each other's faces.

and in no time they are exchanging information. Mr. Manning:

had his little book that he used for mechanical memoranda and measurements in his pocket, and he took it out to write down "straight back," "small muzzle," "deep barrel," and I know not what else, under the head "cow."[12]

while he in turn has to explain a book on dynamics to the minister, after having suggested a new design for a turnip-cutter. Nevertheless when Mr. Manning suggests to Paul that he might do worse than marry Phillis, Paul hastily backs away from the suggestion. Mrs. Gaskell is no longer interested in using her individuals for the sort of neat social solution that concludes *North and South.*

What gives emotional depth to Phillis's suffering is that standards of conduct as well as individual emotion are involved. The contrast is a subtle one worked out in terms of shallowness and depth of character, yet it is at bottom a conflict between true and false values. Holman and Manning can take to each other because they share basic attitudes as well as intellectual curiosity; both are men of integrity and their contrast is of external circumstances only. Phillis and Paul are their fathers' children, inheriting common standards. That is why Paul, the representative of the new world of technology, can find himself at home in the pastoral world of Hope Farm, with its classical outlook (shown in the love

---

[12] *Cousin Phillis*, p. 33. Mr. Manning comes from Birmingham, not Manchester. This change may be delicacy on Mrs. Gaskell's part; an effort not to betray too obviously the character of James Nasmyth. It may also be an unconscious realization of having finally freed herself from the pressure of Manchester.

of Virgil and Dante).[13] He is the perfect narrator, bridging the
two outlooks while we learn through the eyes of his innocence and
gradual experience to distinguish the solid from the superficial.
He is posed between two admirations, the older for his chief, Mr.
Holdsworth, the newer for Hope Farm. When the two are
brought together their standards are tested against each other;
providing the twin framework of opposing values which supports
the idyllic surface of the story.

Some uneasiness is already in Paul's mind when he brings the
convalescent Holdsworth the invitation to stay at Hope Farm,
and Holdsworth is perceptive enough to sense it and chaff him
about it:

> "Manning," said he, "I see you don't think I am half good enough
> for your friends. Out with it, man!"
> "No," I replied boldly. "I think you are good; but I don't know if
> you are quite of their kind of goodness."[14]

The brief exchange pin-points the difference. Holdsworth is, as
Paul says, good in his own way; a generous, kind, intelligent and
cultured man, but lacking the 'seriousness' of Holman and his
daughter. His 'random assertions and exaggerated expressions'
jar on his host; he has to check his conversation while betraying
his essential levity in the private reflection that:

> really it is very wholesome exercise, this trying to make one's words
> represent one's thoughts, instead of merely looking to their effect on
> others.[15]

His lack of discrimination is revealed through his literary taste,
when he suggests sending a copy of *I Promessi Sposi*, 'a capital
novel by Manzoni' to help Phillis improve her Italian for Dante.
He brushes aside Paul's doubts about sending a novel with:

> Pooh! What can be more harmless? Why make a bugbear of a

---

[13] The Dante revival in the early nineteenth century was an important feature of the
cultural scene. See Jack, *English Literature 1813–32*, Clarendon Press, 1963. Dante and
Virgil would indicate a serious participation in the nineteenth-century cultural outlook.
Deborah Jenkyns, we recall, remained with Dr. Johnson.

[14] *Cousin Phillis*, p. 42.   [15] ibid., p. 51.

word! It is as pretty and innocent a tale as can be met with. You don't suppose they take Virgil for gospel?[16]

His many good qualities appeal to the father as well as the daughter, though Holman has reservations about his 'want of seriousness' which prove justified in the injury it causes. He has sufficient sensitivity to respond to Phillis's finer nature, although her influence fades with time and distance, nor can he be blamed for Paul's indiscretion in revealing to her the love he had refrained from putting into words. He is to blame for a want of moral discrimination, for a carelessness about standards rather than a lack of them. He has the finer polish but the coarser sensibility.

The dominant figure in the story is without doubt the Reverend Ebenezer Holman, and he represents in action, as I have suggested, the virtues of the Cranford and Manchester worlds. He has the energy and capacity for work of a successful industrialist, the intellectual curiosity and force of the new breed of self-made engineers. At the same time he has the simplicity of character, honesty and tenderness that make him kin to Captain Brown of *Cranford.* His religion is part of his humanity but as always with Mrs. Gaskell humanity comes first. It is religion worn like an old coat, comfortable, easy, for use rather than show, as far removed as possible from the eager piety of *Ruth.* We can gauge the minister's religion before we meet him; he has nick-named his side door 'the curate', while the front door 'handsome and all for show' is 'the rector'. He will close a day's work with a psalm, interrupt a prayer to make sure a sick animal is being looked after. He refuses to separate religion from honesty of feeling any more than from practical affairs, it is a personal faith that supports him, not the form of it: 'Brethren' he replies to the platitudes of his fellow ministers:

Brethren, God will strengthen me when the time comes, when such resignation as you speak of is needed. Till then I cannot feel it; and what I do not feel I will not express, using words as if they were a charm.[17]

---

[16] *Cousin Phillis*, p. 51. Manzoni's novel was published in 1827, and was greatly admired, but 'pretty and innocent'!   [17] ibid., p. 104.

This is the religion of love that Mrs. Gaskell has postulated in
Mary Barton, the support in distress that had sustained Lois. It is
strong, assured, so that its shallow counterparts can be observed
with the same penetration as Holdsworth's conduct, as part of an
insufficient standard.

There is another sign that Mrs. Gaskell, as a novelist, had come
'home'; for the first time in her serious work she is able to create
the stable, compact family group that she herself had never
known as a daughter. It is fairly obvious that in the portrait of Mr.
Holman and of Mr. Gibson in *Wives and Daughters* she is creating
the missing father of her childhood, endowing them with authority as well as love. It is noticeable that Mrs. Holman is a
shadowy figure on the fringe of the father–daughter relationship.
They are in this sense idealizations, but conceived with a woman's
sharp eye for male fallibility, so that we get intensely individual
and human portraits. Phillis is what she is because her father was
there to guide and teach her, yet as Paul shrewdly realizes there
has been a weakness in the upbringing which has made it easier
for events to take their shape, and for which Holman is responsible. There has been this time an excess of care:

> I could not help remembering the pinafore, the childish garment
> which Phillis wore so long, as if her parents were unaware of her
> progress towards womanhood. Just in the same way, the minister
> spoke and thought of her now, as a child, whose innocent peace I had
> spoiled by vain and foolish talk. I knew that the truth was different,
> though I could hardly have told it now . . .[18]

Hope Farm is Mrs. Gaskell's first real attempt since *Cranford* at
depicting a stable society. It is complete as a family, nobody dies,
and it extends to the farm community. Small as it is, it has its
gradations of duty and class firmly entrenched and generally
accepted; family and workers eat together, but in two rooms
with the door open. It is singularly free from worry; we never
hear of money, neither do we hear of poverty. The minister dis-
misses the half-wit Timothy from natural irritation, he re-employs
him from natural sympathy; love, of family or neighbour or

[18] *Cousin Phillis*, p. 98.

dependent or employer, unites them all, and all that Holman can say at the moment when he realizes the truth is:

Phillis! did we not make you happy here? Have we not loved you enough?[19]

Holdsworth's betrayal of Phillis—for that is the effect of his marriage—can be seen then as a betrayal of the fundamental standards of the community into which he has been accepted.

The course of Phillis's emotions is charted against this background of belief and setting, but to understand the insight behind it we must turn back to biography for a short time. Mrs. Gaskell's daughters were at various stages of the change from adolescence to womanhood when *Sylvia's Lovers* and *Cousin Phillis* were being written; during this period she watched the first of her daughters become engaged and then married, and her letters show that she was an acute as well as an emotionally involved observer. The effect is immediately noticeable in her work. Margaret Hale in *North and South* thinks and behaves like a mature woman; Sylvia Robson, Phillis and finally Molly Gibson are, to use Proust's phrase 'les jeunes filles en fleur'. Phillis is not, however, a repetition of Sylvia; it should be clear by now that Mrs. Gaskell was moving, though on a restricted scale, to a subtler and more complex pattern. Sylvia dominates her setting and is seen from within. Phillis does not stand out in the same way, though the interest in her as an individual is no less; she is part of the setting and both have to be understood if we are to appreciate her. We see her visually, we are constantly given little tableaux in which she is presented as an integral part of the total scene, her calm and confidence both draw from and add to the general impression of tranquillity and stability that is established in the first half of the novel before she and Holdsworth meet. Paul's recollections of her as she was before this meeting:

rise like pictures to my memory, and in this way I can date their succession; for I know that corn-harvest must have come after hay-making, apple-gathering after corn-harvest.[20]

---

[19] *Cousin Phillis*, p. 99.   [20] ibid., p. 54.

The stages of her love and despair are counterpointed with the steady cycle of farm life, and even her passion for learning that she shares with her father is a part of her individuality which is at the same time an essential element in the atmosphere of Hope Farm. When she collapses there is more than her own fate at stake, Hope Farm and all it stands for are involved. Her recovery and determination to:

go back to the peace of the old days. I know we shall; I can, and I will![21]

is not only a personal victory; the 'I' and the 'we' are contained together.

Cousin Phillis is often referred to as an idyll, an evaluation that puts the emphasis on the descriptive setting of pastoral life. The idyllic element cannot be denied, but no idyll would make the impression that *Cousin Phillis* does. The tale of individual sorrow gains its depth and emotional power, as I have tried to show, from having its roots in fundamental issues. Its success depends, of course, on the manner in which it is carried out; the naturalness of the narrative style and dialogue, the precision of detail, the symbolism of the descriptions are all part of the skill which maintains an exceptional unity of mood and tone. The writing appears to have benefited also from the relaxation of strain that has been noticed. The humour which filters through her observations of men and manners and which lightens the texture of the narrative must also be emphasized. *Cousin Phillis* is outstanding in its own right, the finest example of her favourite form, the short novel. It is also the preliminary to her final achievement.

[21] *Cousin Phillis*, p. 109.

CHAPTER XIII

The Final Synthesis: II
'Wives and Daughters'

THE plot of *Wives and Daughters* is complex in detail, for it follows the changes within a number of family groups whose relations with each other are also important. A pattern of parallels and contrasts emerges. In order to make the pattern clear, and to allow discussion without the need for continual explanation, the following brief summary is given.

Molly Gibson is the daughter of Mr. Gibson, the widowed doctor for Hollingford. As she grows up, he feels the need for someone to guide and advise her, and he thinks about marrying again. She is sent to stay with the Hamleys to avoid Coxe, the amorous student-apprentice who woke Mr. Gibson's fears, and Mr. Gibson does nothing further till circumstances make him meet Mrs. Kirkpatrick several times. She is an ex-governess and partial parasite of the Cumnors (who always call her by her maiden name, Clare), now a widow and desperate to escape from the pinching existence of school-teaching. Her superficial qualities of elegance and manners impress the doctor while his anxiety over Molly is fresh, and he proposes without giving himself time for reflection. The adjustment of Mr. Gibson and Molly to life with a vain, selfish and superficial, though not bad, woman is one of the main themes. The marriage also brings Mrs. Gibson's attractive and self-contained daughter, Cynthia, into the household.

Squire Hamley, who has an obsession about his family dignity, pins his hopes for the restoration of the Hamley prestige on his elder son Osborne, who is considered by all to be brilliant: the younger son Roger is regarded as only a steady plodder. Osborne inexplicably fails at Cambridge. The main reason is a clandestine marriage to a Roman Catholic French serving-girl, Aimée, which he dare not mention to his rigidly patriotic, proud and Protestant father. Disappointment and lack of confidence breed an antagonism, and Mrs. Hamley, who might have been able to learn the truth and smooth matters over, dies. In the meantime the Squire has become fond of Molly, short of wanting his sons to fall in love with a doctor's daughter, while Roger has helped her face up to the shock of her father's second marriage. Molly learns by accident of Osborne's secret. While Osborne trifles away his time, Roger emerges as a brilliant young scientist who is asked to the Towers (the Cumnor house) as a man of rising reputation.

Osborne and Roger visit the Gibsons, and Mrs. Gibson busily sets about match-making between Cynthia and Osborne until she eavesdrops on her husband to find out that Osborne is fatally ill. The plans are switched to Roger, the next in line, who is genuinely in love with Cynthia. They become engaged at his request, but Cynthia demands it should not be made public. Molly is slowly realizing that she herself is in love with Roger, who goes off to lead an expedition into Africa.

Cynthia later reveals to Molly that when she was younger she had written some indiscreet letters to Preston, Lord Cumnor's agent, and that Preston is now blackmailing her into marriage. Molly reluctantly agrees to help, but in the process of meeting Preston and finally getting the letters back, she finds herself compromised in the eyes of Hollingford, and becomes the centre of a scandal. Because of the pledge to secrecy she refuses to explain the situation.

The Cumnor family lords it with benevolent patronage over Hollingford, Lady Cumnor being the real power. The heir, Lord Hollingford, is a scientist who is a friend of Roger; the younger daughter, Lady Harriett, has grown to know and like Molly. When she hears of the scandal she parades round Hollingford with Molly on her arm, and so restores her reputation. Then Osborne dies, and Molly feels able to reveal his secret that has been weighing on her. She goes to look after the Squire, Osborne's wife and child arrive, and there is an uneasy reconciliation. Cynthia in the meanwhile reveals that she does not love Roger, and insists on breaking off the engagement, writing to Roger and to the Squire. Molly, worn out physically and mentally by the strain of events, collapses. While she is slowly recovering, Cynthia becomes engaged in a matter-of-fact manner to a wealthy lawyer, whom she fairly quickly marries.

Roger has provided money for the Squire to put the estate in order, and has been secretly helping to maintain Osborne and his wife. He returns home on learning of Osborne's death, to settle affairs and see Osborne's son recognized. He realizes that his love for Cynthia was an infatuation, and begins to fall in love with Molly, whose worth the Squire has also come to value. He has to leave again to complete his African expedition.

When Mrs. Gaskell died the novel was nearly completed, one instalment being required. Her intentions were known; Roger will return to marry Molly, the Squire will be delighted, Osborne's son will carry on the Hamley name. Even without this specific knowledge the lines of the conclusion, with its reconciliations and adjustments, are clear from what was already written. For purposes of discussion therefore I shall talk of the novel as though it were complete, with Roger and Molly safely married.

Wives and Daughters was written in Italy, in France, in Hampshire, but hardly at all in Manchester. The industrial city vanishes entirely, even by reference, from her final work; the rejection is complete.[1] But as I have tried to show, she was rejecting one particular manifestation of change, the industrial city, that created a physical and spiritual meanness for men's lives. Moreover as a novelist she liked to be able to observe human nature with some detachment, and it was difficult to achieve this for a world in which nature was distorted by pressures of poverty and strife, and which depressed her. Dickens had no brief for slum

[1] The novel was also part of a deed of practical rejection. With the help of the £2,000 that Smith offered for it she bought the house at Holybourne in Hampshire where she died while still writing it. Her intention was to persuade her husband to retire and leave Manchester. Such a hope argues either a misconception of her husband's character that persisted through more than thirty years of marriage (an argument sometimes used by those who believe her marriage to have been not particularly successful) or, more probably, a desire to get away from Manchester that led her to use every stratagem possible. It would have been, at the least, a country home where she could spend much of her time.

conditions, but he had an imaginative power that enabled him to handle them creatively by endowing their constituents with qualities of the grotesque and fantastic. This type of creative transfiguration was beyond Mrs. Gaskell; she wrote as an observer about the reality she saw, and found that too harsh and dismal a reality cramped her *as a novelist* (her charitable work never ceased). To say this is to say nothing depreciatory; a novelist selects from all possible aspects of reality those which carry most meaning for him and which he finds to be sympathetic. Reality can too easily be confused with an interpretation of 'realism' that emphasizes the grim and sordid. The reality Mrs. Gaskell finally chose was a perfectly 'real' one even if not contemporary; within it she was able to handle human nature and develop to the full her particular ability as a novelist. Any limitations of that ability must be attributed not to the scene she chooses—George Eliot confined herself often to a similar period and setting—but to the qualities she brought to the handling of it.

She did not, however, reject the idea of change, nor the new knowledge that was transforming society; her retreat into the immediate past helps her to provide oblique commentary on the present. The new forces are symbolized for Hollingford—the final manifestation of the Cranford world—by science. This 'science' is admittedly rather vague and reasonably gentlemanly, something biological and anatomical and not at all dirty or ugly; it harmonizes with the charm and quietness of its surroundings. But it *is* science. The hero, Roger Hamley, will make his way in the world by it instead of being a 'gentleman' and relying on the merit of a name that precedes Domesday; he has the vigour and practical outlook of a new attitude. He will create a social precedent by marrying the daughter of the local doctor, who is himself a man of scientific mind; he will meet on equal terms with the heir of the Cumnors who is also a scientist. These three scientists form a nucleus that is ready to take over from the older generation and lead Hollingford to a newer age.

It is important for this purpose that Hollingford should show a representative social range, and it gives a cross-section of country society from duchess to labourer, concentrating however on the professional and smaller landed classes. The centre of the story is placed in the class Mrs. Gaskell knew best, the professional middle-class; the resulting authority and confident insight into be-haviour and attitude is part of the quality of *Wives and Daughters*. But the inclusion of the Hamleys and the Cumnors brings in the other leaders of social opinion, while the marriage of Roger and Molly recognizes the merging of landed and professional classes in a period of transition. At the same time there is no question of the idea of a social hierarchy crumbling; acceptance of class dis-tinction and class obligations is part of the stability of the com-munity, unlike the industrial scene where mill-worker becomes wealthy industrialist in one generation and commercial success is the criterion of position. Lady Harriet's 'blood has boiled' over her aunt's behaviour, as she tells Molly, because:

Any one who earns his livelihood by any exercise of head or hands, from professional people and rich merchants down to labourers, she calls 'persons.' She would never in her most slip-slop talk accord them even the conventional title of 'gentlemen' . . .

(We can recall Thornton, and his mother's proud boast of his qualities.) Lady Harriet's protest includes the lumping together as well as the inordinate pride; she also attacks the type of people who are 'unnatural in their exaggerated respect and admiration' for hereditary rank. But in adding, to Molly:

You at least are simple and truthful, and that's why I separate you in my mind from them, and have talked unconsciously to you as I would —well! now here's another piece of impertinence—as I would to my equal—in rank, I mean; for I don't set myself up in solid things as any better than my neighbours.[2]

she reveals in perfect simplicity a complex attitude in which the recognition of individual merit and the inevitability of rank distinction merge.

These two elements, of accepted social order and of respect for individual qualities, had been important ingredients of the panacea Mrs. Gaskell had suggested in her first novel for the

[2] *Wives and Daughters*, pp. 184–5.

disordered society of Manchester, with religion as the essential solvent. Sixteen years later, with the urgency of the late forties gone, she contemplates a different society whose behaviour—like that of *Cranford*—is firmly based on Christian ethic and morality; active religion needs little mention. In her diary of her trip to France in 1862, which was written up and published in 1864 while *Wives and Daughters* was being written, she pays tribute to Madame de Circout by making this point:

I think it is Dekker who speaks of our Saviour as "the first true gentleman that ever lived." We may choose to be shocked at the freedom of expression used by the old dramatist: but is it not true? Is not Christianity at the very core of the heart of all gracious courtesy?[3]

The occasional natural prayer, the thought of God in moments of great distress, this is all; the every-day story is concerned with details of every day. There is still the satirical flick at exaggerated religiosity; we note the Methodist cook who refused to prepare French dishes,[4] there is a side glance at the coming of 'muscular Christianity' (another indication of how the contemporary world was in her mind);[5] while the velvet-bound Bible and Prayer Book that are Lady Cumnor's wedding present to Cynthia are also Mrs. Gaskell's final comment on a religion that gives importance to convention and display. Osborne's marriage to the Roman Catholic Aimée raises a more serious issue. Mrs. Gaskell's treatment of religion had always been non-sectarian; a corollary of her dislike of prejudice as well as a facet of the love that was a central feature of her Christianity. Once before, in *North and South*, she had approved marriage to a Catholic, but in that novel Margaret's brother and his wife had stayed in exile. Aimée is similarly not a schemer; our sympathy is demanded for her. Moreover, in letting it be implied that the infant and Protestant heir to the Hamleys of Hamley will be brought up by a Roman Catholic—for this is surely implied in the solution of having the child live with its mother in a lodge on the estate—Mrs. Gaskell shows herself responsive to a further and important aspect of

---

[3] *Cousin Phillis*, p. 643. Mme de Circout, who died in 1863, was a friend of Mrs. Gaskell and well known in French society.

[4] *Wives and Daughters*, p. 203.   [5] ibid., p. 30.

change in social attitudes. She uses the Hamley family throughout *Wives and Daughters* to embody both tradition and, in the person of the squire, resistance to change; the religious aspect of this episode should not be overlooked. On the whole, however, we should note the number of scenes in which there is no appeal to religion but which would have been given some comment in earlier novels; for example the episode in which Molly breaks down on hearing of her father's proposed marriage and Roger comforts her is conducted solely on the level of natural emotion and good advice. Molly's words later to Roger sum up, perhaps, the approach:

I daresay it seems foolish; perhaps all our earthly trials will appear foolish to us after a while; perhaps they seem so now to angels. But we are ourselves, you know, and this is *now*, not some time to come, a long, long way off. And we are not angels, to be comforted by seeing the ends for which everything is sent.[6]

Mrs. Gaskell had travelled a long way from *Mary Barton*, even from *Sylvia's Lovers*, to write that last sentence.

Within this process of change the particular world of *Cranford* is still represented, now seen specifically as an older generation which is to one side of the main stream of progress. The Misses Browning may really be considered as a fourth 'family' in this respect, alongside the Gibsons, Hamleys and Cumnors. They are the leaders of respectable Hollingford society, and it is this society whose moral standards and judgements are the arbiters of conduct. It condemns Molly, and the sceptical self-sufficient Mr. Gibson accepts its 'non-fiat'; it equally condemns the duchess who fails to dress up to her position for the Charity Ball:

Such a shabby thing for a duchess I never saw; not a bit of a diamond near her![7]

as Mrs. Goodenough complains, and Lady Harriett has to force her family into special affability to remedy its guest's refusal to meet the obligations of her rank. Cranford is still powerful. The Misses Browning are guardians and propagators of old but vital

---

[6] *Wives and Daughters*, p. 154.   [7] ibid., p. 338.

principles of integrity—their own trial comes when they feel forced to condemn Molly. Their manners and conventions may be shown to be slightly ludicrous, never their principles.

The treatment of this Cranford element is revealing, for it shows an unconscious shift of attitude by Mrs. Gaskell. There is evidence that as the novel developed so the two sisters began to merge in Mrs. Gaskell's imagination with Deborah and Matty Jenkyns of *Cranford*. At the beginning they are:

tall, handsome women, past their first youth, and inclined to be extremely complaisant to the widowed doctor.[8]

They were friends of his dead wife and are contemporaries of his social circle; Phoebe even has passing hopes of being the second Mrs. Gibson. But the *Cranford* aspect grows; they assume the habits, antiquated customs, and even the speech of the *Cranford* ladies. By the end of the novel they are no longer seen as Mr. Gibson's contemporaries; they have aged beyond the chronology of the story while the Deborah–Matty relationship is pronounced. All these aspects are clearly present in the episode when the elder Miss Browning has boxed Phoebe's ears for reporting the gossip about Molly:

"Phoebe, I'm really sorry I boxed your ears; only I should do it again, if you said the same things." Phoebe sate down by her sister, and took hold of *one of her withered hands*, and began caressing it . . .[9]

They have slipped further back into the past. This has an interesting result, for while working ostensibly with two generations, Mrs. Gaskell spreads her observations of continuity and change over virtually three, so that the younger generation by contrast appears more 'modern'; yet another indication that the contemporary situation is in her mind.

The traditional Cranford world is, then, present in person, as it was not in *Cousin Phillis*. There is little need to enlarge on what

[8] *Wives and Daughters*, p. 9. Molly is twelve when the story begins.

[9] ibid., p. 594—my italics. Molly is now nineteen. Incidentally, it is impossible to give Miss Browning a first name (bearing in mind the convention of calling the eldest daughter 'Miss'). Mrs. Gaskell calls her successively Sally (p. 10), Clarinda (p. 170) and Dorothy (p. 329)—about the best of many examples of her carelessness with names.

has previously been said about the setting. Nature is always close at hand; comforting, influencing, and reflecting with descriptive symbolism the sequence of events and emotions. One passage is worth quoting, for it throws light on Mr. Gibson. The comment occurs as the doctor rides along turning over his problems in his mind:

The country surgeon felt the beauty of the seasons, perhaps more than most men. He saw more of it by day, by night, in storm and sunshine, or in the still, soft cloudy weather. He never spoke about what he felt on the subject; indeed, he did not put his feelings into words, even to himself. But, if his mood ever approached to the sentimental, it was on such days as this.[10]

This is important for our knowledge of this self-contained, logical and outwardly emotional man who is the main ironic observer in the narrative, and of Mrs. Gaskell's attitude to 'sentiment' which will be dealt with shortly.

The details of an antique world, of room ornaments wrapped in cap-paper[11] and of three-cornered notes,[12] are correspondingly diminished, whereas in *My Lady Ludlow*, which had also dealt with change, it was the centre from which change was observed. Similarly the feudal paternalism which Lady Ludlow represented is seen as belonging to the generation of the Misses Browning; the influence of the Towers is on the wane. It flatters the snobbish Mrs. Gibson, but is rejected by Molly until the personal qualities of Lady Harriet recommend themselves; it is held at a distance by Mr. Gibson. Personal relationships such as those between Roger and Lord Hollingford or Molly and Harriet replace the patron-client attitudes.

Professor Kathleen Tillotson has pointed out how much of the quality of certain novels—she quotes *Wives and Daughters* and *Middlemarch*—can be missed by the modern reader not having 'due recognition of their setting in an England forty years before the date of writing'.[13] This quality is one of the excellencies which makes *Wives and Daughters* 'one of the greatest novels about the

---

[10] *Wives and Daughters*, p. 423.   [11] ibid., p. 170.   [12] ibid., p. 511.
[13] *Tillotson*, p. 92.

past'[14] although the relevance of the situation and the occasional reference are, as has been pointed out, contemporary. Mrs. Gaskell is observing with the insight of lived experience and affection; the integration of character, action and background is complete. The opening scene illustrates this; the description of Molly's room moves in and out of an awareness of what it was like to wake up as a young girl in such a room. The detailed description of a bonnet on a stand, while setting the period, is immediately humanized, for:

there was a neat little quilling inside, every plait of which Molly knew; for had she not made it herself the evening before, with infinite pains? and was there not a little blue bow in this quilling, the very first bit of such finery Molly had ever had the prospect of wearing?[15]

The leisurely creation of setting and character that Dickens had grumbled at is never dull, never uninteresting, for the two grow together with a life that absorbs the reader.

We can now sum up the social background and significance of *Wives and Daughters* briefly. Mrs. Gaskell takes an optimistic view; she can see the process of transition occurring without disaster to the social framework. But she avoids any direct dealing with the industrial world; instead she reaches back into the past to the way of life which carried her values and affections, and recreates it in such a way that it is seen moving steadily into the future. From the vantage point of a further hundred years we might interpret this as side-stepping the major issue, seeing Mrs. Gaskell as denying the inevitable in imagining a situation where the world of Cranford in its physical and communal aspects would thrive. There would be some truth in this, but it would ignore the facts that she grasps the central problem and that this world has indeed proved to be vital enough to survive within an industrialized country, its values still important. At least she was the only one of the major Victorian novelists who really knew the industrial city intimately. (London, then as now, was more and less than a manufacturing centre; it is interesting that in her last novel Mrs. Gaskell still sees it as the centre of the fashionable, extravagant way

[14] *Tillotson*, p. 105.   [15] *Wives and Daughters*, pp. 1–2.

of life or of ambition that it had been in *North and South.*) She had appreciated its virtues, and proclaimed that its inhabitants were individuals and human beings. She had accepted that progress, in the technical and scientific sense, was one of the facts of existence, but her nature and her art finally rejected the cities it produced. We may remind ourselves after all that not until the following generation were novelists to suggest that the industrial revolution should be abolished, as Morris did when he dreamed of John Ball.

Wives and Daughters develops as a novel through the social observation of a community and its individual members, related to the close analysis of a young girl's emotions in which Mrs. Gaskell had become interested. The distinction between the two approaches is obviously not a rigid one; Molly's feelings, for example, have social as well as personal consequences which are reflected in her conduct. But it provides a convenient way of looking at the novel. Mrs. Gaskell, as her sub-title implies, is examining every-day behaviour and the attitudes that control it. Admittedly it is not every day that heirs to country estates marry penniless foreign papists, that young girls are blackmailed for foolish promises, or—especially in mid-Victorian England— young scientists set off to explore Africa. Yet the sub-title is accurate in its emphasis. These dramatic features are necessary incidents of plot; the real interest is in the feelings and behaviour between father and son and not in the romance of the marriage; not in blackmail but in the emotions of a young girl apparently caught in a trap. They are types of emotional pressure. And by far the greater part of the novel is concerned with the relationships at the heart of every-day life, those of marriage, family ties and social intercourse.

At the centre is the Gibson family with its unmatched halves and contrasting temperaments. It is the sort of situation that Jane Austen created, stepped down to a lower and less wealthy social level—in this respect Mrs. Gaskell is the less romantic—with the minimum of dramatic incident in order to permit detailed observaation of character. It is difficult not to believe that Jane Austen was an influence on Mrs. Gaskell; in particular the shades of Mr. and

Mrs. Bennett seem to nod behind Mr. and Mrs. Gibson. Miss Hopkins shrewdly comments that:

In the creation of Mrs. Gibson, in *Wives and Daughters*, she has learned what Jane Austen well understood: the art of making stupidity interesting.[16]

It can be added that she had also learned the art of making conduct the vehicle for moral satire. *Wives and Daughters* has this in common with all Mrs. Gaskell's work, that at heart it deals with morality; it is a study of principles, or the lack of them, controlling conduct. It differs in that within the comedy of the novel her satirical gift is allowed full expression. Mrs. Gibson, the main instrument for it, is a not-so-distant cousin of Mr. Bradshaw in *Ruth*, but Mr. Bradshaw is subdued by the predominantly serious and didactic tone of the story in which he appears. Mrs. Gibson blossoms in her environment.

Her importance is that she cares only for the surface aspect of the standards which other characters obey or, when they do not, like Osborne and even Cynthia, suffer for it in their consciences or in the consequences. She carries the weight of Mrs. Gaskell's moral indignation, even though that indignation is tempered by tolerance and a readiness to allow such virtues, for example attempted fairness and a desire to be a good wife according to her lights, as a superficial and selfish character can have. The result is a portrait that rises above the comic; its comedy carries moral judgement, all the more forceful because the author herself on the whole refrains from passing judgement either by comment or by manipulation of the plot. Mrs. Gaskell is, however, careful to avoid attributing any intentional evil to her, for this would be out of place in both the inertia of her character and the Cranford world. Her quality is summed up when she has to discuss Cynthia's return with her husband-to-be. Mr. Gibson's attitude assumes natural maternal affection, Mrs. Gibson's is concerned with the presence of an attractive grown-up daughter:

[16] *Hopkins*, p. 143. In the first of her 'Cranford' type stories, 'Mr. Harrison's Confessions', we find that Jane Austen, Dickens and Thackeray are the three novelists mentioned as being in the narrator's bookcase. *Emma* is quoted in 'Cumberland Sheepshearers' (*Ruth*, pp. 469–70).

Mr. Gibson believed that Cynthia Kirkpatrick was to return to England to be present at her mother's wedding; but Mrs. Kirkpatrick had no such intention. She was not what is commonly called a woman of determination; but somehow what she disliked she avoided, and what she liked she tried to do, or to have.[17]

We catch in this passage an echo of the moral strenuousness that appeared in earlier work. But Mrs. Gibson can do little real harm, for she becomes subject to the restraints that govern the world and the family she enters. The danger of such lack of positive standards lies in the abdication from moral responsibility when there is nothing to replace it, and this we can see in the permanent harm done to Cynthia during her upbringing, a harm aggravated by lack of true affection.

On the whole, however, it is a stable world, its stability resting not only on the traditions of an ordered social hierarchy but in the acceptance by individuals of its standards and in the confidence which is based on family affection and trust. Its conventions are soundly based and it is worth remembering that a woman such as Mrs. Gibson, who has no other restraint to her selfishness, lives by conventions. Cynthia is saved by becoming part of one of the families which create the social climate, and by the restoration of the atmosphere of affection and trust; conversely the greatest Hamley misfortune is the death of Mrs. Hamley, who was the centre of love and trust for her own household and who might have prevented the estrangement between Osborne and his father. Molly says of Osborne's marriage that it had:

a sense of concealment and uncertainty about it all; and her honest, straightforward father, her quiet life at Hollingford, which, even with all its drawbacks, was above-board, and where everybody knew what everybody was doing, seemed secure and pleasant in comparison.[18]

She is herself forced into concealing her actions when dealing with Preston on Cynthia's behalf, with the resulting condemnation by local society and what could have been a breach with her father

---

[17] *Wives and Daughters*, p. 138.   [18] ibid. p. 24

were it not for the affection between them. The comment Molly passes on her own action may serve to mark a distinction which is germane to the narrative point of view:

I'm sure it was not wrong in morals, whatever it might be in judgement.[19]

We are reminded at one stage of the novel that Mr. Gibson:

surgeon though he was, had never learnt to anatomise a woman's heart . . .[20]

The comment occurs after Cynthia's engagement to Roger Hamley, when an invitation from the Squire for lunch is met by Cynthia and her mother with vacillation and apparent indifference, instead of the pleased acceptance that seems obvious to the man. It is an important comment for it suggests that Mrs. Gaskell is doing the anatomizing that is beyond the doctor's logical brain, and that a woman's heart is thought of in connexion with love. The second point is reinforced by a preceding reflection from the baffled Mr. Gibson, who was:

almost ready to vow that he would never again meddle in any affair in which women were concerned, which would effectually shut him out from all love-affairs for the future.[21]

Wives and Daughters is the fullest as well as the final expression of Mrs. Gaskell's attitude to love in the narrower 'romantic' sense and to the various emotions which attach themselves to its label. We may distinguish many varieties in the course of events. There is the romantic love of Osborne and Aimée, jumping barriers of class and religion, and the nostalgically haloed first love of Mr. Gibson for the Jeannie he never married.[22] Infatuation is represented by Roger's love for Cynthia, and in its comic calf-love state by the apprentice Coxe's desperate feelings for Molly. Sexual desire, though it could not be openly stated, is clearly behind Preston's

---

[19] *Wives and Daughters*, p. 603.   [20] ibid., p. 460.   [21] ibid., p. 460.
[22] ibid., pp. 53 and 162. This repeats Mr. Manning's reminiscences in *Cousin Phillis*, p. 36.

pursuit of Cynthia.[23] All these are grouped round the central characters of Molly, whose love for Roger is in the tradition of the quiet, deep and selfless attachment which is the ideal standard, and of Cynthia who is incapable of such depth of feeling and whose emotions have retired behind a protective selfishness that is difficult to throw off.

To complete the picture we need also to include the result of love, which in Mrs. Gaskell's world is marriage (or of course, the memory of what might have been. Miss Matty was only the first of many characters who never spoke their love, or hoped in vain). There are four marriages in the novel; the Hamleys, the Cumnors, the Gibsons and the abortive union of Osborne and Aimée. The last is deservedly a failure by Mrs. Gaskell's standards because Osborne never allows it to become a family unit, it is founded on deceit and separation. The Hamleys are still in love, their marriage has been a happy one, but at the expense of Mrs. Hamley's sacrifice to her husband's prejudices:

She gave up her visits to London; she gave up her sociable pleasure in the company of her fellows in education and position . . . He loved his wife all the more dearly for her sacrifices for him; but, deprived of all her strong interests, she sank into ill-health; nothing definite; only she never was well.[24]

The Cumnor marriage has lost any romantic tinge it may have had, but robustly survives on solid affection, respect, tolerance and, in this case, the wife in control. We learn little about Mr. Gibson's first marriage save that it was not to Jeannie; that he was fond of his first wife but not violently in love, and that she died young. His second is a misalliance that shakes down into a way of life, irritating at the personal level but fulfilling its job at the conventional level by creating a home and looking after the social

[23] Rosamond Lehmann has some interesting remarks on this aspect, and on Mrs. Gaskell's breadth of outlook. She notes 'the insistent sexuality of Preston's manner with attractive women' and comments that 'all this, though interpreted within the literary conventions of the day, is the reverse of a "baffled" approach. We do not need to be told what it is he counts on when he tells Cynthia that he can make her love him after she has married him.'
'A Neglected Victorian Classic', *Penguin New Writing*, No. 32, 1948, p. 94.
[24] *Wives and Daughters*, pp. 45–6.

aspects of upbringing. None of these, it will be noted, are marriages of true minds, none is a properly balanced partnership; this is an omission for Molly and Roger to remedy.

Mrs. Gaskell distinguishes clearly between the emotions of love and the state of marriage, and *Wives and Daughters* is at least as much about the latter as the former. She obviously sees that ideally they can combine, equally obviously her realism recognizes that this is a rare occurrence. Because of this, and because of the vital part played by marriage in the scheme of things, she sees it on the whole as a relationship in which common sense and sound principles are the main elements. If—and the occasional references to early 'true' love suggest it—Mrs. Gaskell was compensating for a romantic nature that had little outlet in the busy household and preoccupied husband in Manchester, it is a romanticism that is not allowed its head. From the very beginning of her work marriage is seen as a sober business bound up far more with the idea of the family than of individual attraction. *Mary Barton*, we may recall, does not end with Mary in Jem's arms, but standing with her child 'watching the return of her husband from his daily work'.[25] Because this relationship is emphasized, man and wife in marriage move within the range of the social observer and become therefore a target for Mrs. Gaskell's irony. Mr. and Mrs. Gibson develop from a succession of husbands and wives, of whom the Bradshaws, the Hales and the Robsons are a fair sample.

Nevertheless one cannot find anywhere in her work the slightest suggestion that marriage can be broken up, unless death does the parting. Her religious beliefs, and her view of the obligation on the home to provide a centre of stability and moral responsibility, would largely account for this. Love as the destroyer of marriage is not considered, but then her descriptions of any love worth considering ignore sexual attraction.[26]

[25] *Mary Barton*, p. 457.
[26] The importance of marriage and the family in Victorian society has often been commented on; see e.g. Houghton, *The Victorian Frame of Mind*, Yale U.P., 1957, Chap. 13. I am concerned here only with Mrs. Gaskell's views, but she is also to be seen as sharing in a common set of opinions, modified by the extent to which she sees one aspect as more important than another.

In its aspect as a love story, *Wives and Daughters* can be clearly seen as a continuation of the analysis begun with *Sylvia's Lovers*. Molly Gibson is yet another study in the temperament and emotions of a young girl growing up and falling in love, although the character is no stereotype. Once again we can link the heroine to the author's observation of her own family; now advanced a further stage, for first love is finally successful. To conclude the biographical element we have to turn to the male side of the story.

Roger Hamley's career is patently based on the public career of the young Darwin, but Darwin would hardly have been the model for a young man in love, even had Mrs. Gaskell known him well enough. The romance of Africa and exploration that was beginning to invade the Victorian imagination is also obviously behind the vague outline of Roger Hamley's journeys; Burton's travel books on his various expeditions were making their impact in the years before *Wives and Daughters* was begun, while Speke's account of the discovery of the Nile appeared in 1863. Africa was news. Yet Africa and exploration provided only the romantic glow behind a solidly detailed character, and that character she abstracted from her son-in-law, Charles Crompton, Q.C., together with many minimally altered details of his career:

He has almost perfect health, and perfect temper. *I* should have said *not* clever; but he was 4th wrangler at Cambridge and is a Fellow of Trinity, and is getting on very fast in his profession; so I suppose he has those solid intellectual qualities which tell in *action*, though not in *conversation*. But his goodness is what gives me the thankfullest feeling of confidence in him . . . Mr. Crompton is not exactly a Unitarian, nor exactly Broad Church,—but perhaps rather more of the latter than the former. He is so good-principled he may be called a religious man; for I am sure the root of his life is in religion. But he has not imagination enough to be what one calls *spiritual*. It is just the same want that makes him not care for music or painting,—nor much for poetry. In these tastes Florence is his superior, although *she* is not 'artistic'. Then he cares for science,—in which she is at present ignorant. His strong, good *un*sensitive character is just what will, I trust, prove very grateful to her anxious, conscientious little heart.[27]

This is an accurate outline for Roger Hamley, not only in the detail of his background, but as a sketch of his character and the basis for his relationship with Molly Gibson. Adapting living people to fiction is a commonplace of novel-writing that needs no special comment in itself; we need note only that Mrs. Gaskell is still the acute observer, sensitive and sympathetic to younger people and attitudes. (Roger Hamley, it need hardly be added, is not simply a description of Charles Crompton; imagination went to work on the characteristics Mrs. Gaskell observed and liked.) The freshness and vitality of *Wives and Daughters* springs as much from its truthfulness to youth, her delight in it and in the optimism and happiness it reflected, as to the delight and renewal of interest she found in recalling the environment of her own youth from the vantage point of experience. The viewpoint and attitudes of both generations are blended in the novel, just as the interests in social history and in the psychology of characters are blended. The author, in stepping back towards her past, is tacitly accepting the climacteric of her own generation and recognizing the growing authority of the next.

Molly Gibson is in many ways the summation of the qualities that Mrs. Gaskell admired and which appear to a varying degree in most of her heroines. She is affectionate, self-reliant, honest and natural, with vitality and intelligence. Mrs. Gaskell does not fall into the error common in Victorian literature, and which mars many of Dickens's novels, of making the heroine little more than a symbol of the feminine principle in a man's world. One reason is that she writes as a woman.[28] A second is that she is too honest and

[27] *Letters*, pp. 105–6, 13 July 1863. The italics are Mrs. Gaskell's. Crompton married Florence Gaskell in September of that year. An outline of *Wives and Daughters*, not yet titled, was ready in May, 1864. Another daughter, Marianne, was engaged to her cousin Thurston Holland (also a barrister) in the later part of 1864. Marianne's family nickname was Polly, and Polly-Marianne is perhaps more than co-incidentally close to the Molly-Mary of her heroine. It is hardly surprising that Cynthia marries into the law.

[28] Not that women were free of the error, they often supported it. Compare Mrs. Gaskell's first description of the grown-up Molly, looking at herself in a mirror:

She saw a slight, lean figure, promising to be tall, a complexion browner than cream-coloured, although in a year or two it might have that tint; plentiful curly black hair,

accurate an observer to accept an abstraction. (It is possible that she was influenced also by the new type of heroine who had emerged in fiction, a woman capable of being an equal partner to a man in marriage.) What sets Molly apart from Sylvia Robson and Phillis Holman is that she is successful. In terms of the novel (i.e. leaving aside the fact that in real life Florence Gaskell had married Charles Crompton) this can be attributed to two causes. The first is that her qualities of temperament and training are in equilibrium. Eagerness, energy, strong emotions, impetuosity, are balanced by self-control, unselfishness, a willingness to learn, and so on. The tension required to maintain the balance, together with the impulses that lead to conduct disturbing the balance, are what make Molly Gibson a singularly successful and interesting portrayal of a good and not particularly complex character. The second cause, which also controls the first, is that circumstances have favoured the way her character has been moulded. If we look back from Molly Gibson down the line of Mrs. Gaskell's heroines, we can see that they have a family resemblance in temperament. Differences in character emerge as to a great extent due to differences in environment and upbringing, while misfortunes are directly related to failure in one or both. Molly is *par excellence* the product of stable surroundings, a secure and affectionate home and a sound upbringing in a well-ordered community.

Which is precisely what Cynthia is not. She is as much the contrast to Molly's upbringing as she is to Molly's character. Her background is one of poverty and pretence, of insecurity and the sense of being unwanted, with, instead of a father to lean on, a

tied up in a bunch behind with a rose-coloured ribbon; long, almond-shaped, soft grey eyes, shaded both above and below by curling black eyelashes. (*Wives and Daughters*, pp. 72-3)

with Mrs. Henry Wood's heroine in *The Channings* (1862):

Constance was standing against the window. She was of middle height, thoroughly ladylike and graceful; her features fair and beautiful, and her dark-blue eyes and smooth white brow wonderfully like [her brother's]. She wore a muslin dress with a delicate pink sprig upon it, the lace of its open sleeves falling on her pretty white hands, which were playing unconsciously with a spray of jessamine while she listened to her brothers as each spoke. (Everyman Edition, 1924, p. 22.)

The first describes an individual, the second an abstraction, even when the cliché-ridden style of Mrs. Wood is discounted.

vain and shallow mother. She has been frightened off love by the result of her adolescent infatuation for Preston, and has grown up fighting her own battles in a world where trust and affection have appeared as traps. Cynthia's problems can be more easily understood today, as can the defensive and prickly reaction.

There is nothing mechanical about the contrast between the two characters; they are created as individuals in their own right. And through Cynthia Mrs. Gaskell has yet another angle of vision for the observation of love. The honesty that leads to the breaking of the engagement with Roger because:

the truth is, I do not love him. I like him, I respect him; but I will not marry him.

makes quite clear for us what Mrs. Gaskell regarded as the essential basis for marriage, while the subsequent remark—which could stand as example for the multitude of comments which show her shrewd discernment of human nature:

It is such a relief to feel free again. It wearied me so to think of straining up to his goodness.[29]

brings even perfection into the observer's range as creating a problem in relationships.

Mrs. Gaskell sets herself one problem that she fails to solve satisfactorily; the treatment of love in *Wives and Daughters* shows a failure to carry the analysis right through and an endeavour to reconcile conflicting attitudes. It is plain that Mrs. Gaskell has in her mind a clear idea of what love and marriage ought to be. Love—which can only be properly considered in terms of marriage —is a deep but not violently passionate relationship, an extension of affection in which the senses have little or no part, founded on mutual attraction of character. It never takes leave of its senses, it rather keeps within hailing distance of common sense. Love and marriage from this point of view, however pleasurable, fall within the pattern of conduct and duty. Yet at the same time she is aware of love as a far more potent and disturbing force. The brain fever that Sylvia, Phillis and Molly all succumb to may be

The Final Synthesis: II 'Wives and Daughters'   225

a conventional way of handling a crisis in a heroine's love life, but the convention provides for a state of mental and emotional conflict which was recognized before the theory of repression was known. Cynthia's fear of Preston and her otherwise exaggeratedly cynical self-control likewise suggest a passionate nature being held in check. In her perception of emotions and reactions, within the range she sets herself, Mrs. Gaskell is as acute and subtle a creator of character as any of her contemporaries.

The romantic streak to her imagination occasionally distorts the sharpness and accuracy of her vision. Luckily this is rare, for Mrs. Gaskell as we have seen avoids whenever possible having to discuss love itself or to depict love scenes. But it does occur. When Cynthia suddenly accepts and quickly marries Mr. Henderson, she comments to Molly after the engagement:

I believe I cared for him when he offered all those months ago, but I tried to think I didn't; only sometimes I really was so unhappy, I thought I must put an iron band round my heart to keep it from breaking, like the Faithful John of the German story—do you remember, Molly?[30]

But the comment is out of character as well as being of dubious application to the agreeable, conventional lawyer we briefly meet; it is a sacrifice of realism on the sacred altar of marriage. The Cynthia of this speech talks like Molly, not like the girl who fears Preston and has developed an armour of irony. Molly's own reflections when she has heard Preston lay claim to Cynthia:

Roger! Oh, Roger!—far away in the mysterious darkness of distance—loving as he did, (ah, that was love! that was the love to which Cynthia had referred, as worthy of the name!)[31]

show passionate feeling that is outside her range. Such forced expressions show by their language that Mrs. Gaskell is trying for an emotion which is beyond the normal range of her analysis. Apart from such rare occurrences she takes good care to keep emotion and sentiment under control.

[30] *Wives and Daughters*, pp. 700–1.   [31] ibid., p. 539.

Wives and Daughters deals largely with emotional matters; its plot develops round love stories and family crises, yet with a few exceptions it triumphantly avoids falling into sentimentality. Sentiment is kept under control by the method of narration and by a strongly anti-sentimental note that is deliberately introduced throughout the narrative and which is part of the attack on false emotions that in places sharpens into satire, mainly at the expense of Mrs. Gibson. At the same time the contrast with honest feeling is made, another of the contrasts by which the novel makes its effect. Mr. Gibson, whose comments play a large part in setting the tone of the narrative, is also willy nilly a lover, acutely conscious of being a widower, who, as Molly observed:

disliked his position as a middle-aged lover being made so evident to the men in waiting as it was by Mrs. Kirkpatrick's affectionate speeches and innuendos. He tried to banish every tint of pink sentimentalism from the conversation, and to confine it to matter of fact . . .[32]

an attitude he maintains into marriage, which he finds can be a reasonably comfortable domestic state, but only:

when Mrs. Gibson was moderately sensible, and not over-sentimental, he mentally added . . .[33]

Any fanciful nonsense about love and marriage is inevitably brought into contrast with this particular wooing and marriage which stays in the foreground of events, while for contrast of a different sort there is the tragedy of Osborne's ill-advised piece of romantic behaviour. And to make her attitude perfectly clear, she grafts her own comment on to Roger's rhapsodic reflections about the perils of his journey and an idealized Cynthia waiting sweetly at home for him:

with all a lover's quickness of imagination and triteness of fancy, he called her a star, a flower, a nymph, a witch, an angel, or a mermaid, a nightingale, a siren, as one or another of her attributes rose up before him.[34]

Nor, it is worth pointing out, do we ever see an actual love scene between either Molly and Roger or Osborne and Aimée, the only

[32] *Wives and Daughters*, p. 151.   [33] ibid., p. 373.   [34] ibid., pp. 429–30.

genuine pairs of lovers in the novel. The emotional tone is subdued
to that of every-day behaviour.

There are however scenes of genuine pathos, such as the death
of Osborne and earlier the death of Mrs. Hamley. Here the touch
is exact, while control is maintained by mediating the scenes
through observers—mainly Molly and Mr. Gibson—and by
constantly shifting from emotion back to the practical level
through action and dialogue.

Molly and Mr. Gibson are more than major characters in the
story. *Wives and Daughters* is too long and too complicated a
novel to be controlled by the narrative device of an observer
within the action, such as Mary Smith in *Cranford* or Paul Manning in *Cousin Phillis*. Nevertheless Mrs. Gaskell keeps her objectivity by retiring often behind the father and daughter; it is
chiefly through their eyes that we see and feel. This double viewpoint has many advantages; they are at the centre of events, and
their own relationship, which is an important part of the action,
is seen from both sides. Between them they set the narrative tone.
Both are emotionally honest, blessed with common sense, have
intelligence. At the same time it is possible for Mrs. Gaskell to
switch from the more ironic and logical remarks of the doctor to
the greater sensibility and sympathy of Molly as occasion demands,
a useful method for handling the psychology of Molly's development. The astringency and irony of the novel owe a great deal to
Mr. Gibson, 'sparing of his words, intelligent, and slightly sar-
castic'[35] whose voice is undoubtedly that of Mrs. Gaskell as
observer of men and manners, as Molly is the voice of her sensitivity.

It would be wrong to leave *Wives and Daughters* without drawing attention to the moral patterning which unites it with her
earlier work. Like *Cousin Phillis* it refrains from drawing conclusions or passing judgements, but its complex plot sets up patterns
which are only faintly discernible in the shorter work, while the
sequence of events that combine into the plot is a moral one.
The lesson of love and forgiveness which Job Legh preached to
John Barton and Mr. Carson after the murder of Carson's son is

[35] *Wives and Daughters*, p. 40.

the same lesson that Squire Hamley learns for himself without changing his character. Reward and punishment follow diversely but without rigidity; Molly is rewarded for her selfless love, Mr. Gibson punished for his selfish motives in the desire to find a substitute mother for her. Behind the moral pattern lies the idea of love. All the different 'loves' that have been discussed have finally to be measured against the greater concept of love that is a pre-condition for a Christian society, and against the tolerance that should accompany it.

But it would be equally wrong to end a discussion of *Wives and Daughters*, even one that is concerned with examining the attitudes behind it, on too heavy a note. It is a novel that lives and will stay alive for the humour and sympathy in the description of characters, incidents and society through whom the author's view of life emerges. We enjoy it, and it moves us, for the same reasons that we enjoy or are moved by the novels of Jane Austen and George Eliot, although enjoyment and emotion are shaped to a different balance. Perhaps we may take the creation of Mrs. Gibson as Mrs. Gaskell's ironic salutation to the imperfect world that, in spite of the suffering it caused, gave her so much amusement to observe.

CHAPTER XIV

The Development of Technique: Form

W HEN Mrs. Gaskell wrote the biography of Charlotte Brontë she had an opportunity to play the critic, yet there is virtually no critical comment in the book, nor do her letters show much concern with theory. Charlotte Brontë's own comment on her has been often quoted:

Do you, who have so many friends—so large a circle of acquaintance—find it easy, when you sit down to write, to isolate yourself from all those ties, and their sweet associations, so as to be your *own woman*...[1]

It is a comment that reflects Mrs. Gaskell's own protestations as she began her career:

Women must give up living an artist's life, if home duties are to be paramount.[2]

and anyone who wishes to show that she was in fact a conscious artist with a fine control of her craft must admit that she lays herself open to adverse criticism in her protestations that being an author is a subsidiary and spare-time occupation. Yet she is not the dilettante that she makes out. There is a growing body of evidence to show that the Victorian novelists as a whole were careful and, at their best, inventive craftsmen in their work, and Mrs. Gaskell was no exception. It would be curious if she were. She wrote for nearly twenty years, was a friend of many of the

---

[1] *Life*, p. 615. Charlotte Brontë's italics
[2] Letter to Tottie Fox, *Haldane*, p. 249, where it is placed after a letter dated March, 1853. But a reference to Watts in a postscript would place it in the first half of 1850. The correspondence on G. H. Watts the artist in *Rylands*, pp. 14–19, makes this clear.

leading writers of her day, and had as her editors and publishers first Dickens and then Thackeray and George Smith.[3] It is difficult to see how she could have avoided discussing her work sometimes at the professional level. Some proof of her awareness can be deduced from her own comments, but the chief evidence must come from an examination of what and how she wrote. Thirty years ago David Cecil said of her:

> Her talent, too, is a Victorian talent, fertile, intuitive, uncritical. Her rambling, unequal, enthralling novels, full of providential chances and comic character-parts and true love rewarded in the last chapter, are typical Victorian novels.[4]

(although he goes on, curiously, to say that she is 'eminently an artist'). We can agree at least on one point; if the skill shown by Dickens, Thackeray, George Eliot and others is the standard, then she is typical of it. It was a high one.

While still talking in general terms we may turn back to the *Life* for initial confirmation of this view. Although Mrs. Gaskell refrained from criticism, she paused when she reached the stage where she had to deal with her friend—and subject—as author as well as individual, and wrote in a paragraph that is patently personal and heart-felt:

> Henceforward Charlotte Brontë's existence becomes divided into two parallel currents—her life as Currer Bell, the author; her life as Charlotte Brontë, the woman. There were separate duties belonging to each character—not opposing each other; not impossible, but difficult to be reconciled. When a man becomes an author, it is probably merely a change of employment to him . . . But no other can take up the quiet regular duties of the daughter, the wife, or the mother, as well as she whom God has appointed to fill that particular place: a woman's principal work in life is hardly left to her own choice; nor can she drop the domestic charges devolving on her as an individual, for the exercise of the most splendid talents that were ever bestowed. And yet she must not shrink from the extra responsibility implied by the very fact of her possessing such talents. She must not hide her gift in a napkin; it was meant for the use and service of others. In a humble and faithful

---

[3] Furthermore her husband and first adviser was a Professor of English. But this is a two-edged piece of evidence.   [4] op. cit., p. 199.

spirit must she labour to do what is not impossible, or God would not have set her to do it.[5]

She adds, 'I put into words what Charlotte Brontë put into actions', but she is rather putting into words her own feelings. In the biography she emphasizes her friend's domesticity and sense of duty, but she overstates the case here. There had been time and solitude for Charlotte Brontë to write in, as her own comment quoted earlier shows. It was Mrs. Gaskell who fretted at not being able to change her employment and who was yet determined not to 'shrink from the extra responsibility'. She was to make a practice of taking her talents away from home in order to exercise them free from domesticity.

In the first chapter I quoted the comment from 'Company Manners' in which she attacks writers who do not bother to 'acquire some expertness' in the art of telling a story. To study her novels is to see how she developed her own art. Most of her own comments are concerned with style rather than structure, yet the most interesting and subtle changes are in the structure and the narrative method. Like her great contemporaries she made form significant by careful thought and craftsmanship, changing it to suit her ends before ever the doctrine of significant form had been formulated.

Because Mrs. Gaskell shaped her fiction to express her themes, it has already been necessary to say a good deal about method. What follows will attempt to build on what has been previously said while tracing the development of her art. And just as a discussion of her thought involved considering her method, so an examination of the method will come back to the content it presents. Manner and matter derive eventually from the same creative impulse.

Structure and Pattern

When writing to Mrs. Greg about *Mary Barton*[6] Mrs. Gaskell reinforced her apologia by a long account of how the novel was written:

[5] *Life*, pp. 348–9.   [6] See ante, p. 131.

The whole tale grew up in my mind . . . imperceptibly . . . I can
remember now that the prevailing thought in my mind at the time
when the tale was silently forming itself and impressing me with the
force of a reality, was the seeming injustice of the inequalities of
fortune . . . I fancied I saw how all this might lead to a course of action
which might appear right for a time to the bewildered mind [of her
hero] but that this course of action, violating the eternal laws of God,
would bring with it its own punishment of an avenging conscience far
more difficult to bear than any wordly privation . . . [The book
originally formed itself round John Barton] . . . *the* person with whom
all my sympathies went, with whom I tried to identify myself at the
time . . . Mr. Greg has exactly described . . . the very treatment which
I am convinced is needed to bring such bewildered thinkers round
into an acknowledgment of the universality of some kind of suffering,
and the consequent necessity of its existence for some good end. . . .

[The novel was conceived and begun in illness and sorrow] . . . It
is no wonder then that the whole book seems to be written in a minor
key; indeed, the very design seems to me to require this treatment. I
acknowledge the fault of there being too heavy a shadow over the
book; but I doubt if the story could have been realized without these
shadows. The cause of the fault must be looked for in the design;
and yet the design was one worthy to be brought into consideration.

[The rest of the letter recounts her protest at having to add material
later—probably most of Chap. 37—to make up the required number of
pages.][7]

The question of purpose has already been dealt with, our concern
here must be with what Mrs. Gaskell calls the 'design'. It is an
ambiguous term, for it comprehends design as intention (i.e.
demonstration of the eternal laws) as well as structure; the two
are inseparable in her mind.[8] There are several interesting points
in the letter; the evidence of a creative imagination ('the whole
tale grew up in my mind') of identification with a character, and
of stylistic control (the 'minor key'). Of immediate relevance is
the evidence of conscious control ('how all this might lead to a
course of action'). The plot structure is developed as a vehicle for

[7] *Mary Barton*, pp. lxiii–lxiv.
[8] Paley's argument by design, when he compared the universe to a watch that proves a
maker, inevitably comes to mind. It was an argument often quoted in the heated theo-
logical discussions of the period.

the thematic structure, which is the moral pattern of the intention. The pattern is a linear one, not completed until the narrative itself is concluded, it is the pattern that also controls *Ruth*. Its broad features, the demonstration of retribution and reward and the movement towards understanding and reconciliation, are ones that occur consistently throughout Mrs. Gaskell's work. It is a pattern that is shaped by a moral vision and which allows expression to the various beliefs that go to make up that vision. But, and this must be emphasized, the vision is not straight-jacketed into a framework, we do not get a tract. 'The whole tale grew up,' the creative imagination is at work while the conscious control shapes the action and selects the style.

The original plan was in fact extensively modified and elaborated, as can be seen from a study of the rough sketch of the plot that Mrs. Gaskell drew up originally.[9] Apart from changing round the names of the two central families of the Wilsons and the Bartons (which makes the first reading of the outline a disconcerting experience), there have been radical changes in development and detail. The whole of the section covering the alibi and trial for example, more than a fifth of the book, seems to have grown out of a brief heading: 'How she proves an alibi by Margaret Clegg's help.' This entailed not merely the invention in detail of a major episode but the creation of the necessary plot clues long beforehand. The novel as we have it, though it retains the basic story and its pattern, is a work of the narrator's art.

The outline sketch also shows that the original conception was organized much more closely round John Barton's catastrophe, which is the pattern of an individual life confirming the existence of universal moral law. Although such a plot line, with its retribution and reward, can be found in all of Mrs. Gaskell's novels, it can be said to control only three of them, *Mary Barton*, *Ruth* and the later *Sylvia's Lovers*, in which we have seen that the balance of interests controlling the author's imagination was changing, and that the pattern had for once to be imposed. But there is another

[9] A transcript by Clement Shorter is in the Brotherton Library, 15 q., 10. See Appendix.

sense in which we can say that Mrs. Gaskell moves naturally towards a design within her structure, and this is in her inherently
powerful sense of contrast and balance. The early novels show
something of this in the way in which characters are contrasted,
Alice Wilson with Mrs. Wilson, Jem with young Carson, Mr.
Benson with Mr. Bradshaw. It first comes out fully in *North and
South* with its highly wrought pattern, and it creates its own
problems. That novel was, as we have seen, shaped from the beginning into a study of contrasts based on the feeling between
Margaret Hale and John Thornton. The plot acts like a zipper to
the two sides of the pattern, interlocking them while moving
forward. It cannot have the inevitability in its conclusion that
can be contrived for the history of one central character; we
know the two sides will come together at a convenient point, but
there seems no good reason why any particular point is chosen,
other than convenience or a desire to finish. The contrivance of
the conclusion is imposed on the pattern that the creative imagination has formed.[10]

In *Wives and Daughters* Mrs. Gaskell solves her problem by
synthesizing the two approaches, as she had synthesized her
interest and attitudes. The moral patterns are themselves balanced
and contrasted. The linear pattern is carried in the various histories
with their sequences of action and consequences. The conclusion
to Squire Hamley's history is a delicate balance of reconciliation
and merited retribution, equally so in its way is Cynthia's marriage. So we could go on; justice, moral justice, is seen to be done
to all, except for Mrs. Gibson who remains pattering on as Mr.
Gibson's retribution. Yet the framework which holds these histories presents a social pattern, in equilibrium; its representatives
keeping station while they suffer their individual fortunes. If we
are ever to talk about significant form, then *Wives and Daughters*,
for all its apparently casual manner, must be considered as an
early and excellent example.

[10] Mrs. Gaskell claims in her preface that the pressures of serialization spoilt the end, in
spite of amplification in the book version. Yet she had wanted to add even another
balancing element with its sub-plot (see Chap. 8). I cannot believe that Mrs. Gaskell could
have rounded off her conception naturally at that stage of her development, she sees the
conclusion but has to jump to reach it.

The Moral Pivot

When Miss Benson suggests that Ruth 'be passed off as a widow', the author interrupts the action to comment:

Ah, tempter! unconscious tempter! Here was a way of evading the trials for the poor little unborn child, of which Mr. Benson had never thought. It was the decision—the pivot, on which the fate of years moved; and he turned it the wrong way.[11]

She adopts the term 'pivot' for a device which she was to use many times to set the pattern of the action; many times, as in *Ruth*, it is a moral pivot, controlling both the moral pattern and the plot. Ruth's early history and seduction are the necessary introduction on which the plot structure can be raised; the drama of discovery and consequence is inevitable from the moment of the pivotal decision.

This early and conscious example contains the essential qualities of the moral pivot as Mrs. Gaskell often used it. The decision *is* a moral one (to acquiesce in a lie and a deception). The motives behind the decision are not necessarily bad (to save Ruth from public censure and her child from a bastard's position) but at the same time they lead to an evasion of the duty to accept the consequences for an action (on Benson's part of sheltering a 'fallen woman', on Ruth's part of facing her shame) and betray an element of selfishness. Furthermore the decision is not made by the main character but the consequences fall chiefly on her. The use of the moral pivot is easily recognizable in much of Mrs. Gaskell's work, though its position in the plot may vary. In *North and South* it is placed early in Mr. Hale's decision to leave the church and Helstone, it is relatively early in *Wives and Daughters*, in Mr. Gibson's decision to marry and solve the problem of Molly. In *Mary Barton* and *Sylvia's Lovers* it is more centrally pivotal; the circumstances which lead up to Barton's agreement to murder must be presented, while a full presentation of character and background precedes Philip's decision to keep quiet about the press-ganging of Kinraid. But in each case the decision, once taken,

[11] *Ruth*, p. 121. The sentence reads as though the pivot was turned, an abnormal use of the word—unless it is 'the fate of years' that is turned.

locks the pattern into position, demonstrating not simply that actions have consequences but also that they carry a heavy responsibility for the lives of others who may be affected by them. Each pivot moreover is germane to its particular context. In *Ruth* we are reminded by the author's comment that morality is linked to sin, for although the tempter is immediately Faith Benson, the very word suggests that Satan is near by. Barton's decision is similarly accompanied by religious apostrophization. In two cases, those of Manasseh Hickson's demand that Lois marry him and of Philip's decision, sin and sexuality are linked together, whereas Paul's impulsive decision to tell Phillis that Holdsworth loves her is purely an emotional one, reflecting his inexperience. The 'morality' activating the pivot changes with the interests activating the novels.

Plot

It would have been impossible to handle this type of inter-relation between theme and plot structure without a more than ordinarily capable command of plot construction and a correspondingly fertile imagination for story and incident. Invention came easily to Mrs. Gaskell, she puts into Faith Benson's mouth her own mock apologia:

I do think I've a talent for fiction, it is so pleasant to invent, and make the incidents dovetail together; and after all, if we are to tell a lie, we may as well do it thoroughly, or else it's of no use.[12]

Mrs. Gaskell took to fiction as to the manner born. Her progress can be seen as partly a long education in curbing and controlling to her needs a facility for the invention or appropriation of incident, particularly of the dramatic type, and subordinating it to the analysis of character, emotion, or relationships. One suspects that her short stories often acted as a safety-valve for a melodramatic streak. She began dramatically enough, her ideas possibly coloured by the popularity of the sensation novel and certainly affected by the new and thrilling art of detection. She wrote one of the early articles in praise of 'the Detective Police' and noted that:

[12] *Ruth*, p. 149.

there could be no more romances written on the same kind of plot as Caleb Williams; the principal interest of which, to the superficial reader, consists in the alternation of hope and fear, that the hero may, or may not, escape his pursuer.[13]

She was wrong, of course; cops and robbers carry on an eternal chase, although now it is the hero (mainly) who pursues; the detective story is the modern morality. But she was forecasting her own future. Such adventures were not to be her staple. *Mary Barton* was luckily written before she consigned the chase to oblivion; for a hundred pages we follow Mary in pursuit of the witness who will prove her lover innocent, down the river after the boat that is carrying him away, while:

full of the spirit of the chase, though as yet ignorant of Mary's motives, the men sprung to hoist another sail.[14]

and watch him burst into the court-room in the nick of time. Nothing quite so exciting or self-contained as an episode appears again in the novels, if we except the complete digression of story-within-a-story in *My Lady Ludlow*, but scenes of high drama still occur. Margaret flings herself in front of Thornton to save him from the rioters, Daniel leads the destruction of the press-gang's headquarters, but such incidents although dramatic have not the self-justifying element of sheer excitement that was worked into the first novel, where murder, fire and rescue are the prelude. Mrs. Gaskell turns more and more to analysis. By the end, in *Wives and Daughters*, there is little of such drama left.[15] The villain, if he is impressive enough to deserve the name, has his share in the minor mystery, but is tamed on an evening walk by the threat of being reported to his employer.

The love of a mystery remained, however, even though melodrama was relegated. *Mary Barton* qualifies also as an early detective story, complete with false clues, circumstantial evidence, wrongful arrest and an alibi. Typically the mystery is not kept long from the reader, but an element of suspense is involved in the

---

[13] 'Disappearances' (1851), *Cranford*, p. 412.   [14] *Mary Barton*, p. 342.
[15] But it still appears in her more off-hand work. 'Crowley Castle' has murder, jealousy, revenge, dissipation, remorse and passion as its ingredients.

nature of its solution. In *Ruth* we wait to see how the heroine's secret will be revealed, and whether her seducer will be able to harm her. The detective reappears in *North and South* with Frederick Hale's return and the mysterious death of the threatening porter. We have Kinraid's disappearance in *Sylvia's Lovers*, while in *Wives and Daughters* there is not only Cynthia's guarded secret but that of Osborne's wife. These are examples of a mystery used to create or promote action in the plot, and to give us the suspense of 'when' or 'how', with Mrs. Gaskell laying the clues with care. If we turn to her shorter fiction we find the interest clearly marked in such stories as 'The Squire's Story' (a straight detective story), 'The Poor Clare', 'The Manchester Marriage' and the long suspense of 'A Dark Night's Work'. The creation of a mystery, with its effect on those involved, becomes an element in the moral pattern. When Margaret Hale lies to Thornton about her brother, it is to preserve the necessary secrecy about his being in England, but the lie works against her after the need for secrecy has gone. Cynthia Kirkpatrick's case is an even clearer one; her whole life is one of deception and misery that cannot be lifted until the mystery that is the cause— the promise to Preston—is cleared up.

The gradual disappearance of coincidence as a spring to release action is another sign that motivation and conduct were becoming steadily more dependent on character and natural circumstance. It is only too easy to point out the workings of coincidence, to ask why Ruth's lover must return, why Thornton has to ride by the station to see Margaret and Frederick and why the porter should be one of Frederick's crew, why Philip should see Kinraid captured and then hear gossip about him every time he is prepared to reveal what happened. Coincidence is a staple of the beginner, and some is necessary in any action, but clumsy chance is less and less obvious as Mrs. Gaskell gains control of her medium. In *Wives and Daughters* there is only the blurting out of Osborne's marriage when Molly is present, which hardly affects the action but is used to give the reader a piece of necessary information.

Nor was the progress of 'the whole tale' affected by the

demands of serial publication. Even though, of the works we have been considering, *Cranford, North and South*, 'Lois the Witch'. *Cousin Phillis* and *Wives and Daughters* appeared serially, they were not conceived as serials. Mrs. Gaskell had produced two full-length novels before she was induced to agree to serial publication for *North and South*, which has already been discussed at some length. It would be untrue to say that she altogether ignored the realities of serialization. The MS. of 'Lois the Witch' is headed 'Lois the Witch/Part 1st', and in the top left-hand corner is added 'In 3 parts', the three sections each being numbered afresh from 1. But they have respectively 25, 33, and 58 pages, hardly a concession to editorial planning, and they follow the natural stages of Lois's life.[16] Nor do the episodes pay much attention to that other aspect of serial publication 'which normally demands an "effect" of some sort at each monthly fall of the curtain',[17] they close undramatically but appropriately. *Cousin Phillis* has four sections for the four numbers of the *Cornhill* which similarly mark stages in the story without any sense of climax. In the 'nouvelles', with the distinct technique that the shorter form calls for, such stages are more naturally and necessarily marked, but the movement is still a quietly continuous flow rather than a series of climaxes. In the long novels, with their common pattern of introduction and development, it is hardly possible to point to one rather than another as having been written for serialization.

The continuity and cumulative effect of time, with its accompanying stream of experience, is a positive feature in Mrs. Gaskell's work, although she does not consciously manipulate it, and for a creator of elaborately detailed plots she is peculiarly unable to follow time through the calendar. She is not happy with actual dates, she does not visualize the actual passing of days and hours as Jane Austen did; even when she works from the archive material for *Sylvia's Lovers* the dating sequence is impossible.

[16] The MS. is in the Houghton Library, Harvard University. It was not written for Dickens (the last section may have been meant as a double one), but it was published in *AYR* in its three sections.
[17] From *Fraser's* review of *Vanity Fair*, 1848, quoted in G. Tillotson, *Thackeray the Novelist*, C.U.P., 1954, p. 23.

She sees change but is not concerned to mark it off on the calendar; she is aware of the process of dissolution and alteration, of the perspective of tradition; the social historian in her is sensitive to the fact that society and manners and conduct alter with it. So 'Morton Hall' begins with the statement:

Our old Hall is to be pulled down, and they are going to build streets on the site.

and moves backwards and forwards over two hundred years to its conclusion:

the street they are going to build right through the rooms through which Alice Carr was dragged . . . is to be called Carr Street.[18]

which creates a continuity even in destruction. We recall the opening of *Ruth*, of the *Life*, of *Mary Barton*. Mrs. Gaskell is as intensely aware of time's continuum as any novelist. This is no less so when she concentrates on the 'present' of a novel, she sees her characters moving along and being altered by time's stream. We find therefore that it is always clearly marked, but as periods of development rather than as segments of a calendar. The seasons as they pass are sometimes her measure, as in *Cousin Phillis*, sometimes historical or social events are used, and always there is the growth of the heroine to maturity as a gauge of innocence and experience. The eternal laws reveal themselves on earth, in time, but:

reckoning time by events and thoughts, and not by clock or dial-plate.[19]

Narrative Method

Mrs. Gaskell begins as a moralizing author who is prepared to step forward and point the moral, as an author who intervenes to tell us how we should interpret a character or an action. She proceeds, in other words, by the method of authorial commentary, using the novel as a screen behind which she could speak, as she admitted to Furnivall when asked to support by public letter the protest at Maurice's dismissal from King's College:

[18] *Cranford*, pp. 446 and 488–9.   [19] *Mary Barton*, p. 389.

I could not—physically *could* not, I believe, speak out more than a blurting sentence of abuse, tantamount to the box on the ear,—a "That's a downright falsehood," I might say,—or even *worse*, not *more*. It is different when speaking as the character in a story—or even as the author of a book. Do you think I cᵈ say or write in a letter (except one that I was sure would be regarded as private by some dear friend) what I have said both in Mary Barton and Ruth. It may seem strange and I can't myself account for it—but it *is* so.[20]

She ends by withdrawing almost completely from the narrative, her authorial omniscience reserved with few exceptions for the task of unfolding the story. I have already drawn attention to the way in which the Cranford world demanded another, more intimate and personal narrator; there is something more to be said of this. But we need to know also how she handled what was then the standard technique of commentary before we can see clearly how she fuses the two types of narration in *Wives and Daughters*.

In the novels of religious and social purpose she steps in as author to augment what the characters can themselves say, at the same time identifying herself with the reader, and both herself and the reader with humanity at large, with comments such as:

He was like too many of us: he did not place his future life in the hands of God . . .[21]

Many examples of exhortation or moral lesson have been given in previous chapters, and this point I shall not labour. My concern is with the extent to which this authorial presence persists.

The example just given is from a later novel; the comment is cast into a form which assumes, and therefore helps to create, a sense of common ground for the reader and the author, who has stepped humbly back to be one of 'us'. The author as commentator separates herself in this way from the more impersonal author

[20] Letter to F. J. Furnivall dated 9 Dec. 1853, Huntington Library, ref. FU.312. Frederick Dennison Maurice (the son of a Unitarian minister) was dismissed in 1853 from his post as Professor of English at King's College, London, because of unorthodox views on eternal punishment. The 'abuse' would be for Maurice's opponents. In a later letter (FU.314) she agrees to collect signatures for a testimonial.
[21] *Sylvia's Lovers*, p. 187.

as narrator, the one who talks about 'he'. But the narrator's voice in the early work is that of the story teller talking to her audience, eager to strike up a personal relationship:

> I must tell you; I must put into words the dreadful secret which she believed that bit of paper had revealed to her.
> Her father was the murderer.[22]

Or she adopts the tone of familiar knowledge and shared background, with the artless air of passing on a story or a piece of gossip that suggests equality of experience in the reader as well as understanding:

> I need not tell you how the mother spent the weary hours. But yet I will tell you something.[23]

This is probably the most naïve form of narrative comment, and disappears from her work as she gains control of her medium, although the sense of human kinship is maintained by the occasional statement such as:

> you, reader, I, writer, have each our great sorrow bearing down on us.[24]

The omniscient author remains, however, to take short cuts in explanation:

> There is always something aggravating in being told, that the mood in which we are now viewing things strongly will not be our mood at some other time . . . Mr. Bradshaw was not soothed by this last remark of Mr. Benson's.[25]

explanation which can move through a generalization on human nature into an item of character analysis that moves us back into the main stream of the narration. Such generalizations on humanity and society persist to the end, brief observations which are the irreducible minimum of comment that Mrs. Gaskell could not dispense with, which are part of her flavour, often used briefly to illuminate a scene which does not permit of expansion, as

---

[22] *Mary Barton*, p. 282.   [23] 'Lizzie Leigh', *Cranford*, p. 214.
[24] 'A Dark Night's Work', *Cousin Phillis*, p. 434.   [25] *Ruth*, p. 402.

when the labourer's daughter-in-law has told Squire Hamley that the man is dying:

Poor people acknowledge the inevitableness and the approach of death in a much more straightforward manner than is customary among the more educated. The Squire was shocked at her hardheartedness . . .[26]

The easy style and tone is that of the observer, not the moralist, and unless we are too rigidly conditioned by the twentieth-century reaction against direct authorial comment, the ease and illumination of such remarks are part of the attraction Mrs. Gaskell has to offer.

She remains also consciously in control of the progress of her narrative, although unobtrusively and for the most part impersonally so, giving as much as possible of its development over to dialogue. The length of *Wives and Daughters* is partly due to the fact that we spend so much time listening to what people have to say, and how they say it. But she is prepared to be forthright when necessary, though skilful in her manner:

Molly grew up among these quiet people in calm monotony of life, without any greater event than that which has been recorded—the being left behind at the Towers—until she was nearly seventeen.[27]

The reference back is made to connect with the new events, and to introduce a new aspect of the Towers in Lord Hollingford's relationship to Mr. Gibson. 'Time passes' in a quietly workmanlike way. But at one time she openly admits her problem and her method while revealing a detachment from her creation:

These changes in humour and disposition, here described all at once, were in themselves a series of delicate alterations of relative conduct spread over many months—many winter months of long evenings and bad weather, which bring out discords of character, as a dash of cold water brings out the fading colours of an old fresco.[28]

We can see her beginning to stand away from her work and her readers in this fashion in *Sylvia's Lovers*, when the analysis of con-

---

[26] *Wives and Daughters*, p. 388.   [27] ibid., p. 38.   [28] ibid., p. 482.

duct and feeling began to be the major interest. She turns there to look at the characters she has created:

At this hour, all the actors in this story having played out their parts and gone to their rest, there is something touching in recording the futile efforts made by Philip to win from Sylvia the love he yearned for.[29]

or she can address them direct from the observer-commentator's height:

Ay! go in to the warm hearth, mother and child, now the gay cavalcade has gone out of sight, and the chill of night has succeeded to the sun's setting! Husband and father, steal out into the cold dark street, and seek some poor cheap lodging where you may rest your weary bones, and cheat your more weary heart into forgetfulness in sleep! The pretty story of the Countess Phillis, who mourned for her husband's absence so long, is a fable of old times; or rather say, Earl Guy never wedded his wife, knowing that one she loved better than him was alive all the time she had believed him to be dead.[30]

Such comments are exceptional. They suggest, with some allowance for the rhetoric which opens the second one, the voice of Thackeray, and his influence is a probable one. It may be more than coincidental that the girl Kinraid marries went to a school run by a Miss Dobbin, and that the selfish and handsome heir of Squire Hamley is called Osborne. Mrs. Gaskell admired him and was moving into the *Cornhill* influence, though it is possible that his manner is also transmitted through Charlotte Brontë.[31] The fact that they occur at all is a mark of her growing awareness of the process of creation.

The use of the observer within the action has been traced from *Cranford* (although the slightly earlier story of 'Mr. Harrison's Confessions' shows by its use of a narrator 'hero' that the process of identification had begun), but it was a method that imposed itself gradually. The first paper of *Cranford* looks backward in method and tone to the discursive eighteenth-century essayist of

[29] *Sylvia's Lovers*, p. 141.
[30] ibid., p. 497. Did this suggest the title name for *Cousin Phillis?*
[31] 'A new chapter in a novel is something like a new scene in a play, and when I draw up the curtain this time, you must fancy . . .' (*Jane Eyre*, World's Classics, 1955, p. 107) and 'You expected bread, and you have got a stone; break your teeth on it, and don't shriek because the nerves are martyrized . . .' (*Shirley*, World's Classics, 1947, p. 103).

manners, appropriately for the old-fashioned society described; the 'I' of the narrator is the friendly and ironic descendent of Mr. Tatler, of an age with the people she describes and talking of them as an equal. Imperceptibly this 'I' changes. Miss Jenkyns dies, the years pass, but the narrator grows younger; she becomes dependent on a father for permission to visit her friends; she becomes the 'poor girl! she did her best I've no doubt,'[32] who brought the 'pretty, neat, middle-aged cap'[33] which disappointed Miss Matty. She takes on an identity, introducing herself three-quarters of the way through the series and explaining her presence:

I must say a word or two here about myself. I have spoken of my father's old friendship for the Jenkyns family; indeed, I am not sure if there was not some distant relationship.[34]

finally to answer to the name of Mary Smith when the long-lost Peter returns. The objective narrator has arrived. Such a character should not however be confused with the type of narrator that Isherwood imagined as a camera. Mary Smith, who sets a precedent for those that follow, is one with the group she describes, her sympathies are actively involved, but she can stand sufficiently apart from the central issues to report them clearly, her own views and comments touching the narrative with irony.

It was a method natural to the social observer and easily developed to deal with a range of people and emotions by altering the character and interests of the narrator. It was used for articles and for occasional stories, such as 'Morton Hall' and 'My French Master', and when the major effort of the *Life* was called for, Mrs. Gaskell adopted it naturally, leaving characters to speak for themselves in their letters and quietly describing background or linking the narrative together with little direct intervention. By the time of *My Lady Ludlow* the narrator is fully introduced as a character. Margaret Dawson is established in her own right and has a story of her own. With *Cousin Phillis* the narrator has become a major character. Paul Manning is catalyst to the action as well as observer, his own mind and feelings are important. Mrs. Gaskell has moved from the observer to the central intelligence.

[32] *Cranford*, p. 99.   [33] ibid., p. 98.   [34] ibid., p. 141.

Wives and Daughters, as I have pointed out, was far too complicated and too long to be narrated in the first person. The omniscient author controls it, starting it off and setting the tone of easy and comfortable familiarity:

> To begin with the old rigmarole of childhood. In a country there was a shire, and in that shire there was a town, and in that town . . . and in that bed there lay a little girl.[35]

The moralist however is almost entirely absent, even the social historian as commentator is very much in the background; the author as narrator moves the story calmly along, supplying background, setting scenes, introducing characters, but keeping her personality out. To supply the standard and provide a consistent viewpoint from within the novel we have, fully developed, the 'fine central intelligence' that was to become a feature of Henry James's technique. Not surprisingly James had admired *Wives and Daughters*, and before he had himself set up as a novelist had drawn attention to 'The gentle skill with which the reader is slowly involved in the tissue of the story.'[36]

Mrs. Gaskell did not control her 'central intelligence' as rigidly as James was to in his later novels; her treatment of Molly is closer to the idea that James applied to *The Portrait of a Lady*, where he was concerned about 'positively organising an ado about Isabel Archer,'[37] and retrospectively analysed why he came to see the need to concentrate on:

> the view of her relation to those surrounding her. Make it predominantly a view of *their* relation and the trick [of avoiding too direct a concentration on the heroine] is played . . . "Place the centre of the subject in the young woman's own consciousness," I said to

---

[35] *Wives and Daughters*, p. 1.
[36] op. cit., p. 153. One wonders whether a phrase in the novel stuck in his mind. Molly we learn is 'Seventeen. Its a very awkward age for a motherless girl.' (p. 114.) The phrase is used again in a precise context by the precocious Cynthia, about herself and her mother: 'As soon as the holidays came round, she was off to some great house or another; and I daresay I was at a very awkward age for her to have me lounging about in a drawing-room, when callers came. Girls at the age I was then are so terribly keen at scenting out motives . . . they've no distinct notion of what are the truths and falsehoods of polite life.' (p. 545.) This is the basic situation of James's *The Awkward Age*.
[37] *The Art of the Novel*, Charles Scribner's Sons, 1950, p. 48.

myself . . . Stick to *that*—for the centre; put the heaviest weight into *that* scale, which will be so largely the scale of her relation to herself. Make her only interested enough, at the same time, in the things that are not herself, and this relation need n't fear to be too limited.[38]

I am not of course claiming that Mrs. Gaskell approached a novel, as James did, looking for interesting difficulties; my point is that in creating a form to contain Molly Gibson and the themes that wove themselves into the total vision, she found and successfully used a method that enables us to quote from his theory to describe a key feature.

In the process of developing the appropriate method for this, Mrs. Gaskell's most complex novel, the 'I' of the first person narrator is merged with the author's narrative omniscience. By the use of an oblique form of interior monologue that shades from third person to first person and back, we share Molly's feelings and thoughts while following Mrs. Gaskell's analysis of them in one continuous process. It is a method that develops from the close description of thought and feeling, the sense of identification, that was present from the start; we can see it coming into use in *North and South*:

Margaret turned to the envelope: it was marked "Too late." The letter had probably been trusted to some careless waiter, who had forgotten to post it. Oh! what slight cobwebs of chances stand between us and Temptation! Frederick had been safe, and out of England twenty, nay, thirty hours ago; and it was only about seventeen hours since she had told a falsehood to baffle pursuit, which even then would have been vain. How faithless she had been![39]

The narrator begins the description, but it concentrates on Margaret's reactions; only the pronoun 'us' in the first exclamation indicates that the author has come in with a generalization; while the 'she' of the second exclamation is as much Margaret's as the author's. In each case the sudden change to speech-like exclamation identifies it with the train of Margaret's thought that surrounds it. By the time of *Wives and Daughters* this type of oblique monologue is used consistently and for relatively long

[38] *The Art of the Novel*, p. 51.   [39] *North and South*, p. 339.

stretches, as in the scene where Molly learns of Osborne's marriage, of which the following passage is a small part:

These and similar speeches had given Molly the impression of the future Mrs. Osborne as some beautiful, grand young lady . . . Osborne too, who had spoken with such languid criticism to Mrs. Gibson about various country belles, and even in his own home was apt to give himself airs—only at home his airs were poetically fastidious, while with Mrs. Gibson they had been socially fastidious—what unspeakably elegant beauty had he chosen for his wife? Who had satisfied him, and yet, satisfying him, had to have her marriage kept in concealment from his parents? At length Molly tore herself up from her wonderings. It was of no use: she could not find out . . .[40]

The author is present to indicate stages in Molly's reflection, but for most of the time is so closely identified with Molly's disturbed mind that its uneven flow takes over the structure of the English and its direct questions mingle with the stream of thought. Mrs. Gaskell has slipped into Molly's consciousness and speaks from it. Sometimes she will use the same device for another character as the viewpoint shifts, and the centre of interest moves away for the time from Molly; this shift of viewpoint and its accompanying comment is one of the chief sources of Mrs. Gaskell's irony. The result is that we are fully in possession of emotions as well as facts as the relationships develop; in each episode the reader can draw his own conclusions. Our attitude is obviously controlled in other ways also, by the style and by the selection of events and characters presented. But as far as the reader's relation to characters and incident is concerned, the author rarely interferes. Once indeed she comes in with a quick thrust at slanted narration when she comments on Molly's embarrassment at having to tell the Misses Browning of her visit to the Towers while conscious of her step-mother's 'critical listening':

She had to tell it all with a mental squint; the surest way to spoil a narration.[41]

In making these claims for a controlling art that moulds the structure of Mrs. Gaskell's work, and that develops to accom-

[40] *Wives and Daughters*, p. 243.   [41] *Wives and Daughters*, p. 726.

modate her changing purpose as a novelist, I cannot claim that every step and every practice had been deliberated upon; I would be very surprised if that were the case. It is possible to show however that we are dealing with a writer who is aware of her craft and whose achievement is based on a conscious practice of it. This consciousness is far easier to demonstrate where style is concerned.

CHAPTER XV

The Development of Technique: Style

THE development of the novelist is reflected interestingly in her use of language, although it would give a wrong impression to talk simply of a development in style. The novelist of the Manchester world moves immediately into dialect, while the novelist of the Cranford world records the accents of educated and genteel English. The distinction is obviously not clear cut, as the narrative element of the dialect novels is written in educated English while even in *Wives and Daughters* a small dialect stratum survives in the speech and invitation notes of Mrs. Goodenough and her circle. It is easier and more accurate to think of Mrs. Gaskell as a writer who uses 'appropriate language'[1] rather than as a conscious stylist, in spite of her great interest in words and usage. Her style can be compared within its own range to Wordsworth's. It can be flat and undistinguished when energy and imagination fail to fill it, can become ludicrous when the writer strains for effect, or allows sentiment to escape the scrutiny of observation or thought. But also, like Wordsworth's, it can achieve a surprising fitness and effectiveness when the author's imaginative power and creative energy fill it. In *Cranford*, 'Lois the Witch' and *Cousin Phillis*, different as those stories are from each other, we could not imagine or wish them written otherwise. *Cranford* probably owes something to being written without strain and without the pressure of a publication date, in episodes when the author felt like writing. The other two are

---

[1] I borrow the term from Professor Quirk, whose inaugural lecture on 'Charles Dickens and Appropriate Language' (Univ. of Durham, 1959) covers much ground in a few pages. I give the term a slightly different use for my purpose.

'nouvelles', a form in which she could sustain a creative effort without flagging. But when she was not on form, or when her stamina came under strain, the style could flag. Only in the *Life of Charlotte Brontë*, when a sustained creative spell was inspired by personal sympathy and a desire to know and present the truth, does the style hold out at its best over a long work. Yet in its own way *Wives and Daughters* is also successful. There has been criticism of its style even by those who admire it, and it is in fact fairly easy to point to weaknesses. Yet much of this criticism seems to me to be misplaced, for the easy, sometimes gossipy and seemingly every-day prose is appropriate to the tale being told, heightening only when the emotional level rises.

To think in terms of appropriate language helps to explain the non-dialect as well as the dialect work. It emphasizes Mrs. Gaskell's awareness that all forms of English, particularly of spoken English, whether those of a Lady Ludlow or a Bessy Higgins, are 'dialects'. This awareness of the varieties and social distinctions revealed by the use of language crops up constantly in references throughout her work, such as the one she puts into the mouth of Philip when he answers Sylvia's complaints about the hard road to literacy:

"I'm sure I wish the man were farred who plagues his brains wi' striking out new words. Why can't folks just ha' a set on 'em for good and a'?"
"Why! you'll be after using two or three hundred yoursel' every day as you live, Sylvie; and yet I must use a great many as you never think on about t' shop; and t' folks in t' fields want their set, let alone the high English that parsons and lawyers speak.[2]

When considered as appropriate language the use of dialect falls into its place in Mrs. Gaskell's development as a novelist, reflecting the shift of her interest away from the Manchester world along with her sociologist's observation of the features which dis-tinguish social groups from each other.

The way in which dialect is used demands a closer look, but it must be thought of in relation to the use of her natural style, which needs to be considered first. This is to be found most

[2] *Sylvia's Lovers*, pp. 113–14.

obviously in her essays when she speaks in her own person, but it is also the prose of the narrative element in her novels. Its distinguishing register[3] is that of informative ease, the note of an intelligent but unpedantic observer. It is the note of the 'salon' and of educated gossip that she admired in the letters of Mme de Sévigné, whose biography she had hoped one day to write. It is the note she ascribes to Bellingham when he comes to Eccleston as Mr. Donne; anticipating linguistic definition in the way she separates the tone of his breeding from outward signs of wealth and rank:

It was nothing like this; it was something indescribable—a quiet being at ease, and expecting every one else to be so—an attention to women, which was so habitual as to be unconsciously exercised to those subordinate persons in Mr. Bradshaw's family—a happy choice of simple and expressive words, some of which it must be confessed were slang, but fashionable slang, and that makes all the difference—a measured, graceful way of utterance, with a style of pronunciation quite different to that of Eccleston. All these put together make but a part of the indescribable whole which unconsciously affected Mr. Bradshaw . . .[4]

A more stylistic description of this ideal, one that points back to *Cranford*, is found in her praise of a fragment of Branwell Brontë's work, whose characters she describes as drawn:

in perfectly pure and simple language which distinguishes so many of Addison's papers in the 'Spectator.'[5]

while her view of language as individual expression is implicit in her criticism of Mrs. Gibson's speech, whose words:

were always like ready-made clothes, and never fitted individual thoughts.[6]

Her style reflects her sense of good manners in the relationship between author, subject and reader. Sometimes, as in the *Life*, she is more serious, the biography demanding a certain touch of

---

[3] I use 'register' in the technical sense it has in linguistics, to indicate the social relationship which is reflected in the use of language, e.g. of teacher to pupil. Linguistics also uses 'style' in a limited sense, but this limited use can create difficulty and I therefore use 'style' in its generally accepted sense.

[4] *Ruth*, p. 259.   [5] *Life*, p. 185.   [6] *Wives and Daughters*, p. 355.

solemnity or emotion appropriate to the story it has to tell, just as it calls naturally for the full range of vocabulary of the educated biographer. In other cases, as when Paul Manning narrates *Cousin Phillis*, the language is simpler, its overtones those of the speech appropriate to narrator and setting. The author behaves, linguistically, according to the situation. One need hardly add that success depends on the situation being one that the author can behave naturally in.

This relationship to behaviour is clearly marked in 'Company Manners', an essay where comments on social behaviour include scattered remarks which amount to as near a statement of Mrs. Gaskell's general aims as a writer as we have. I have already quoted her comments on the obligations of a narrator; another comment discusses the sense of being at ease. Noting that some people 'put on their agreeableness with their gowns,' she finds that certain people are:

more pleasant in society in their second-best than in their very best dresses . . . With their best gowns they put on an unusual fineness of language; they say "commence" instead of "begin;" they inquire if they may "assist," instead of asking if they may "help" you to any-thing.[7]

One tendency of Mrs. Gaskell's work is steadily away from an 'unusual fineness.'

This basic narrative style, which is to be distinguished from the prose of the author as moralist or commentator, and to some extent from that of a narrative character, is adequate without being remarkable; it does not obtrude while its flow carries the reader smoothly along. In the prose of connecting narrative these are virtues, but they can lead to faults. The chief of these is that fluency is not checked by sufficient control; her style sometimes needed pruning and more care taken over its vocabulary. Mrs. Gaskell admits to having 'a very runaway kind of mind,'[8] it is reflected in the flow of detail and the temptation, too often un-resisted, to accept the handiest word or phrase instead of searching for something more fitting or less hackneyed. The following

[7] 'Company Manners', *Ruth*, p. 506.   [8] *Letters*, p. 12.

Mrs. Gaskell

extract from *Sylvia's Lovers*, written when she was experienced
and claimed to be taking particular care, demonstrates these
points:

It was different with Sylvia. She was going to choose her first cloak:
not to have an old one of her mother's, that had gone down through two
sisters, dyed for the fourth time (and Molly would have been glad had
even this chance been hers), but to buy a bran-new duffle cloak all for
herself, with not even an elder authority to curb her as to price, only
Molly to give her admiring counsel, and as much sympathy as was consistent with a little patient envy of Sylvia's happier circumstances.
Every now and then they wandered off from the one grand subject of
thought; but Sylvia, with unconscious art, soon brought the conversation round to the fresh consideration of the respective merits of grey
and scarlet. These girls were walking bare-foot and carrying their shoes
and stockings in their hands during the first part of their way; but as
they were drawing near Monkshaven they stopped, and turned aside
along a foot-path that led from the main-road down to the banks of the
Dee. There were great stones in the river about here, round which the
waters gathered and eddied and formed deep pools. Molly sate down
on the grassy bank to wash her feet; but Sylvia, more active (or perhaps
lighter-hearted with the notion of the cloak in the distance), placed her
basket on a gravelly bit of shore, and, giving a long spring, seated herself on a stone almost in the middle of the stream. Then she began
dipping her little rosy toes in the cold rushing water and whisking them
out with childish glee.[9]

It flows easily, carrying the reader on, but there is a monotony in
the repetitive construction, with its pattern of statement and extension, and the contrast of the 'but' repeated four times. The
detail creates the scene, but the descriptions—adjectives and
phrases—are not precise. The simplicity of scene and character
is blurred by the formal clichés of educated language such as 'elder
authority,' 'was consistent,' 'fresh consideration of their respective
merits,' while when a simple freshness is tried for it appears as the
sentimental cliché of 'little rosy toes.'

Such narrative sequences rarely continue for many pages, Mrs.
Gaskell relies greatly on dialogue. But when they come they may
pay for their ease by a slackening of attention in the reader as he

[9] *Sylvia's Lovers*, pp. 12–13.

drifts on to the next scene, and a consequent lowering of tension or interest.

The style alters with the relationship of the novelist to the story. The informative, descriptive ease develops firmness and factual authority when she slips into the vein of the social historian, while as moralist or commentator she sometimes steps forward with a conscious rhetoric that draws on the style of the pulpit, and stands out sharply from the unobtrusive run of the narrative:

To whom shall the outcast prostitute tell her tale? Who will give her help in the day of need? Here is the leper-sin, and all stand aloof dreading to be counted unclean.[10]

But this note, with its overtones of sermon or of the Bible, dies away as the novels cease to be vehicles for indignation or exhortation; the last echoes sound in *Sylvia's Lovers*.

A more serious weakness has already been mentioned in earlier chapters. Mrs. Gaskell fails, sometimes grotesquely, when she tries to convey the actual force of passionate emotion or dramatic intensity, instead of observing the behaviour it causes. It is a peculiar limitation, for she can write powerfully as long as she remains objective. There are few novelists who could have described the scene of misery in the Davenports' basement with the controlled effectiveness of detail that she shows in *Mary Barton*, or could have etched with such quiet sympathy Lady Ludlow's grief at the death of her last son. But when she tries to show the actual magnitude of Higgins's grief for his daughter's death, she loses touch with reality. The image created is ludicrous:

throwing his body half across the table, he shook it and every piece of furniture in the room, with his violent sobs.[11]

The passion of Thornton, proposing and being refused, produces another ludicrous image dressed in cliché:

He held her hand tight in his. He panted as he listened for what should come. He threw the hand away with indignation as he heard her icy tone.[12]

[10] *Mary Barton*, p. 182.   [11] *North and South*, p. 260.   [12] ibid., p. 231.

I have said that in drawing Margaret Hale she drew a heroine for a love story without at the time having interest in or insight into young love. The result is an abstraction to match the one quoted from Mrs. Henry Wood:

She sat facing him and facing the light; her full beauty met his eye; her round white flexile throat rising out of the full, yet lithe figure; her lips, moving so slightly as she spoke, not breaking the cold serene look of her face with any variation from the one lovely haughty curve; her eyes, with their soft gloom, meeting his with quiet maiden freedom.[13]

Fashions in beauty and description have changed, but it is reliance on cliché and stereotype, not change of fashion, that kills the description for a modern reader.

In these quotations we see Mrs. Gaskell out of her depth, writing of what she has either not observed or not felt, and without the self-criticism or stylistic sensitivity that would have made her visualize what she had described. *North and South* is a more artificial novel than her others, it is true; for that reason the faults inherent in her style show up more clearly. Her final work to a great extent creates a strength from her limitations. The description of Molly has already been given; we can add the description of her grief when she hears of her father's impending marriage:

When she had once got to the seat, she broke out with suppressed passion of grief. She did not care to analyse the sources of her tears and sobs—her father was going to be married again—her father was angry with her; she had done very wrong—he had gone away displeased; she had lost his love; he was going to be married—away from her— away from his child—his little daughter—forgetting her own dear, dear mother. So she thought in a tumultuous kind of way, sobbing till she was wearied out, and had to gain strength by being quiet for a time, to break forth into her passion of tears afresh. She had cast herself on the ground—that natural throne for violent sorrow—and leant up against the old moss-grown seat; sometimes burying her face in her

---

[13] *North and South*, p. 71. We also hear of 'her beautiful lip curled in a slight disdain' (p. 31), and her 'flashing eye and dilating nostril' (p. 53), among other characteristics of a proud heroine.

hands; sometimes clasping them together, as if by the tight painful grasp of her fingers she could deaden mental suffering.[14]

This is appropriate to Molly, it is natural and its detail of behaviour rings true. We need not pretend too much for it, but it is effective in its context and the faults are under control.

The gift for inventing and describing detail is present from the beginning, a reflection of her own delight in observation and curiosity. Mary Smith's hardly suppressed impatience with Miss Matty's comments:

Oh dear! how I wanted facts instead of reflections, before those letters were concluded![15]

echoes her own impatience; the novels of the Cranford world in particular are built up with the density of detail she herself demanded from life:

Our Times of today has taken away my breath—Who—What, Where, Wherefore, Why—oh! do be a woman and give me all the possible details.[16]

she wrote about an unexpected engagement—to a man, a woman would not need the request.

It is possible to understand the justification behind Dickens's reaction when Mrs. Gaskell refused to accept his editing of the proofs of *North and South*. He had, as he told Wilkie Collins with some self-righteousness:

gone over the proofs with great pains—had of course taken out the stiflings—hard plungings, lungeings [sic] and other convulsions—and had also taken out her weakenings and damagings of her own effects. "Very well," said the gifted man, "she shall have her own way. But after it's published show her this Proof, and ask her to consider whether her story would have been the better or the worse for it."[17]

Some of the blue pencil must have been at work on the novel's length and wealth of incident, but much of his scorn is obviously directed at the type of effect that has been discussed. The stiflings and other convulsions disappear from her later work with the

---

[14] *Wives and Daughters*, p. 128.   [15] *Cranford*, p. 56.
[16] *Brotherton*, 15 q. 9. Letter to Mr. Fox, 1859.   [17] Quoted in *Hopkins*, p. 149.

attitudes that nourished them, but one is left with a feeling that a little editorial discipline might have done some good where the weakenings were concerned.

Dialect

When Mrs. Gaskell decided to use the Lancashire dialect she was able to draw on a considerable local tradition of dialect study and literature to supplement her own interest. In particular there was the work of John Collier, who as 'Tim Bobbin' had written 'His View of the Lancashire Dialect' three-quarters of a century earlier.[18] Collier's work was well known (it can be recognized behind Job Legh's story of his journey from London with the baby); Samuel Bamford, the literary weaver whose 'God Help the Poor' is quoted in full in *Mary Barton*, issued a new edition in 1850 with a revised glossary and grammatical notes. Other writers, such as Bamford himself and the artisan coterie that called itself the 'Poets of Lancashire' kept the tradition alive, while song, story and proverb were in use around her as part of the dialect.

She had as well the advice of her husband. We have seen that the Rev. William Gaskell took a close interest in her earlier work; the verse chapter headings of *Mary Barton* and *North and South* are almost certainly mostly his. When the fifth edition of *Mary Barton* appeared in 1854 it carried as an appendix his 'Two Lectures on the Lancashire Dialect,' a monograph that draws heavily on 'Tim Bobbin' and other local literature for its material. His approach to the study of dialect is that of the comparative philologist which was normal at the time, concerned mainly with words, meanings and derivation, and there can be little doubt that many of the more erudite footnotes to *Mary Barton* were supplied by the husband. But the ear for dialogue is her own.

The use of dialect in literature that was meant for general consumption had a respectable ancestry in Scott, an early and abiding favourite of Mrs. Gaskell's. Scott had emphasized the importance of dialogue as against narrative, and much of that dialogue had been put in the mouths of dialect-speaking characters who had

---

[18] Collier's dates were 1708–86. *The Miscellaneous Works of Tim Bobbin Esq.* were first published in 1806 by H. D. Symonds.

nevertheless a serious and important part in the Waverley novels.[19] But the Scottish peasantry were at least picturesque and romantic as Scott presented them, which could hardly be said of Lancashire mill-workers. Dialect was still largely the province of comic writers when Mrs. Gaskell published *Mary Barton*. Distinctions of dialect were far greater than they have become in a B.B.C. and cinema age; the speech of one area of England would have been largely unintelligible to another, and would have been re-garded as uncouth and degraded by the ordinary educated reader, as Charlotte Brontë knew when she defended *Wuthering Heights*.[20] But the use of dialect less seriously, or for minor characters, goes back to Fielding, while the example of Dickens, Thackeray, Lever, Jerrold and others had made the use of it familiar, sometimes in a serious context.

Mrs. Gaskell had then a certain amount of precedent behind her, but her originality was great enough. It was a new speech in an unromantic setting; her heroes and heroines are and remain working class. Novels of factory life had already been written, but *Mary Barton* was the first to be written from a linguistic level appropriate to the characters.

Nevertheless Mrs. Gaskell came to her task as a novelist first, as an amateur of dialect second. Had she attempted to present genuine Manchester speech her novel would have been un-readable, as she hints when she comments on the song 'The Old-ham Weaver' that Margaret sings:

Do you know "The Oldham Weaver?" Not unless you are Lancashire born and bred, for it is a complete Lancashire ditty. I will copy it for you.[21]

which she does, in a tolerable attempt at phonetic transcription, with the warning at the end:

[19] I draw here on Professor Jack's discussion, op. cit., pp. 210–12. Mrs. Gaskell's love of Scott is mentioned in *Chadwick*, p. 94; and see *Wives and Daughters*, pp. 78 and 191.
[20] In her preface to the 1850 edition: 'the language, the manners, the very dwellings and household customs of the scattered inhabitants of those districts must be to such readers in a great measure unintelligible, and—where intelligible—repulsive.' (World's Classics, O.U.P., 1950, p. xxv.) But Heathcliffe and Catherine do not pour out their passion in broad Yorkshire, dialect is for the servants.   [21] *Mary Barton*, p. 37.

To read it, it may, perhaps, seem humorous; but . . . it is a powerfully pathetic song.[22]

Samuel Bamford too, while praising the power and honesty of *Mary Barton*, told the anonymous author that 'the dialect I think might have been given better'.[23] What Mrs. Gaskell gives us is appropriate language; appropriate to the environment and yet appropriate also to the comprehension of the reading public and to the dignity of the characters. As dialect it can be faulted in many ways. It is not consistent, its syntax is largely standard, it is more concerned to give specimens of dialect vocabulary and idiom, inflexion and contraction, than to present the genuine manner of speech that 'Tim Bobbin' tries to, and that Mr. Gaskell quotes in his lectures.

But to criticize Mrs. Gaskell's presentation of dialect because it is not an accurate transcript would be ludicrously misplaced criticism. It is not what she sets out to do, nor what a reader could accept in a novel. Even Shaw dropped his Cockney transcript in the printed form of *Pygmalion* after giving his readers a taste of it. Mrs. Gaskell uses dialect to place her characters in a particular social setting, that of the Manchester artisan. She had to gain the reader's sympathy for them while preserving their essential humanity and dignity; had she moved fully into dialect she would have run the double risk of putting the reader off by its difficulty, and of arousing the wrong emotions instead of sympathy because of the conventional association of dialect with comedy and low life. (Nor, we might add, is it easy in practice for anyone to think or write fluently and naturally in the accent of another class when that accent has not at some period been native to the writer.) Her characters speak grammatical English, with occasional variations to indicate a lower class but not enough to elicit the feeling of snobbery or humour that is even today a common reaction of the educated to uneducated speech. The vocabulary employs enough dialect words and forms to indicate 'Lancashire' although the number of items that has to be glossed is not large. The reader is given continuous hints from the language to keep the speakers firmly placed in class and locality; the language they speak is

[22] *Mary Barton*, p. 39.   [23] *Rylands*, p. 8.

appropriate to them in the context of the novel. It is symbolic dialect rather than true dialect.

How far from an actual transcript it was, and incidentally how much it shared in the general want of detailed care, can easily be seen in a representative passage from *Mary Barton*.

You'll wonder, chaps, how I came to miss the time this morning; I'll just tell you what I was a-doing. Th' chaplain at the New Bailey sent and gived me an order to see Jonas Higginbotham; him as was taken up last week for throwing vitriol in a knob-stick's face. Well, I couldn't help but go; and I didn't reckon it would ha' kept me so late. Jonas were like one crazy when I got to him; he said he could na get rest night or day for th' face of the poor fellow he had damaged; then he thought on his weak, clemmed look, as he tramped, footsore, into town; and Jonas thought, maybe, he had left them at home as would look for news, and hope and get none, but, haply, tidings of his death. Well, Jonas had thought on these things till he could not rest, but walked up and down continually like a wild beast in his cage. At last he bethought him on a way to help a bit, and he got the chaplain to send for me . . .[24]

A fairly long extract is necessary to represent it fairly, but to cover all the linguistic points would take too long. In general, the complex sentence construction, carefully placed adjectives, and general balance are those of written and practised prose; the majority of the sentences or parts of sentences are standard English, the 'wild beast' image is a literary one. The spelling—and therefore the pronunciation that echoes in the reader's mind—is with minimal exceptions (ha', th', na) standard spelling; deviations from normal syntax are few. Two dialect words, 'knob-stick' (blackleg) and 'clemmed' (starved), support the indications of dialect, but these indications have no regularity about them. We get 'couldn't', 'could na' and 'could not'; 'th' chaplain' and 'the chaplain'.

For the same reasons we find that Mr. Carson and the other masters speak educated English, though we are told that Mr. Carson had begun life as a mill-hand; his speech indicates his

[24] *Mary Barton*, p. 218.

social position, not his pronunciation. And when Mary comes to make her public confession of love for Jem from the witness-box, there is not a single non-standard contraction in the long speech, not a single piece of non-standard syntax, only two or three mildly marked expressions (e.g. 'I'd a deal to bear', 'I'd fain have done so') to maintain the indication of her manner of speaking. The heroine at an emotional climax needs dignity of expression as well as dignity of emotion.[25] So does the repentant and dying Barton.

A little more control over the presentation of the dialect used is to be found in *North and South*. Mrs. Gaskell was a more skilled writer by then, while the dialect characters are now secondary to and in contrast with the central 'educated' ones; there was also now the example of writers as diverse as Charlotte Brontë and Charles Kingsley who had begun to mingle dialect in serious work. In *Sylvia's Lovers* she took exceptional care to make the dialect accurate, and Yorkshire as distinct from Lancashire, for the first time using such devices as doubled vowels to indicate pronunciation. Yet even in *Sylvia's Lovers* the underlying vocabulary and syntax are near normal, though Mrs. Gaskell is at pains to mark the greater education and refinement of Philip by giving him a less marked dialect speech than Sylvia and her family, as being more appropriate to his position.

The dialogue of the dialect novels employs basically the simple, colloquial style that is Mrs. Gaskell's natural prose medium, but kept to the simplest end of its scale; its very simplicity and the range of reference of its vocabulary mark it out from the dialogue of a higher social class. This is indeed language relevant to the context of situation (to use Malinowski's phrase), but a situation with two distinct sets of reference. On the one hand there is the social, educational, and geographical setting; on the other hand the demands made on the novelist by the conventions of the contemporary novel and its readers. Neither Mrs. Gaskell's courage and originality as a writer, nor the accuracy of the dialect elements she used, should be ignored or played down because she had to meet these double and to a great extent conflicting demands.

[25] *Mary Barton*, p. 377.

The Development of Technique: Style 263

When Hardy saw this problem looming up in *Tess* he got round it by looking it squarely in face, and then side-stepping:

Mrs. Durbeyfield habitually spoke the dialect; her daughter, who had passed the Sixth Standard in the National School under a London-trained mistress, spoke two languages; the dialect at home, more or less; ordinary English abroad and to persons of quality.[26]

I have not attempted a full examination of Mrs. Gaskell's style, although the main characteristics have inevitably been discussed in following its adaptation to her varying purposes as a novelist. The faults are obvious enough, but they are rarely those of pretentiousness or artificiality. They spring from too easy a facility of expression, and from the attitude she adopts in establishing the relationship between author and reader. It is the attitude which prompts Mr. Gibson's advice to the vicar on parish visiting:

"you shouldn't try to make talk when you go into the cottages, but just talk."

"I don't see the difference," said the vicar, a little querulously; "but I daresay there is a difference, and I have no doubt what you say is quite true."[27]

We have seen that she is by no means artless; she could have been more careful. It suited her to write in the ease of her second-best gown, but the gown could have been smartened up a little. Yet the faults have to be balanced against the total effect, and we need to remember the many cases in which her limitations and ease become positive virtues. Henry James called the style of *Wives and Daughters* a 'homely prose'. 'Homely' is a dubious term, even allowing for the more complimentary meaning it would have had a hundred years ago, but it catches one aspect of Mrs. Gaskell's style, an aspect James needed for the contrast he wanted with the pretensions of 'fine writing'. Its context is one of considerable praise, and praise from James is worth quoting. It will make a

[26] *Tess of the D'Urbervilles*, Macmillan (Wessex ed.), 1912, p. 22. But like Mrs. Gaskell, he anticipates modern theory in the psychology of language.
[27] *Wives and Daughters*, p. 42.

fitting conclusion to note the qualities which he recognizes as being within her range:

If an author can be powerful, delicate, humorous, pathetic, dramatic, within the strict limits of homely prose, we see no need of his "dropping into poetry," as Mr. Dickens says.[28]

[28] op. cit., p. 159.

Appendix

THE ORIGINAL ROUGH SKETCH FOR *MARY BARTON*

(This is presumably the rough sketch mentioned in the account of the Knutsford edition that has been quoted from the *The House of Smith Elder*. A copy of it is with the papers that Clement Shorter compiled and that are now in the Brotherton Library.)

1st Chap. Scene in G H—Spring Evening—Wilsons and Bartons—The Wilsons speak of Esther's disappearance—are joined by the Bartons and etc.

2nd Chap. 4 years passed away. Changes. The strong Alice Wilson and healthy Thomas Barton dead—while the feeble and less healthy remain behind—no news yet of Esther.

Good times—How flourishing Wilson is—How he joins a Chartist club at the instigation of Job Leigh—How he apprentices Mary to a dress-maker. How Widow Barton strives on to keep her delicate twins with the help of her son Thomas and succeeds.

How Thomas Barton in his way to work always meets Mary, and what arises therefrom.

How Mr. Chadwick Junior on his way home to dinner always meets Mary and what arises therefrom.

A Father and daughter's talk over the fire; Past life—gone and dead.

The old always homing to the past, the young looking to the future. Plans for the day at Dunham and Whitsun week.

The day at Dunham.

Rumours of bad times—Bad times.

Bradshaw and Co. fail. Wilson dismissed.

Mrs. Barton's sorrows.

Wilson engaged at Chadwick and Co.'s Mill.

How Chartism from a theory becomes an action in bad times.

END OF VOL I

How Mary suffers from the bad times.

Margaret Clegg and Mary have mourning to make.

Death at the Bartons'. Mary and Aunt Esther sit up by turns.

Mary's first love.

How in the midst of much sorrow, Mary is happy in her own individual world of love.

Poor Thomas Barton.

Thomas and Mary quarrel. His despair.

Mary's bliss. Her conscience—struck by visit to poor Widow Barton. Aunt Esther.

Mary's downfall of heart. Mr. Chadwick's threat.

Fanny's first visit to Wilson—her tale—her warning regarding Mary.

Mary undeceived. Who was listening.

Trades Unions, and desperation.

Mr. Chadwick murdered.

VOL. III

The police on the scent.

Barton arrested.

Mary's revulsion of feeling. Goes to see widow Barton.

Accompanies her to prison.

Barton in prison.

Mary's determination to prove Barton's innocence.

Discovers the murderer.

Fanny.

Agony.

Visits Widow Barton. Aunt Hester's childishness.

A sympathising and advising friend, Job Leigh.

How she proves an alibi by Margaret Clegg's help.

Interview with Barton. *He* knew too.

Father's death of remorse—Widow Barton's.

Aunt Hester's death.

Marriage—Sail for America.

Notes

Many names were altered for the final version:

(a) The names of Wilson and Barton as family names were changed round, e.g. Wilson becomes John Barton, Thomas Barton becomes Jem Wilson.

(b) Chadwick becomes Carson.

(c) Margaret Clegg becomes Margaret Jennings (Job Legh's granddaughter) while Leigh becomes Legh.

(d) Aunt Hester becomes, probably, Aunt Alice Wilson.

(e) Fanny and Esther are combined.

(f) Bradshaw becomes Hunter. But there is an echo of the name. Esther lodges with a Mrs. Bradshaw (*Mary Barton*, p. 5).

The sketch bears out Mrs. Gaskell's claim that 'the whole tale grew up in my mind' but it completely contradicts the statement that follows it:

I cannot trace back now why or how such a thing was written, or such a character or circumstance was introduced.[1]

It substantiates her comment that the plot was originally built round John Barton but the changes made in the final version provide a wider range for the theme of punishment inevitably resulting from sin, which she gives as the initial controlling idea.

The pattern of transgression, repentance and reconciliation is developed by the changes in the plot. It becomes the mill-owner's son who is murdered, leaving the mill-owner to repent his own lack of sympathy for the workers and to share Barton's remorse in the reconciliation scene at his death-bed. Margaret is rewarded by marrying Will Wilson—a new character introduced for the new alibi and pursuit section—the marriage balancing Mary's marriage to Jem. Esther's remorse and secret help are also carried through to repentance and reconciliation; it appears that Esther takes over the part allotted to Fanny in the draft. Barton's responsibility for his own fate is increased by

[1] *Mary Barton*, p. lxiii.

making Job Legh benevolent and neutral, not the man who introduces Barton to the Chartists' club.

Another example of the care and sense of proportion that went to the making of the book can be seen in the removal of the 'Day at Dunham' episode. This was not wasted; it appears as the short story 'Libbie Marsh's Three Eras' published in 1847. This incidentally helps us to see more clearly the beginning of Mrs. Gaskell's writing career. *Mary Barton* was begun first, 'Libbie Marsh's Three Eras' developed out of it as her first short story, to be followed by the other stories under the pseudonym of Cotton Mather Mills—'The Sexton's Hero' and 'Christmas Storms and Sunshine'—before the novel was completed and published.

The change round of names is difficult to understand. But Mrs. Gaskell was not a great inventor of names, which she normally borrows from life (although not necessarily borrowing the personalities). Barton and Wilson were probably recollected from families she had come across. She may have begun by merely using the names, and then found that the characteristics of the families she had in her imagination were more suited to the opposite names. She always relied heavily on her observation and remembrance of local detail. The virtual elimination of Bradshaw, who turns up as a major character in *Ruth*, is probably another case of the name remembered. But Mrs. Gaskell often repeats names for characters, and places; Gibson, Dixon, Coxe, Hamley are examples. Dixon, we may note, is used for superior servants, Hamley is associated with places (in 'A Dark Night's Work' and with the Hamleys of Hamley in *Wives and Daughters*).

The original plot called for three volumes. The final version was in two volumes in spite of the additional material. One can only guess at what happened to the intention. It seems likely that for her first long novel Mrs. Gaskell was unwilling or unable to rely on local and domestic detail to hold the interest of her readers, and was concerned about having enough incident and excitement. She may well have begun also to feel her power of creating incident and plot. The new detail, the alibi and the chase and trial, bring *Mary Barton* much closer to the contemporaneous sensation novel than her other serious work. This would be an understandable effect of local and particular circumstance, although she never lost the need for the strong situation entirely.

One thing is certain; that between this rough sketch and the completed novel Mrs. Gaskell laid the foundation for her command of technique.

Bibliography

I. Novels, Stories, Articles, etc. by Mrs. Gaskell

The Works of Mrs. Gaskell, 8 Vols. John Murray, 1919–1920. (This is the Knutsford Edition. For details of contents see pages xiii–xiv.)

The introduction also contains:
'Sketches Among the Poor, No. 1.' *Blackwoods Magazine*, Vol. 41 January 1837.
'On Visiting the Grave of My Stillborn Little Girl.' (A sonnet written on Sunday, 4 July 1836.)

The following items are not included in the Knutsford edition:
'The Scholar's Story', *Household Words*, 22 October 1853. (Translation by William Gaskell of a Breton ballad introduced for a chain story for Mrs. Gaskell.)
'A Christmas Carol', *Household Words*, 27 December 1856. (Poem)
'The Cage at Cranford', *All the Year Round*, 28 November 1863.
'Robert Gould Shaw', *Macmillan's Magazine*, December 1863. (Article)

The Life of Charlotte Brontë, Haworth Edition; Smith, Elder, 1914.

There were also introductions to the two following books:
Maria S. Cummins, *Mabel Vaughan*, Sampson, Low & Co., 1857.
Col. C. A. Vecchi, *Garibaldi at Caprera*, Cambridge, 1862.

II. Published correspondence

Letters on Charlotte Brontë, privately printed, 1916.
Letters of Mrs. Gaskell and Charles Eliot Norton, 1855–1865, edited by Jane Whitehill, O.U.P., 1932.
Letters Addressed to Mrs. Gaskell by Celebrated Contemporaries, edited by Ross D. Waller. Reprinted from the *Bulletin of the John Rylands Library*, Vol. 19, No. 1, January 1935.
Other letters are quoted in some of the books in Section IV.

III. The Collections in the following libraries have been used:
The British Museum.
The Brotherton Library, University of Leeds.
The Houghton Library, Harvard University.
The Huntington Library, California.
The Manchester Central Library.
The Arts Library, Manchester University.
The John Rylands Library, Manchester.
The Library of the University of California, Los Angeles.

IV. The following books and articles are referred to in the text:
Allen, Walter, *The English Novel*, Penguin, 1958.
Arnold, Matthew, *The Poetical Works*, O.U.P., 1942.
Briggs, Asa, *Victorian People*, Odhams, 1954.
Brontë, Charlotte
    Jane Eyre, World's Classics, O.U.P., 1955.
    Shirley, World's Classics, O.U.P., 1947.
Browne, Sir Thomas, *Religio Medici*, Everyman, 1940.
Browning, Elizabeth Barrett, *The Poetical Works*, O.U.P., 1951.
Carlyle, Thomas, *Past and Present*, Chapman & Hall, 1905.
Carpenter, S. C., *Church and People, 1789–1889*, Seraph Books, 1959.
Cary, Joyce, *Art and Reality*, C.U.P., 1958.
Cazamian, Louis, *Le Roman Social en Angleterre, 1830–1850*, Didier, Paris, 1935.
Cecil, Lord David, *Early Victorian Novelists*, Constable, 1935.
Chadwick, Mrs. Ellis H., *Mrs. Gaskell: Haunts, Homes and Stories*, Sir Isaac Pitman & Sons, Ltd., 1913.
Clark, G. Kitson, *The Making of Victorian England*, Methuen, 1962.
Collier, John, *The Miscellaneous Works of Tim Bobbin, Esq.*, H. D. Symonds, 1806.
Collins, H. P., 'The Naked Sensibility', *Essays in Criticism*, Vol. 3, Jan. 1953.
Collins, Philip, *Dickens and Crime*, Macmillan, 1962.
Conrad, Joseph, *Notes on Life and Letters*, Dent, 1949.
Crabbe, George, *Crabbe's Poetical Works*, John Murray, 1823.
Darwin, Charles, *The Autobiography of Charles Darwin*, edited by Frances Darwin, Dover (New York), 1958.
Dickens, Charles,
    Bleak House, Oxford Illustrated Dickens, O.U.P., 1951.

Christmas Books, Oxford Illustrated Dickens, O.U.P., 1954.
Hard Times, Oxford Illustrated Dickens, O.U.P., 1955.
Charles Dickens as Editor. Letters edited by R. C. Lehmann, Smith, Elder, 1912.
Disraeli, Benjamin, *Sybil,* Penguin, 1954.
Dunn, W. H., *James Anthony Froude: A Biography 1818–1876,* O.U.P., 1961.
Eliot, George, *The George Eliot Letters,* edited by Gordon S. Haight, Yale, Vols 1–3 1954, Vols 4–7, 1956.
Elliot-Binns, E. L., *Religion in the Victorian Era,* 2nd ed., Lutterworth Press, 1946.
ffrench, Yvonne, *Mrs. Gaskell,* Home and Van Thal, 1949.
Gaskell, William,
 The Lancashire Dialect, Illustrated in Two Lectures, Chapman & Hall, 1854.
 Protestant Practices Inconsistent with Protestant Principles, R. Hunt, 1836.
 Some Evil Tendencies of the Popular Theology, West Riding Tracts, 1847.
 Unitarian Christians Called to Bear Witness to the Truth, Edward T. Whitfield, 1862.
Gettman, Royal A., *A Victorian Publisher,* C.U.P., 1960.
Greg, William R.,
 Review of *Mary Barton* in the *Edinburgh Review,* Vol. 180, April 1849.
 'The False Morality of Lady Novelists', *Literary and Social Judgements,* Trübner, 2nd ed., 1869.
Haldane, Elizabeth S., *Mrs. Gaskell and her Friends,* Hodder & Stoughton, 1930.
Hardy, Thomas,
 Tess of the D'Urbervilles, Macmillan, 1912.
 The Mayor of Casterbridge, Macmillan, 1920.
Holt, Raymond V., *The Unitarian Contribution to Social progress in England,* Allen & Unwin, 1938.
Hopkins, Annette B.,
 Elizabeth Gaskell: Her Life and Work, John Lehmann, 1952.
 'Dickens and Mrs. Gaskell', *The Huntington Library Quarterly,* Vol. 9, 1946.
Houghton, Walter E., *The Victorian Frame of Mind,* Yale Paperback (New Haven), 1963.

House, Humphry,
  The Dickens World, Oxford Paperbacks, 1960.
  'Wordsworth's Fame', *English Critical Essays, Twentieth Century,
  Second Series*, World's Classics, O.U.P., 1958.
The House of Smith, Elder, printed for private circulation, 1923.
Howitt, William, *Visits to Remarkable Places*, Longmans, 1840.
Jack, Ian, *English Literature 1815–1832*, Clarendon Press, 1963.
James, Henry,
  The Art of the Novel, Scribners, 1950.
  Notes and Reviews by Henry James, Dunster House, Cambridge,
  Mass., 1921.
  The Portrait of a Lady, Houghton Mifflin & Co. (New York), 1891.
  William Wetmore Story and His Friends, Thames & Hudson, n.d.
Klingopulos, G. D., 'Notes on the Victorian Scene', *Pelican Guide to
  English Literature*, Vol. 6, Penguin, 1958.
Latourette, Kenneth Scott, *Christianity in a Revolutionary Age*, Vol. 2,
  Eyre & Spottiswood, 1960.
Lehmann, Rosamond, 'A Neglected Victorian Classic', *Penguin New
  Writing*, No. 32, 1948.
Mottram, R. H., *Portrait of an Unknown Victorian*, Robert Hale, 1936.
Payne, George A., *Mrs. Gaskell and Knutsford*, Clarkson & Griffiths,
  Ltd., Manchester, 1900.
Pollard, Arthur, 'The Novels of Mrs. Gaskell', *Bulletin of the John
  Rylands Library*, Vol. 43, No. 2, March, 1961.
Pope, Alexander, *Pope's Poetical Works*, Macmillan, 1897.
Quirk, Randolph, *Charles Dickens and Appropriate Language*, University
  of Durham, 1959.
Shaen, Margaret J., *Memorials of Two Sisters*, Longmans, 1908.
Tillotson, Geoffrey, *Thackeray the Novelist*, C.U.P., 1954.
Tillotson, Kathleen, *Novels of the Eighteen-Forties*, Oxford Paperbacks,
  1961.
Times Literary Supplement, The, 11 August, 1961.
Trollope, Anthony, *Autobiography*, World's Classics, O.U.P., 1941.
Wellek, R. and Warren, A., *Theory of Literature*, Harvest Books (New
  York), 1960.
Willey, Basil, *Nineteenth Century Studies*, Chatto & Windus, 1949.
Williams, Raymond, *Culture and Society 1780–1950*, Penguin, 1961.
Woodward, E. L., *The Age of Reform, 1815–1870*, O.U.P., 1954.
Wordsworth, William, *The Poetical Works of Wordsworth*, O.U.P., 1926.
Young, G. M., *Portrait of an Age*, O.U.P., 1953.

V. *The following is a brief selection of other books and articles referring to Mrs. Gaskell:*

Allot, Miriam, *Elizabeth Gaskell*, Longmans, 1960. (Writers and Their Work, No. 124.)

Dodsworth, Martin, 'Women Without Men at Cranford', *Essays in Criticism*, Vol. 12, No. 2, April 1963.

Eliot, T. S., 'Review of "Letters of Mrs. Gaskell and C. E. Norton",' *The New England Quarterly*, Vol. 6, No. 3, 1933.

Green, John A. *A Bibliographical Guide to the Gaskell Collection in the Moss Side Library*, Manchester Reference Library, 1911.

Hopkins, Annette B.,
'Mrs. Gaskell in France, 1849–1890', *Publications of the Modern Language Association*, 1938.
'Mary Barton: A Victorian Best Seller,' *The Trollopian*, 1948.

Lane, Margaret, *The Brontë Story*, Heinemann, 1953.

Laski, Marghanita, 'Words from Mrs. Gaskell', *Notes and Queries*, September 1961, December 1961, January 1962.

Northup, Clark S., Bibliography to 'Sanders, *Elizabeth Gaskell*'.

Payne, George A., *Mrs. Gaskell: A Brief Biography*, Sherrat & Hughes, Manchester, 1929.

Quiller-Couch, Sir Arthur, *Charles Dickens and Other Victorians*, C.U.P., 1925.

Sanders, G. de Witt, *Elizabeth Gaskell*, O.U.P., 1929. (See Northup.)

Shorter, Clement K.,
The Brontës, Life and Letters, Hodder & Stoughton, 1908.
The Brontës and Their Circle, Dent, 1914.

Waller, Ross D., *Times Literary Supplement*, 25 July 1935. (Letters on *Cranford* and its relation to 'The Last Generation in England'.)

Whitfield, Archie S., *Mrs. Gaskell: Her Life and Work*, Routledge & Kegan Paul, 1929.

A Chronological List of the Writings of Mrs. Gaskell

Items are listed in order of the date of first publication. Where a book was originally published in serial form, it appears under the date of the first instalment, the title is in italics and the date of book publication is given in brackets at the end of the entry. Introductions written by Mrs. Gaskell for other authors are noted. The three posthumous items can hardly be considered as written for publication, and are therefore listed at the end.

The following abbreviations are used:—

    H.W.—*Household Words*
    A.Y.R.—*All the Year Round*
    C.M.—*The Cornhill Magazine*
    *—Collections of stories originally published in periodicals.
    †—Stories later renamed. These are given a reference to the
       later title.

1. 1837 Sketches Among the Poor, No. 1, *Blackwood's Magazine*, Vol. 41 (poem written in collaboration with her husband)
2. 1840 Clopton House (published as an anonymous contribution by William Howitt in *Visits to Remarkable Places*, Longmans)
3. 1847 Libbie Marsh's Three Eras, *Howitt's Journal*, i.
4. 1847 The Sexton's Hero, *Howitt's Journal*, ii.
5. 1848 Christmas Storms and Sunshine, *Howitt's Journal*, iii.
*6. 1848 *Life in Manchester* (items 3, 4, 5)
7. 1848 *Mary Barton*, Chapman and Hall.
8. 1849 Hand and Heart, *The Sunday School Magazine*, July.
9. 1849 †The Last Generation in England, *Sartain's Union Magazine* (America) July. (Revised, see item 17)
10. 1850 Lizzie Leigh, *H.W.* 30 Mar.–13 Apr.
11. 1850 †Martha Preston, *Sartain's Union Magazine* (America) June (revised, see item 34)

12. 1850 The Well of Pen-Morfa, *H.W.* 16–23 Nov.
13. 1850 *The Moorland Cottage*, Chapman and Hall.
14. 1850 The Heart of John Middleton, *H.W.* 28 Dec.
15. 1851 Mr. Harrison's Confessions, *The Ladies' Companion and Monthly Magazine*, Feb.–Apr.
16. 1851 Disappearances, *H.W.* 7 June
17. 1851 *Cranford, H.W.* 13 Dec and irregularly to 21 May, 1853. (1853, Chapman and Hall)
18. 1852 Bessy's Troubles at Home, *The Sunday School Penny Magazine*, Jan.
19. 1852 The Shah's English Gardener, *H.W.* 19 June.
20. 1852 The Old Nurse's Story, *H.W.* Christmas No.
21. 1853 Cumberland Sheep-Shearers, *H.W.* 22 Jan.
22. 1853 *Ruth*, Chapman and Hall.
23. 1853 Bran (poem), *H.W.* 22 Oct.
24. 1853 Morton Hall, *H.W.* 19–26 Nov.
25. 1853 Traits and Stories of the Huguenots, *H.W.* 10 Dec.
26. 1853 My French Master, *H.W.* 17–24 Dec.
27. 1853 Introduction to 'The Scholars Story' (poem translated by husband), *H.W.* Christmas No.
28. 1853 The Squire's Story, *H.W.* Christmas No.
29. 1854 Modern Greek Songs, *H.W.* 25 Feb.
30. 1854 Company Manners, *H.W.* 20 May.
31. 1854 North and South, *H.W.* 2 Sep.–27 Jan., 1855. (1855, Chapman and Hall)
★32. 1855 *Lizzie Leigh and Other Tales*, Chapman and Hall, (items 3, 4, 5, 8, 10, 12, 14, 15, 16, 18, 20, 24, 25, 26, 28, 30)
33. 1855 An Accursed Race, *H.W.* 25 Aug.
34. 1855 Half a Life-Time Ago, *H.W.* 6–20 Oct. (see item 9)
35. 1856 The Poor Clare, *H.W.* 13–27 Dec.
36. 1856 A Christmas Carol (poem) *H.W.* 27 Dec.
37. 1857 *The Life of Charlotte Brontë*, Smith, Elder & Co.
38. 1857 Introduction to *Mabel Vaughan* by Miss Cummins, Sampson, Low, Son & Co.
39. 1858 The Doom of the Griffiths, *Harper's New Monthly Magazine* (America), Jan.
40. 1858 My Lady Ludlow, *H.W.* 19 June–25 Sep. (1859 in item 44)
41. 1858 The Half-Brothers, *Dublin University Magazine*, Nov.
42. 1858 †The Sin of a Father, *H.W.* 27 Nov. (renamed 'Right at Last' in item 48)

43. 1858   The Manchester Marriage, *H.W.* Christmas No.
*44. 1859   *Round the Sofa*, Sampson, Low, Son & Co. (items 33, 34, 35, 39, 40, 41)
45. 1859   Lois the Witch, *A.Y.R.* 8–22 Oct.
46. 1859   †The Ghost in the Garden Room, *A.Y.R.* Christmas No. (renamed 'The Crooked Branch' in item 48)
47. 1860   Curious if True, *C.M.* Feb.
48. 1860   *Right at Last and Other Tales*, Sampson, Low, Son & Co. (items 42, 43, 45, 46)
49. 1861   The Grey Woman, *A.Y.R.* 5–19 Jan.
50. 1862   Six Weeks at Heppenheim, *C.M.* May.
51. 1862   Introduction to *Garibaldi at Caprera* by Colonel Vecchj, Macmillan & Co.
52. 1863   *A Dark Night's Work*, *A.Y.R.* 24 Jan.–21 Feb. (1863, Smith, Elder & Co.)
53. 1863   An Italian Institution, *A.Y.R.* 21 Mar.
54. 1863   *Sylvia's Lovers*, Smith, Elder & Co.
55. 1863   The Cage at Cranford, *A.Y.R.* 28 Nov.
56. 1863   *Cousin Phillis*, *C.M.* Nov.–Feb. 1864 (1865, see item 61)
57. 1863   Robert Gould Shaw, *Macmillan's Magazine*, Dec.
58. 1863   How the First Floor Went to Crowley Castle, *A.Y.R.* Christmas No.
59. 1864   French Life, *Fraser's Magazine*, Apr.–June.
60. 1864   *Wives and Daughters*, *C.M.* Aug–Jan. 1866 (1866, Smith, Elder & Co.)
*61. 1865   *Cousin Phillis and Other Tales*, Smith, Elder & Co. (items 4, 15, 30, 56)

Posthumous Publication

62. 1835–38   *My Diary: The Early Years of My Daughter Marianne*, Privately printed, 1923.
63. 1836   On Visiting the Grave of My Stillborn Little Girl (Sonnet), in introduction to *Mary Barton*, Knutsford edition.
64. n.d.   Two Fragments of Ghost Stories, in *Cousin Phillis*, Knutsford edition.

Index